For James

Clues in the Calico

A GUIDE TO IDENTIFYING AND DATING ANTIQUE QUILTS

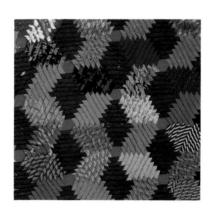

BARBARA BRACKMAN

EPM PUBLICATIONS, INC.

ACKNOWLEDGMENTS

I am grateful to many people and institutions for assistance with this book, in particular to Carol Gilham, Virginia Gunn and James Liles for their advice and thoughtful suggestions. Many friends have shared their quilts and quilt-related materials, among them Cuesta Benberry, Bets Ramsey, Wilene Smith, Merikay Waldvogel, Marilyn Woodin and Sally Garoutte, who gave me access to her file of date-inscribed quilts and much advice over the years. The staff and volunteers at three quilt projects, The Kansas Quilt Project, Quilts of Tennessee and the North Carolina Quilt Project, were generous in sharing their findings with me. The staff at the University of Kansas's Spencer Museum of Art has been most helpful as has the staff at the Smithsonian Institution and the Daughters of the American Revolution Museum. I am also grateful to Larry Schwarm for his help with photography.

Cover and book design by Stephen Kraft.

The frontispiece photograph
of an end-of-the century fabric
was obviously inspired by patchwork,
although the pattern is not a typical quilt design.
Collection: Wilene Smith.

Library of Congress Cataloging-in-Publication Data
Brackman, Barbara.
Clues in the calico: a guide to identifying and
dating antique quilts / Barbara Brackman.
p. cm.
Includes bibliographical references.
ISBN 0-939009-27-7
1. Quilts—United States—Identification.
2. Quilts—United States—Dating.
I. Title.
NK9112.B66 1989
746.9'70488—dc20
89-16873
CIP

TABLE OF CONTENTS

Feathered Star quilt made by Sarah Rannabarger Snouffer in Frederick County, Maryland. Estimated date: 1825–1850. Pieced and quilted. Cotton. Collection: Woodin Wheel Antiques.

The color scheme of red and green on a white background seems a natural outgrowth of the colors popular in chintzes like the one in the border. According to a story that will quicken the pulse of any collector, this neverwashed quilt was found abandoned in a storage shed behind a house in Iowa.

1

THE QUILT DETECTIVE

Too few quiltmakers have been blessed with the foresight to sign and date their work, so most antique quilts can be dated only by an educated guess. Determining age is a matter of finding enough reliable clues in the quilt to build a case for a date. This book is designed to teach you how to read the clues, how to analyze them and how to make a truly educated guess as to the dates they reveal—how to become a quilt detective, in other words.

I have no formal education in textile science; my training is in art education and special education, a background that may seem irrelevant to the dating of antique quilts. However, much of my interest in education is in human perception and memory—how we name, classify and recall the things in our universe. Perception and memory have great relevance to quilt dating, if we think of comparative dating as a system for defining categories.

While collecting old quilts, I realized I was learning to categorize them by colors, patterns and styles and that the categories correlated with certain dates. I learned to listen to my intuition about a quilt's age, and I listened as well to dealers and collectors who had seen far more quilts than I. Their quick judgments about a quilt's age often amazed me. How did they know, I'd ask. Just a feeling or intuition, they would say. It seemed to me (to use terms I used in my education classes) that they had good visual discrimination skills and good visual memories. They had learned to notice details most people might consider insignificant and to file different details of border, print or texture into mental categories, storing them neatly on the right sides of their brains. But very few dealers and collectors used the left sides of their brains—the verbal side—to give names to the categories. When they did, the names were usually non-descriptive and vague, names like "those old reds" or "that sleazy feel" or "those thirties' prints". If pressed to tell how they distinguished

one old red from another, they'd fall back on "just a feeling".

I knew from my experience in teaching children with learning problems that assigning what psychologists call "verbal mediators" (an awkward term for "names") to categories, improved learning and retention. I felt that if I could find names for some of these categories, and use the left side of my brain as well as the right to talk about what I was seeing, I could create a system for quilt dating that I could rely on better than intuition alone and one that could be taught to others.

This book tells not only what I have learned about dating quilts from my own classification system but also summarizes recently published information about quilts and related textiles on which I based my system. It deals first with the history of American quilts from 1750 through 1950 from the perspectives of social influences, technological developments, and fashion, household decoration and artistic taste. Subsequent chapters discuss quilts in terms of fiber, fabric, color, techniques, style and pattern, assigning names whenever possible, organizing categories and evaluating clues. In these chapters we view the different aspects of quilts from three major perspectives: names, categories and clues.

Names

When I began formalizing quilt dating I looked for names for everything, names for colors like a particularly bright blue that seems to appear only in pre-Civil War quilts; names for fabrics like the twill weave with cabbage roses that appears on the back of turn-of-the-century quilts; names for techniques like the standard applique used today. My first choice would be a period name, gathered from textile history books and antique diaries, dye manuals and fashion magazines. I hoped always to find the names used by the women who made the quilts and actually found more than one in some categories. If a blue is known as Lafayette Blue, Prussian Blue or Napoleon's Blue, the reader can make a choice. In the absence of a period name I was occasionally forced to make up a name. I call the applique technique, for example, "conventional applique" to distinguish it from cut-out chintz and reverse applique.

After reading the names in the book, you should learn to use them. Take along a friend when you go looking at quilts and talk about why you think one quilt is older than another, whether a red print is Turkey red or claret red, whether an embroidery thread is a chenille or a filoselle, whether a dye is fugitive or fast. By verbalizing about what you're seeing, you are using both the left and the right sides of your brain and improving your discrimination skills and memory.

Categories

Red, green and white quilts and whole-cloth wool quilts, you will discover, form obvious categories. Others require more thought about similarities and differences to categorize. Many categories correlate with specific eras; whole-cloth wool quilts, for example, fell out of favor in the decades before the Civil War. Using categories as clues for dating is another way of looking at what is called comparative dating; comparing the quilt in question to those you know more about. There are obviously many ways to categorize quilts. Those I have chosen—color, fabric, technique, style, pattern—are the most relevant to dating.

I made a computer file of nearly 900 American quilts, all known to have been made before 1950 by the dates inscribed on them. To supplement my informal observations about how these categories have come in and out of fashion, I classified each quilt in 13 ways (see Appendix 2 for a list) including, for example, color scheme, border style, and method used to sign and date the quilt. The computer could select the quilts made in any one style category and give me a print-out of them in chronological order. Patterns of popularity were easily discerned in style characteristics, such as stuffed-work quilting and fringed edges, found on the earliest quilts in the data base but rare after the Civil War. Other styles, like the album sampler and the Crazy Quilt, showed obvious birthdates (album samplers in the early 1840s, Crazy Quilts

in the 1880s). Many styles showed no patterns of popularity at all; binding the quilt with straight-grain, applied fabric was standard for nearly 200 years. I found so few examples of some styles, I couldn't draw any conclusions about them. I had only one instance of a ruffled quilt, for example, with a date on it and only seven applique quilts constructed of four large blocks. With many style characteristics, however, the computerized data-base enabled me to draw useful conclusions. In this book I have made a point of distinguishing between conclusions drawn from observation and those drawn from the database.

In Chapter 7 I have included a guide to the distinctive styles such as the silk show quilt, the red, green and white cotton quilt and the whole-cloth wool quilt. As it summarizes information presented in other chapters, the guide can be used as a quick reference for identifying and dating quilts.

Clues

My interest in computers and visual perception may have influenced the way I look at quilts, but I must confess my childhood fascination with girl detective Nancy Drew may have influenced me more. Each undated quilt I see as an unsolved mystery that summons the quilt detective in me.

Comparative dating means basing the case for the quilt's age on bits of evidence, much as a detective or a prosecutor would. Neat cut off points in the computer data make good clues. Because stuffed quilting drops off so markedly after the Civil War it is strong evidence of a quilt's date before 1865. Some clues are good simply because they are so easy to recognize. It doesn't take much experience to learn to recognize a cotton print with a black background; these prints were used most often in the years between 1890 and 1925. Other clues are good because they indicate a short period of time. The black-ground cottons are a reliable clue to that period of about 35 years, a rather compact era compared to a clue like Turkey red cotton, which was used over a span of 100 or more years.

Weaker clues can help build a case for a date, but one shouldn't rely on them too heavily. For example, scalloped edges were popular between 1925 and 1950, but scalloped quilts also appeared in earlier eras. To help you organize the characteristics of a quilt into strong and weak clues I have developed a form which you will find in Appendix 1.

Comparative dating works best if you think in blocks of time. It is tempting to try to narrow a quilt's date to a single year, but unless the quilt is date-inscribed I would avoid it. Even knowing something as specific as the date a pattern was published or a scrap of fabric printed cannot tell you exactly when the quilt was made. The Winterthur Museum owns a date-inscribed quilt from 1793 that has a piece of English copperplate print in it attributed to the years 1765-75 (1). The Spencer Museum of Art owns one dated 1848 that has a Hewson print in the center identical to fabric in another quilt owned by the St. Louis Art Museum, dated 1807-09 (see page 85). Women saved fabric for years and sometimes for generations.

Many scholars use a date of "circa 1875", which implies a ten-year span on either side of the date. A 20-year span is often too narrow, so I prefer to use a span with earliest to latest date, for example, 1865-1890.

For the purposes of this book I divide the history of American quilts into six periods of time.

☐ **Before 1800**   ☐ **1800-1840**   ☐ **1840-1865**   ☐ **1865-1900**   ☐ **1900-1925**   ☐ **1925-1950**

The boundaries coincide with natural points like the turn of a century as well as with important changes in quilt styles. In many cases these blocks of time are useful boundaries for dating.

I have limited the book to quilts made before 1950 because it seems necessary to gain a perspective through hindsight. The recent past has seen so many changes that it will be decades before we have a comprehensive view of quilting in the last half of the twentieth century. I also deal primarily with quilts made in the United States, as I rarely see English, Canadian or other foreign-made quilts.

I do not discuss appraisals or the monetary value of antique quilts. The market is currently escalating so quickly that any book describing prices is soon out-of-date. For current market values, check weekly and monthly periodicals that list sales and auction prices.

Practicing Your Detective Skills

Reading this book and using it for a reference can help you get started in dating old quilts, but your most important asset is going to be your own experience with antique quilts and fabrics. You need to build a personal mental file of quilts. You can start with a notebook file if you like. Photocopy pictures of quilts from books and magazines and file them in chronological order. Collect old blocks and fabrics and organize them by similar prints and colors. Keeping a notebook of quilt blocks with red fabric in them will show you how red fabrics changed over the years. Take close-up photos of old quilts, and always be on the lookout for a quilt with a date. Memorize details about dated quilts for they are the most reliable references for comparative dating.

The best way to learn any skill, including dating quilts, is by practicing the skill and getting feedback—in other words, guessing and checking to see if you are right. When you are at a quilt show or an antique shop and spot an old quilt, make a guess about the date *before* reading the label. Go through your quilt books and guess the dates *before* reading the caption. You will find yourself improving with practice. There will come a time when you begin to outguess the caption writer. Trust your judgment. There are many mistakes in print and more than a few exaggerations in family stories.

In this book I hope to give you some facts and some opinions to start you off as a quilt detective. After you've read the book, the next step is to begin reading the clues.

Hexagonal Pineapple comforter (detail). Maker unknown. Estimated date: 1880–1925. Pieced using the foundation method. Wool and silk. Collection of the author.

This seldom-seen variation of the Log Cabin is based on a hexagonal block rather than the square. Each piece was individually stuffed with cotton as it was stitched to the foundation fabric. The silk has deteriorated in spots near the center, but they have been stabilized with a covering of net.

2

AN OVERVIEW OF AMERICAN QUILTMAKING

Quilts Before 1800

The American patchwork quilt, like the United States, has its roots in many cultures. We can trace the technique of quilting—the stitching together of two or three layers of fabric to provide warmth—back to the ancient Egyptians and through the Middle Ages in Europe and Asia. Patchwork—the cutting of fabric into pieces and recombining them—is also common to many cultures. We see influences from Africa, Japan and China, India and the European countries. Seeds sown from around the world have flowered into the American patchwork quilt.

America was colonized by refugees and adventurers from several cultures. The English had the strongest influence, leaving their mark in areas both lofty and mundane, from the American language and legal system to furnishings, food and bedding. Descriptions of the bedding of the early colonists, those who settled here in the sixteenth and seventeenth centuries, cannot be drawn from the textiles themselves because very few survive. Researchers rely instead on written records such as newspaper advertisements, import orders, invoices, wills and inventories of the deceased. These last records, required of estates in certain regions, often listed blankets, quilts and other textiles among the cows, bedsteads, sheep and cooking utensils.

The colonists kept warm with blankets, bedrugs, coverlets, spreads and quilts, although quilts were few until after the colonial period. Historians Sally Garoutte (1), who examined New England records, and Gloria Seaman Allen (2), who studied Maryland records, found that quilts before 1800 were rare and expensive, valued higher than blankets or bedrugs (heavy pile or shaggy cov-

erlets). In Providence, Rhode Island, for example, the average blanket was valued at 10 shillings, the average bedrug at 15 1/2, and the average quilt at 52 (3). Quilts, because of their value, were more likely to be owned by the rich than by the middle class or poor. Such findings about American quilts during the colonial era parallel conclusions about English quilts, drawn by Dorothy Osler, who has studied written records of the sixteenth, seventeenth and eighteenth century (4).

The image of quilts as a luxury contradicts the popular idea that quilts were developed out of necessity by the poor colonists who patched threadbare blankets with scraps of cloth into random patchwork design. The quilts in use in America during the seventeenth century were far different from the patched-together utility quilts that the myths describe. Terse descriptions in the written records give us an idea of the styles of the times. The quilts were probably one-piece or whole-cloth quilts, covered with one or two or more pieces of the same fabric. They were made of cotton, silk, wool, linen or of a fabric combining fibers. A 1655 reference to an East Indian quilt probably describes a quilted piece of chintz, imported as a finished quilt from India (5). A 1685 inventory inclues a quilt of "calico, colered and flowrd", probably a similar Indian quilt. The same document describes a large white quilt (6). A 1689 will bequeaths "my silken quilt" (7).

Written accounts of "quilts" may refer to quilted petticoats rather than to bedquilts (a word that is sometimes used in eighteenth-century and earlier references to distinguish between these two quilted items). In the mid-eighteenth century, fashion in England and America dictated a skirt split in front to reveal a decorative quilted petticoat. Like the bedquilts, petticoats were of whole

Whole-cloth silk quilt made by Sarah Smith, Hannah Callender and Catherine Smith in Philadelphia, Pennsylvania. Inscribed in the quilting: 1761. Quilted. Silk. Collection: Independence National Historical Park.

Three women collaborated on this light blue silk quilt, one of the few American quilts surviving from the colonial era. The backing is tan and brown block-printed cotton; the batting is cotton; the quilting thread silk. A closely-quilted filling pattern causes the motifs, similar to crewel or Jacobean embroidery, to stand out in relief. Along the top is the inscription, "Drawn by Sarah Smith. Stiched (sic) by Hannah Callender and Catherine Smith in Testimony of their Friendship. 10 mo 5th 1761".

cloth, often of silk or glazed wool, quilted with designs such as feathers and flowers. The fashion for exposed quilted petticoats dated from about 1710 to 1780 in England. Two surviving American examples are dated 1750 and 1758 in the quilting (8).

In 1770 Boston schoolgirl Anna Green Winslow wrote her mother to ask if she might give her "old black quilt to Mrs. Kuhn for aunt said it is never worth while to take the pains to mend it again" (9). Anna was probably discussing a petticoat; other women of the time, rather than giving away their worn petticoats, opened them up and recycled them into bed quilts; a number of whole-cloth quilts appear to have been petticoats once.

Specific references to bedquilts with patchwork designs do not appear until the eighteenth century. Kent County, Maryland, appraisers first use the word "patched" to describe a quilt in 1760 (10). In Boston in 1763, Rebecca Amory advertised that she sold English and India patches, which may have been intended for bedcovers

(11). There are earlier references to patchwork in Europe. By 1726 in England the word was common enough that Jonathan Swift described Gulliver's clothes as looking like "the patchwork made by the ladies in England, only that mine were all of a colour" (12). A patchwork quilt dated that same year is in the collection of the McCord Museum in Montreal (see photograph below). This silk, linen and cotton quilt, the oldest date-inscribed quilt on the North American continent, was likely made in England in the early eighteenth century and brought to Canada in the early nineteenth century (13).

The McCord Quilt. Quiltmaker unknown. Made in England. Inscribed in applique: 1726. Pieced (English-style template piecing) and appliqued. Silk, linen and cotton. Collection: McCord Museum of Canadian History. M972.3.1

Acknowledged as the oldest patchwork quilt on the American continent, the McCord Quilt was probably brought from England.

At least fifteen date-inscribed quilts from the eighteenth century, attributed to American makers, survive. Four are of whole cloth, similar to the quilts described in the records of the previous century. Eleven, all dating from after 1770 are patchwork, both pieced and appliqued. The Saltonstall Quilt, previously credited as the oldest American patchwork, has been recently re-examined; its supposed 1704 date is in doubt. Ann Farnham, curator of the Essex Institute in Salem, Massachusetts, where the quilt is now preserved, believes it to date from sometime between the late-eighteenth and the mid-nineteenth centuries despite the date of 1701 on the papers basted behind the pieces. Although the pattern and style are consistent with eighteenth-century quilts, the fabrics appear to be from the mid- to late-nineteenth century (14).

The dated quilts and those uninscribed quilts reliably attributed to the last quarter of the nineteenth century do much to refute the assertions of some earlier quilt historians like Ruth Finley who, in her 1929 book *Old Patchwork Quilts and the Women Who Made Them*, wrote, "The art of quiltmaking in America was as highly developed in 1750 as it was in 1850" (15). We have much evidence that eighteenth-century quiltmakers used styles, techniques and patterns that were far more limited than those of their descendants one hundred years later. The early patchwork quilts fall into two general categories, pieced scrap quilts and applique designs of cut-out chintz. The styles shared several design characteristics, especially a medallion format, with a central focus contained by a series of borders or a secondary field of patchwork. Nine of the 11 date-inscribed quilts made between 1770 and 1799 have a central design focus, and only two are based on the grid or block format. The makers combined large-scale chintzes with small-scale prints and were also likely to combine fabrics of different fibers. They combined decorative techniques, using embroidery, applique and piecing in the same quilt. Seamstresses who appliqued their designs generally cut the floral motifs, birds or butterflies from chintz, and fastened the figures to a background. Those who pieced designs used simple patterns, primarily squares and triangles. A few complex patterns featuring stars adapted to a square or circular form were in the repertoire of the more advanced seamstresses.

Although patterns became more sophisticated and styles more diverse through the generations, a few design conventions established in these early quilts have continued important until today. Early quiltmakers showed a preference for stars and floral motifs and for borders of vines and swags, motifs with long and healthy histories in earlier textiles such as Jacobean crewel embroidery, counted stitch samplers and Indian palampores. Quiltmakers from the eighteenth century to the present have shown a preference for a light background behind their applique, a design idea that developed in the palampores and chintzes from which the early applique was cut. Styles in quilting designs, both plain and fancy, were also established early. Plain motifs, like grids and parallel lines, and fancy ones, like feathers and pomegranates, can be traced back to the earliest sur-

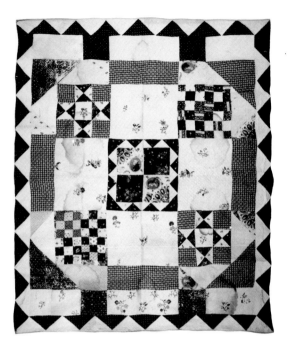

Chintz quilt. Maker unknown. Estimated date: 1791–1820. Pieced and quilted. Collection: Smithsonian Institution, Negative # 45821b.

The chintz in the center commemorates the Treaty of Pillnitz between Austria and Prussia in the early 1790s. The quilt may have been made soon after; it has several style characteristics typical of late eighteenth-century quilts: simple patchwork designs, a combination of small scale and large scale prints, a medallion format with a focus on the central design, and Jacobean-style embroidered motifs in the plain spaces.

viving whole-cloth bedquilts and petticoats.

Both written records and surviving quilts strongly suggest that the patchwork quilt is an eighteenth-century development that did not become common or practical in America until the time of the Revolution, but the popular press (and some scholarly writers) continue to furnish imaginary colonial homes with patchwork quilts. One reason for the anachronism is the quantity of inaccurate, out-of-date and out-of-print literature still in libraries. Another is that the quilt stories have become myths. They answer a contemporary need to view our ancestors as brave and resourceful survivors of everything from an inhospitable New England climate to Depression farm prices. As long as quilts provide a tangible link to our family and national heritage, their history will continue to be romanticized.

Writing about quiltmaking seems to have been colored by nostalgia from the beginning. An early published description of the social conventions surrounding quilting was T.S. Arthur's fictional "The Quilting Party" in *Godey's Lady's Book* in September, 1849, in which the narrator pined for his

Woman's World magazine suggested updating traditional patterns in 1929 with black cotton sateen behind reproduction calicoes—a color scheme that never caught on. The headline, "Designs of Colonial Origin", exaggerated the age of the patterns, most of which can be traced only to the mid-nineteenth century.

younger days 20 years earlier when young ladies knew "the mysteries of the Irish chain, rising star, block work or Job's trouble." Nostalgia persisted throughout the nineteenth century despite quilt-making's vitality. Even though the craft and the social conventions associated with it thrived, writers looked longingly at the past. During the colonial revival in architecture and decorating that began in the l890s, Americans developed a new respect for their history with a tendency to overly romanticize it. Quilting was no exception. Writers attached a colonial pedigree to all aspects of the craft. Patterns like the fan or the pieced tree, designed in the 1870s and '80s, were sold as "colonial" designs with connections to colonial heroes such as Martha Washington and the Minutemen. Typical of the prose of the l930s is Carrie Hall's description of the Log Cabin pattern in her book, *The Romance of the Patchwork Quilt in America.* "No Colonial home was complete without one or more of the geometric arrangement of scraps" (16). Technically, a colonial quilt would be one made before the Revolution of 1776, but

Hall and her contemporaries used the term "colonial" rather loosely as a synonym for "pioneer", which refers to the era from 1830 until the end of the century when the west was settled. If we substitute "pioneer" for "colonial" in Hall's description of the Log Cabin pattern, we still have a romantic generalization but one that is more accurate.

In truth, the patchwork quilt demands a certain minimum level of affluence and material goods, rather than poverty or scarcity, since patchwork requires a diversity of fabric. Our contemporary concept of making a quilt from the smallest scraps left over from domestic sewing calls for far more domestic sewing than colonists did. Before the nineteenth century, fabric was so scarce that the average person had few changes of clothes; poor people and those who economized made garments from simple square-cut patterns that used an entire width of cloth selvage to selvage, leaving no scraps to be incorporated into other projects. It took the development of factory-produced cotton (and later factory- produced woolens and silks) to provide fabric cheap enough to afford the poor and the growing middle class the luxury of a larger wardrobe and the accompanying luxury of cutting fitted clothing from rectangles of fabric, leaving leftover scraps. We do not see a democratization of patchwork quilts until the industrial revolution made fabric affordable and commonplace.

Reading the written records of the eighteenth century also gives us a glimpse of how quilts fit into the lives of American women. Like the design conventions, some social conventions in the making of quilts seem to have been established early. The piecing and applique work that decorated the top was generally the province of a single maker, but the quilting was a separate step, which might be done by the woman who sewed the top, or by a professional quilter or jointly by a group of friends.

Professional quilters predate patchwork in England and America. In 1721, Pennsylvanians Elizabeth and Sarah Coates recorded expenses paid for quilting, possibly for Elizabeth's wedding quilt, which she described as a "silk bed quilt" in her 1753 will (17). Quilters advertised their services; in 1749 Anne Griffith of Annapolis said she did "plain or figured, coarse or fine quilting in the best and cheapest manner in her house" (18). In 1776, Elizabeth Evans let New Yorkers know she "wrought quilts" (19). Any of these women might have quilted petticoats in addition to bedquilts.

Quilting petticoats and bedquilts as a social event was also well established by the end of the eighteenth century. In 1758 Elizabeth Drinker recorded in her diary that she "dined and spent ye afternoon at Betsy Moode's. Helped to quilt" (20). A 1768 diary mentions "quilting at my house", the earliest use of "quilting" as a noun to refer to the social event, according to the *Oxford English Dictionary* (21). On July 3rd of that year Elizabeth Porter Phelps recorded that her aunt came to stay "to have me go to quilting for Miss Patty" (22). In 1773, Molly Cooper noted in her diary that her daughters were hurrying to a quilting frolic (23). Martha Ballard in 1790 wrote of a quilting where her daughters entertained 15 women who quilted between 3 P.M. and 7, whereupon a dozen young men arrived for tea, followed by dancing (24). Frances Baylor Hill in 1797 recorded several quilting occasions at her home. Like Elizabeth Drinker, she considered the dining an important part of the event. "Fine eating and merry quilting," she wrote one day in July and the next day: "Mrs. Garlick and Sally came. Spent the day agreable eating drinking and quilting" (25).

Both patchwork and quilting were taught at needlework schools. In 1771, Boston newspapers advertised schools that taught French quilting along with embroidery, darn work, plain sewing and knitting (26). In 1771, 12-year-old Anna Green Winslow, who boarded with her aunt while attending Madam Smith's sewing school, among other Boston schools, recorded that she "exchanged a piece of patchwork which had been wrought at my leisure intervals with Miss Peggy Phillips, my schoolmate for a pair of curious lace mitts with blue flaps . . . I had intended that the patchwork should have grown large enough to have covered a bed" (27).

We find many later references to the needlework curriculum at finishing schools along the east coast when needlework was the major emphasis in a girl's education. After learning the basics of reading, writing and computation, she spent her time practicing plain sewing (clothing and household linens) and fine sewing (decorative needlework). These were the skills that made a girl marriageable; an academic education was considered unimportant. I found no references to patchwork in eighteenth-century curricula, but we can assume it was taught in the schools. Patchwork was considered plain sewing, a way to teach young girls the construction skills they would need to clothe their future families.

Quilts from 1800 to 1840

During the first decades of independence, cultural and economic changes affecting the entire American society took place. One of the most significant was the increasing industrialization of the textile industry, the first shots in America's industrial revolution. As mechanized spinning and weaving of cotton replaced the hand production of linen and wool, cotton cloth and thread became cheaper and more commonplace. In the years between independence and the 1840s, cotton became the signature fabric for the American quilt.

During the first decades of the nineteenth century, women continued to make quilts in the styles that had become standard. Appliqued tree-of-life and floral motifs were cut out of chintz; pieced quilts were made of all types of printed and plain fabrics. Whole-cloth quilts in wool, linen and silk showcased a seamstress's quilting skills. With the availability of cotton fabric and cotton sewing thread, however, new styles developed. Whole-cloth quilting could be worked on plain white cotton with cotton thread; functional and relatively inexpensive cotton thread on the market meant seamstresses could add more quilting to their designs and could incorporate stuffed and corded details (28).

Cheaper fabrics gave them the option of controlling color schemes and fabric choices. Some bought yardage in two or three colors specifically for their quilts, while others continued to incorporate dozens of dressmaking and furnishing prints in all colors into their designs. As quiltmaking became increasingly widespread, fabric printers in Europe and America catered to the market with chintzes designed specifically for quilts. The motifs could be cut out and appliqued to another fabric or they could be pieced into the design, giving the look of cut-out chintz with less work.

Although the medallion format continued strong, the block format, a single design unit repeated over the surface of the top, gained popularity. The number of pieced patterns increased with simple innovations appearing in the square and star designs. Stars sprouted serrated edges called feathers and grew to cover the entire top in the Star of Bethlehem design. Squares were organized into Irish Chains, and triangles into Sawteeth. Circular patterns fractured into Mariner's Compasses and Sunflowers. Hexagon mosaics, pieced over papers, showed off scraps of woodblock, plate prints and the new roller-printed cottons.

Irish Chain quilt, made by Margaret Lowery Wills in Leonardtown, Maryland. Estimated date: 1800–1825. Pieced, appliqued and quilted. Cotton. Collection: Smithsonian Institution, Negative #33846.

The Irish Chain is one of the oldest block patterns; several date-inscribed examples from the early nineteenth century survive.

Seamstresses began to show a freer hand with applique, constructing their own images of patterned or plain fabric. Eagles, popular for all kinds of decorative arts in the Federal period, were among the first free-hand applique designs, in both reverse and conventional applique. Appliqued feathers and plumes, probably adapted from quilting designs, also began to appear in the center of patchwork quilts.

We know little about how the growing repertoire of patterns was communicated from quiltmaker to quiltmaker and community to community. Needleworkers had embroidery pattern books dating from the early seventeeth century, but such books for quilt designs were not published until the end of the nineteenth century. The first quilt design published in the United States (a hexagon pattern) appeared in *Godeys' Lady's Book* in January, 1835; but periodicals did not become a significant source for patterns until the last quarter. We can assume that the teachers who included patchwork in their curricula taught standard patterns such as the nine-patch, which would have been appropriate for novices. We can also assume that patterns were traded at quiltings and other social events where one quiltmaker may have traced a design off another's newly finished top.

Fairgoers may have been inspired then, as they are today, by novel ideas from quilts on display. The first American agricultural fair is attributed to Pittsfield, Massachusetts, in 1810 (29). It is unlikely that quilts were exhibited there, but over the next few decades the quilt exhibit became a standard class at the American agricultural fair along with the flora and fauna. Ladies' fairs were another important nineteenth-century social event. Women exhibited and sold their needlework such as pincushions, pen wipers and quilts, raising funds and consciousness for anti-slavery and other causes. The Boston Female Anti-Slavery Society began holding fairs in 1833; the Philadelphia branch began its annual fair in 1836 (30).

We have little idea what the women who made these quilts called their designs. The appraisers who described eighteenth-century patchwork for estate inventories described them minimally. Women writing their wills and diaries were rarely specific as to quilt names. In 1798 Eliza Bowne Southgate wrote about her "pieced geometrical" and a "Mariner's Compass" (31). Sarah Robert Lawton's 1832 will listed an "eagle quilt", her "best hexagon quilt", a "coffin quilt" and a "new patchwork quilt" (32). *Godey's* gave three names to the hexagon pattern they printed in 1835, "Hexagon", "Six-Sided" or "Honeycomb" patchwork. What little written information we have from the era indicates that the poetic names like "Mariner's Compass" or "Honeycomb" are the exceptions, with more prosaic names the rule.

During the early decades of the nineteenth century, quilts were made and owned by a wider cross section of the population. In Kent County, Maryland, in 1820, 63% of the estates included quilts, compared to 28% in 1760 (33). The decline in fabric prices and increasingly available fabric, plus a rising middle class with money to spend on fabric, made the quilt a more universal bed covering, although it still retained a higher value than blankets and coverlets. An 1803 Pennsylvania inventory lists seven quilts averaging $3.71 and three blankets averaging $1.66. An inventory dated 1839 lists nine quilts averaging $2.85 and a blanket valued at $1 (34).

The expansion of quilts and quiltmaking into everyday American life is reflected in memoirs of

Chintz Basket quilt, made by Mrs. James Lusby in Washington, D.C. Date attributed is 1837–8. Appliquéd, quilted. Cotton. Collection: Smithsonian Institution, Negative # P63340.

Mrs. Lusby cut birds and flowers from printed cotton chintz and appliqued them to a plain cotton background. The quilt is attributed to the end of the era when such cut-out chintz or Broderie Perse quilts were popular. The appliqued dog-tooth border was also fashionable before the Civil War.

the period. Girls growing up in these decades later recalled their first experiences with patchwork at home and at school. Lucy Larcom who learned at six in the 1830s, remembered her struggles with the squares of cotton that were scraps from family dresses (35). A contemporary of hers, who wrote her memoirs as Grandmother Brown, pieced a Nine Patch in l835 also at age six (36).

Quilting continued to be a source of income for working women. Chloe Samson of Pembroke, Massachusetts, who earned money in domestic service, recorded that she spent three days making a bedquilt and earned one shilling in 1822 (37). Miriam Davis Colt, who was 19 in 1836, taught school that year and sewed and quilted in the evenings for extra money (38). The Female Society for the Relief and Employment of the Poor in Philadelphia employed otherwise destitute women at their House of Industry to do knitting, spinning and quilting. In 1831 the best quilters received 15 cents per day; ''most others received 12 1/2 cents'' (39).

Quilting afforded entertainment as well as income. Many writers recorded quilting frolics, quilting parties, quilting bees or quilting matches (40). One author unimpressed with such American cultural experiences was the English visitor Mrs. Trollope, who wrote a satirical sketch entitled "The Day of A Lady in The West", in which the fictional Mrs. Cob and her unattractive family prepared for an evening quilting frolic. Refreshments included tea for the ladies and whiskey for the gentlemen guests (41). Quilting parties offered diversion for young and old, community socializing, romancing and matchmaking. Chastina Walbridge and Alfred Rix were only one couple of many who met at a quilting; they recalled their meeting in a diary they kept together after they married in 1849 (42).

Any analysis of how the quilt has come to be so important a part of the fabric of American life should weigh the significance of the quilting bee. Nostalgia for the neighborhood parties, with their matchmaking possibilities, undoubtedly influenced much of the later sentimental writing about quilts.

Quilts From 1840 to 1865

In the decades between 1840 and the end of the Civil War, quilts took on new meaning as women began using them to raise funds and to symbolize political issues and friendship. Technological progress brought even more affordable new fabrics with improvements in roller printing and dye chemistry. The sewing machine, patented in 1846, was commonplace by the end of the era, freeing women from the tediousness of constructing clothing by hand and from the handicap of an education based primarily on sewing.

Among the important developments was the social fad for album quilts. Bound paper albums to be inscribed with verses, drawings, and autographs had been popular since the 1820s; around 1840 the custom was adapted to quilts. Friends might each sign a block for a quilt made up of squares of an identical pattern worked in different fabrics; or they might each contribute a block in a different design. Because so many of these quilts are dated as well as signed they are among the easiest styles to trace. In the database there were 249 signature album or friendship quilts. The earliest is dated 1839. Two are dated 1840, three 1841, fifteen 1842, ten 1843 and eighteen 1844,

with over a dozen a year through the 1840s. In the 1850s the numbers drop off. There are only 11 in the whole decade of the 1860s and fewer in the 1870s. The fad seems to have been strongest in the late 1840s and early 1850s, after which it faded becoming—as fads sometimes do—a classic, popular to this day. The album quilt craze surfaced in the mid-Atlantic area from Trenton, New Jersey, down through Philadelphia and Delaware to Baltimore, Maryland. By 1845 the signature quilt idea spread north to New York and New England and south to Virginia and the Carolinas, and later to the rest of the country.

The album quilts undoubtedly inspired an increasing variety in patterns as friends strove to contribute something clever and unique to the group effort. Pieced patterns diversified as stars blossomed from pots into Cleveland Tulips and North Carolina Lilies. Whig's Defeat and Rocky Mountain designs took triangles to new heights. Plain patterns such as the Nine Patch became complex with additional seam lines, and the Mariner's Compasses and other intricate patterns became even more complicated. In the 1840s, applique designs evolved into block-size bouquets and wreaths of chintz flowers, scaled down from the medallion format. By the end of the era most seamstresses were cutting their applique from calicoes and plain cottons, constructing their own flowers using conventional applique. Many based their designs on variations of a simple rose, arranging the flowers with great ingenuity in urns and baskets, wreaths and bouquets. Cut-out chintz became an almost forgotten style, along with stuffed work and whole-cloth quilts.

Quiltmakers incorporated the new fabrics on the market into their new styles. Scraps of Turkey red calicoes and other multicolor roller prints, printed plaids, and rainbow prints wound up in cotton quilts. Silks were sometimes combined with fine wools and cottons; more often they appeared alone in the silk quilts advocated by the magazines of the time. More quilters purchased fabric especially for their quilts, limiting their choices to a few popular colors. A taste developed for green and Turkey red cottons on a white background. The two-color quilt—navy on white, red on white or green on white—became another standard that endured for generations.

With the increase in patterns we see some evidence of an increasing use of imaginative names. In the published material and private letters of the time we find more references to names such as Job's Troubles (43), Flowering Almond (44) and Bonaparte's Retreat (45). (My guess is these are the designs we today call Grandmother's Flower

Album sampler quilt, made for Mary E. Mannakee (1827-?) in Montgomery County, Maryland. Inscribed in ink: 1850–1851. Appliqued. Cotton. Collection of the Daughters of the American Revolution Museum, Washington, D.C. Gift of Mrs. Benjamin Catching.

The sampler quilt using conventional applique techniques and a red, green and white color scheme is a style that developed in the early 1840s and faded soon after the Civil War. The fact that there are only three signed blocks (two by Mary and one by William Thomas Johnson), the homogeneity of the fabrics and the peculiar grace of the blocks suggest that a single hand worked on this quilt. Mary may have made the blocks herself, intending to obtain more signatures from her friends. Similar wreaths and bouquets are found in other applique samplers and single pattern quilts of the period.

Garden, Coxcombs and Currants, and Burgoyne Surrounded.) We also see a slight but steady increase in published quilt patterns. *Godey's,* the leading periodical for women in those years, printed a number of designs in the fifties and sixties, as did competitors *Graham's* and *Peterson's.* The American magazines often printed identical designs, since plagiarism was common. The magazine patterns owed much to English patchwork; even the designs that were not blatantly copied from English magazines followed English-style construction and design in what may have been an editorial attempt to uplift the common patchwork quilt (46). The typical magazine pattern of the era advised the use of silk fabrics in a mosaic-style construction. The average quiltmaker, who

Floral Basket quilt, made by Mary C. Pickering (Bell) (1831-?) in St. Clairsville, Ohio. Estimated date: 1850–1860. Appliqued with buttonhole stitch, stuffed and quilted. Cotton. Collection: Smithsonian Institution, Negative # 81.5765.

Design characteristics typical of the 1840–1865 era include applique constructed of calico prints and plain cottons (rather than applique cut out of chintz), block format, red, green and white color scheme, fine buttonhole stitch outlining the applique, stuffed work, stipple quilting and the use of a sampler of quilt patterns in the plain blocks.

did not get her patterns from any printed source, was more likely to use cottons and a block-style construction. Reading about quilts in mid-century magazines reveals only a portion of what was actually happening at the time.

During the pre-Civil War decades we see some evidence of regionalism in the spread of patterns. Recent research, facilitated by the State Quilt Projects that record quilts in the context of their family histories, has discovered a regional provenance for some of the more unusual applique designs. Jan Murphy has traced a circular geometric pattern to the Carolinas (47), Merikay Waldovogel has found several examples of an applique wreath in Tennessee (48), and Katy Christopherson and Louise Townsend have noted examples of a carnation and pineapple design with a connection to Garrard County, Kentucky (49). There is limited evidence that quiltmakers in different areas were

partial to different designs for their friendship quilts, with Chimney Sweep album patterns common in New York (50) and Rolling Stone a favorite in Pennsylvania.

Evidence of such specific regional differences is unusual. More typically, designs seem to have popped up simultaneously all over the map. In the mid-1840s, Cleveland Tulips were made in Ohio, New York and Maryland; Caesar's Crowns in New York, New Jersey and Pennsylvania. The network of friends trading album blocks across state lines probably helped the patterns to spread rapidly, as did the waves of women emigrating west, taking their quilts and family designs with them. Our ideas on how patterns were communicated are mostly speculative. We have little tangible evidence beyond the very limited magazine designs. An exception is a set of letters from members of the Shaw Family, written to and from Nebraska in the 1850s and 60s, containing quilt blocks (51). We assume that other letter writers traded patterns between new homes and old.

Most of our current information about quilts in these years deals with quilts made east of the Mississipi rather than in the new western territories. Precious few quilts made on the road west or on the frontier survive. Of 312 quilts in the database made between 1840 and 1860 not one was made in a territory, and only eight are attributed to makers living west of Ohio (two each in Indiana, Illinois, Missouri and Texas, all of which were states by that time). We have written evidence that women made quilts and comforters in the west. Early California settlers recorded an 1846 quilting party (52). In the first months of Kansas settlement in 1856, Hannah Anderson Ropes mentioned visiting a woman who was "sewing together the breadths of a comforter" (53). Weeks later Ropes noted a curious combination of items hanging from the beams of another Kansas cabin. Next to the dried venison and beef and the baskets of beans and potatoes was a workbasket of patches (54). What these quilts and comforters looked like and where they are today is unclear. They may have been used and used up. Pioneer women write of using quilts and other bedding for cabin doors and windows, for wagon covers to protect their families from the weather and from Indian attacks, to cover the crops in grasshopper plagues and to bury the dead in cholera plagues. Yet many older quilts, made in the East and carried to new homes, survived the trip west and the years on the frontier—possibly because they were special souvenirs of another life and lost family and friends. It is also possible that few quilts were made on the frontier due to lack

Goose Tracks quilt, made by Mary Ellen Neese in Ohio. Inscribed in chain stitch embroidery: 1861. Pieced and appliqued. Cotton. Collection: Kansas Museum of History.

Mary Ellen Neese brought this quilt with her to Kansas when she emigrated in the 1870s. The colors—red, green and yellow-orange on white—were popular for pieced quilts as well as for applique in these years. The colored piping inserts (between the border and the blocks) are found primarily on mid-nineteenth century quilts.

representation of Union or Republican sentiment, but we find little corroborating evidence of such symbolism recorded in either published or un-published writings during these years. Most of our theories on mid-nineteenth century politics and quilts remain speculative, despite all the pattern names—Kansas Troubles, Underground Railroad, Whig's Defeat and Tippecanoe and Tyler Too— recorded after 1880 that seem to speak of mid-nineteenth century political ideas. One design with published political references is a stars and stripes design printed in red, white and blue in *Peterson's Magazine* in July, 1861, at the beginning of the Civil War. Although quilts made in this design (and there were many) may appear to us today to be merely patriotic, they were also likely political (a distinction that becomes more subtle

Patriotic quilt. Maker unknown. Estimated date: 1861–1875. Pieced, appliqued and quilted. Cotton. Collection: Smithsonian Institution, Negative # 36635.

Peterson's Magazine printed a colored illustration for this red, white and blue quilt in June, 1861, under the caption "A Patriotic Quilt", hoping to inspire readers to quilt their Union sympathies. The 34 stars in the center and in the border represent the 34 states in the Union including those that had seceded. A number of examples survive, one a baby quilt, some full-size, and several made as blocks for album quilts.

of time and materials. More research into quilts made in the early years of western settlement is called for.

While quilts served basic bedding and sheltering functions on the frontier, they developed functions of a different sort back in the east. Album quilts, described earlier, symbolized ties of community, family and friendship, and during the troubled decades before the Civil War quilts began making political points. A cradle quilt was inscribed with a poem describing the anguish of a slave mother separated from her baby. The quilt, sold at the 1836 Boston Female Anti-Slavery Society Ladies' Fair, is now in the collection of the Society for the Preservation of New England Antiquities. It is one of at least three surviving quilts inscribed with anti-slavery sentiments (55).

Presidential partisanship seems evident in several quilts that picture the log cabin of William Henry Harrison's 1840 campaign. Because most are dated later than Harrison's death (a month after his inaugural) they may be memorial rather than political quilts. The familiar pieced Log Cabin, which apparently dates from the second log cabin presidential campaign (Abraham Lincoln's in 1860), may have begun as a symbolic

in wartime). During the Civil War women incorporating 34 stars into their quilts to represent all the states, North and South, were undoubtedly expressing Union sentiments.

The Civil War's profound effect on life in the Confederate and Union states extended to quilts, as fabric became scarcer, especially in the south.

The physical realities of war destroyed many of the old quilts, not only in the southern states where they were lost in the burning and looting of civilian homes, but also in the north where relief organizations solicited quilts to use as hospital and field blankets. During the month of May, 1863 alone, the United States Sanitary Commission issued 1,203 quilts to Virginia soldiers. Some of these quilts were made especially for the troops, and some were family quilts sacrificed for the cause (56).

During the Civil War women raised money for war relief through fairs where needlework, including quilts, was sold. Some northern fairs featured quilting demonstrations in colonial costume, a scene recorded in an engraving from Frank B. Goodrich's *The Tribute Book: A Record of the Munificence, Self-Sacrifice and Patriotism of the American People During the War for the Union.*

Quilts From 1865 to 1900

The decades between the end of the Civil War and the end of the century brought about radical changes to America. In the north, the generally gay and prosperous postwar years were flawed by economic ups and downs and the problems of a growing lower class. In the rural south the shattered economy began to industrialize when the northern fabric mills moved south to to take advantage of cheaper labor and nearby raw material. The west boomed with postwar migration that resulted in nine new stars on the American flag.

Hexagon or Honeycomb quilt, made by Emma St. Clair Whitney. Inscribed: 1876. Pieced. Silk. Collection: Smithsonian Institution, Negative # 76.1097.

The design we call *Grandmother's Flower Garden* today dates from the early nineteenth century. This show quilt is pieced of the weighted silks of the late Victorian era. The heavy silks and the distinctive black color scheme are clues to a date later in the century, rather than earlier, a guess confirmed by the signature which says, "1876, Emma St. Clair Whitney. Centennial."

Quilts continued to reflect regional circumstances, but styles became more homogeneous through the influence of national magazines and national exhibits like the 1876 Centennial exhibition. New styles and patterns appeared in response to changes in economics, technology and taste. Silk show quilts became more prevalent as silk prices dropped. The variety and complexity of pieced patterns increased with each decade; many of today's standards like the Drunkard's Path, the Ocean Wave, the Schoolhouse and the Pine Tree appeared. The popular Log Cabin pattern, built on a foundation fabric, led to other foundation designs like the Pineapple, the String Quilt and the Crazy Quilt.

We can track the Crazy Quilt fad during the l880s and '90s through the thousands of remaining examples, many of which are dated. We can

A turn-of-the-century Wichita, Kansas woman spent her leisure time working squares of a Crazy Quilt. She is identified only as Florence M. on the reverse of the photo.

also track trends through the popular press of the time. Editors encouraged (and when they'd seen enough—discouraged) the making of Crazy Quilts. Filled with missionary zeal, some editors hoped to inspire readers to more tasteful needlework by introducing styles such as outline embroidery and patterns like the Fan, inspired by current trends in decorating and fine art. Other editors responded to popular taste by printing patterns and instructions reflecting the quilts actually being made by their readers. For the first time, a significant number of block-style, pieced designs appeared in print, sometimes under captions such as "An Aesthetic Quilt" or "Design for Patchwork", but also under fanciful names like Bird's Nest and Kaleidoscope, published in *The Ohio Farmer* magazine in 1894.

The spread of patterns entered a new age in 1889 with the publication of *Diagrams of Quilt, Sofa and Pincushion Patterns*, a catalog of patterns for sale from the Ladies' Art Company. Women, who ordered their yard goods by mail from Montgomery Wards and Sears, Roebuck and Company in Chicago and their dress patterns from Madame Demorest and Butterick in New York, could send a dime to St. Louis and receive a paper pattern

for any of three hundred designs. Those who preferred to copy a fabric example could order a full-size block of, say, the Rose Album design in cotton for 75 cents or in silk for $1.40.

America's 1876 Centennial celebration marked an industrial coming of age, when handcraft gave way to mass production. Around that time roller printing peaked, supplying seamstresses with cottons abundant in detail, fast in color and modest in price. Block and plate printing all but disappeared as printers learned to use rollers to print up to eight colors on both sides of a fabric. By the end of the century synthetic dyes were well on their way to dominating the dye industry, producing more and brighter colors than natural dyes. Designer William Morris led a minor backlash against the garish run-of-the-mill fabrics, advocating a return to hand-printing methods and natural dyes with muted, secondary shades. Morris's esthetic influence can be seen in some of the subdued rusts, ochres, olives and wine-colored cottons that wound up in end-of-the-century quilts, but the average quiltmaker was happy to combine these more tasteful prints with vivid chrome oranges, Turkey reds and double-pink calicoes.

Fabric manufacturers, like other industrialists, learned that profits demanded increased productivity, which translated into a decline in quality. In quilts from the last decade of the century we see the results; print detail, color range and thread count were sacrificed to keep prices low.

Individual craftsmanship suffered similar declines in these years as the sewing machine and the growing ready-to-wear garment industry freed women from making all the family clothing and freed girls from learning the necessary hand-sewing skills. Although exceptions occurred, especially in the category of silk Show Quilts, late-nineteenth century cotton quilts generally show lower levels of hand workmanship. Applique designs turned simpler, and many seamstresses appliqued on the machine. End-of-the-century quiltmakers were less likely to use finishing details like corded binding. Quilting became sparser, and time-consuming, subtle designs like stuffed work, cording and stippling disappeared, leaving only a few exceptions. The trend was to fewer quilting lines per square foot and to thicker batting, resulting in longer stitches and in a type of quilt with a homely, rather crude look. Log Cabins, Crazy Quilts and other foundation patchwork patterns were often not quilted at all; tying the layers to make a comforter (also called a comfort or comfortable) became a common time-saving option.

We find more surviving tied comforters and more thick, coarsely-quilted quilts from the last decades of the nineteenth century than from earlier periods, evidence that traditional quilts were no longer important as expressions of a young woman's artistic and needlework skills but were seen as functional bedding for the rural middle and lower classes. In 1862, Dolly Lunt Burge wrote that "Lou {her stepdaughter} is making a bed quilt but she says she is never going to cut up peices (sic) again for such work, that only poor white folks make bed quilts, that the rich buy blankets" (57). Cheap cottons, plentiful scraps from both home and factory clothing production, machine sewing and tying rather than quilting made late-nineteenth century patchwork quilts and comforters an economical alternative to blankets. The 1890-91 Montgomery Ward catalog listed their cheaper gray wool blankets from $2.25 to $8. Purchased quilts (probably whole-cloth rather than patchwork) ranged from 65 cents to $4.65. Components for homemade quilts included quilt batting that ranged from 28 cents to 77 cents; quilt backing at around 75 cents (3 yards of 90-inch cotton at 25 cents per yard) and the 6 yards of cotton the patchwork might take at 36 cents (6 cents per yard). The materials for a patchwork quilt with a mid-price batting and store-bought calicoes would thus be about $1.60, less than the cheapest wool blanket. The abundance of inexpensive cotton and wool scraps from home clothing production meant that one could piece the top for little or no actual cash outlay. When considering the relative value of quilts versus blankets one has to factor in the time required to make a quilt, but during this era the time spent in sewing and assembling the three layers was minimal. Quilts, in the post-Civil War years, did become the cheap bedding that the myths now describe.

Tastemakers denounced traditional quilts as ugly, common and a menace to the public health. Particularly caustic was the advice offered by the anonymous author of an 1874 article titled "Bed-Rooms and Beds" in *The Household* magazine. "Neither the unhealthful thing called a comfortable nor the unsightly covering known as a patched quilt should be seen on a bed in this day" (58). Nearly a decade later *Arthur's Home Magazine* noted with disgust that "3/4 of the bed coverings of our people consists of what are miscalled 'comfortables' " (59).

Sampler album quilts, in which each contributer chose her own pattern, declined in popularity, although single-pattern friendship quilts remained fashionable. In 1870 *Hearth and Home* magazine described the making of a friendship quilt in an article about a sewing circle where women old and young made a quilt "designed for Mrs. Blake . . . every square bears in indelible ink a different name. At one of our Sewing Circles several weeks ago, Jessie Pride busied herself in cutting out patches for making the square . . . and distributing them among the members. The best calico and the most durable white muslin compose them, and they are set together with great taste so as to form both harmony and contrast in coloring when viewed as a whole" (60).

Other styles expressed a woman's taste and skills with a needle, although new standards for excellence and beauty developed in the 1870s and 80s. Late nineteenth-century trendsetters who discounted the subtle design of stuffed work quilting and the almost invisible buttonhole applique stitch valued contrast in color and texture, opulent fabrics and showy stitching. The ultimate adaptation of the Victorian esthetic to quiltmaking was the Crazy Quilt in which seamstresses painted the lily by overlaying every seam in their silk quilts with bold embroidery. The fashion for excess and the abundant, cheap fabrics resulted in new styles in cotton quilts too. The charm quilt with 999 different prints and the postage stamp quilt with thousands of scraps measuring less than an inch apiece led to extravaganzas like Martha Haggard's 1893 *Wonder Quilt*, containing over 70,000 minute pieces.

Because magazines and the Ladies' Art Company catalog recorded pattern names, we know that patterns were being named for contemporary events, commemorating Admiral Dewey and his victory in the Spanish American war of 1898 (The Philippines and the Dewey Dream Block), the temperance movement (WCTUnion), and presidential elections (Cleveland Lilies) and assassinations (Garfield's Monument). Most of these patterns seem more patriotic than political; the presidential designs commemorate a sitting president, perhaps, rather than a candidate, since there are no patterns for losers Hancock, Blaine, or Bryan. Or it may be that patterns named for also-rans were not recorded in print, as we would expect the publications to screen out the unpleasant and the partisan as well as the less genteel.

Temperance was one political issue that inspired both patterns and fundraising quilts. We find many records of women making quilts to raise money for favored causes, especially those having to do with support for churches. Ladies' aid societies paid for church carpeting, missionaries' transportation, hymn books, roof repair and new sanctuaries with money earned by quilting tops for hire, by assembling quilts to be raffled or auc-

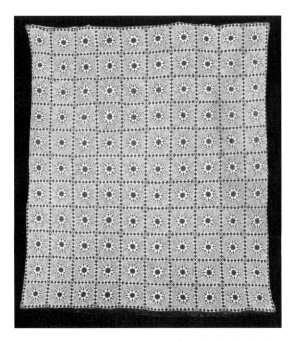

Carpenter's Wheel (variation) spread, made by Martha A. Haggard (1815–1899) in White Cloud, Kansas. Attributed date: 1895–1897. Pieced, bound and backed. Cotton. Collection: Helen F. Spencer Museum of Art, the University of Kansas. Gift of Louise Langworthy.

On the back of this quilt is stamped a record of Martha Haggard's achievement, noting that the quilt contains "62,948 seperate (sic) pieces". It may indeed contain more; calculation based on multiplying the pieces per block results in a figure of 79,950. In 1945, Albert Small made a quilt with 123,000 hexagons, the current world record.

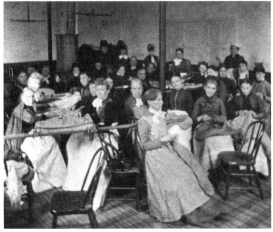

Using quilt frames propped on chair backs, the Ladies' Aid Society of the First Methodist Episcopal Church in Lawrence, Kansas quilted to raise funds for a new church, built in the 1890s.

tioned and by organizing signature quilts in which community members donated a dime or a quarter to have their names embroidered or inked into the quilt's design.

Group quilting—whether for recreational or fundraising reasons—remained important in the lives of many women in the post-Civil War decades. However, as American life grew more diverse and more sophisticated, and as social opportunities for young people expanded, reports of dancing, men and refreshments (especially alcohol) at quilting events disappeared. Quilting bees seem to have become an exclusively female domain, social circumstances that continue in the twentieth century.

Quilts From 1900 to 1925

We know far more about twentieth-century quiltmaking. Not only do we have more twentieth-century quilts to study, we are still able to talk to people who recall the first decades of the century, and their memories have been recorded in recent years by folklorists, oral historians and volunteers for state and regional quilt projects. We also have an enormous body of quiltmaking literature from the popular press.

Many trends that had begun in the late nineteenth century continued beyond World War I: Crazy Quilts, wool and cotton comforters, foundation patchwork, thick, functional quilts, a preference for dark color schemes based on blue and black and two-color quilts of blue and white or red and white. Outline embroidery remained popular; during these years an increasing variety of colorfast cotton threads stimulated a fashion for multicolored embroidery, although Turkey red thread on white remained the standard for pictorial embroidery and signature fundraising quilts. Applique work, close quilting and fine hand detailing stayed in decline.

The fabrics used in quilts continued to deteriorate in quality. Synthetic dyes, especially the greens that were so unreliable that quiltmakers stopped using them, presented problems with colorfastness. Low thread count and poor print quality kept calico prices low. The inexpensive printed cottons in a limited color range of blues, gray, black and maroon were the common choices for quilts.

As silk prices rose due to Chinese and later worldwide war, silk quilts became scarcer. The Crazy Quilt, which had originated as a spectacle

A man at the quilting frame inspired an affectionate and amused glance at this turn-of-the-century quilting bee. The group is actually tying a comforter. Notice the ball of yarn on the patchwork top.

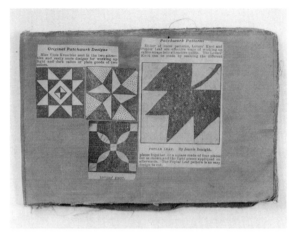

Quilters clipped sketches and photos of blocks from magazines and newspapers. The frugal collector of these patterns made her needlework scrapbook of scraps of salvaged green window shades, bound on her sewing machine with a line of stitches. Author's collection.

of silk scraps and plentiful embroidery, evolved into a serviceable wool comfort with sparse decorative stitching.

Magazines that had begun printing patterns in the nineties expanded their quilt pattern offerings, asking readers to share original and traditional designs in such columns as *Hearth and Home's* "Useful and Fancy Work" and *The American Woman's* "The Needle-worker". The standard magazine format at the time was a black and white sketch or photo of the finished pieced block (applique blocks were rarely pictured) with a short paragraph containing color suggestions, the pattern name and the hometown, name or initials of the contributor. Many magazines also had a mail order pattern department similar to the one found in *American Woman*, as explained by Editor Edna Chalmers Monroe in an open letter to Daisy C. of Huntsville, Pennsylvania around 1910:

"Any Quilt Pattern published in our department, no matter how long ago, will be sent you for five cents. A large book of quilt blocks, nearly 200, may be had for a dime. I am glad you are so interested in this department and trust you will introduce the paper to many of your friends for I am sure you have a host of them."

The book of quilt blocks was probably similar to the Ladies' Art Company catalog, which by 1907 had been revised at least ten times and offered 500 pieced and applique patterns (61). Competition among magazines and pattern companies undoubtedly did much to increase the number of new designs and the diversity of pattern names. A long-time Ladies' Art Company advertisement spoke in strange superlatives that must have sold

quilt patterns: "Every quilter should have our book of 400 designs, containing the prettiest, queerest, scarcest, most grotesque patterns from old log cabin to stars and puzzle designs" (62).

Quilts and tied comforters continued to form a good deal of America's bedding, a fact that offended tastemakers who preferred the uncluttered look of a manufactured white spread. *Cutler's Red Book of Ready Reference* offered a compromise in this 1903 advice to the housewife:

"A few quilts for summer covering are convenient, but for cold weather good, thick comfortables, with a white counterpane on the outside make a bed look well and it is warm and more easily made than one with too many quilts. A counterpane is more easily washed and looks better than a quilt, and costs less if we can count our labor anything" (63).

Oral histories recalling the era remind us that women's labor was indeed counted very cheaply. An up-to-date white bedspread was unaffordable for many families, but quilts, which often required no cash outlay, provided not only bedding but livelihood. In a 1986 interview Thelma Brown Waldrop recalled that her mother raised $7.50 for Thelma's graduation class ring in 1918 by piecing 15 quilt tops of scrap fabric, which she sold for 50 cents a piece (64). References are frequent to quilting "on shares", a method of obtaining the fabric to piece a top when scraps were few and far between. The more affluent customer would supply enough material for two sets of blocks, two tops or two quilts. The quiltmaker kept one and gave one to the customer. Many, many unquilted tops survive from this era; possibly they were set aside to be finished later when the quiltmaker could afford to buy the batting and backing.

Magazines of the era catered to their quilt-making audience. The women's pages in farm magazines and some of the women's and needle-work magazines included patterns and instructions for the inexpensive scrap quilts that quiltmakers seemed to favor. But patchwork quilts were also gaining favor with writers for upscale magazines, who advocated decorating in the fashion of the Colonial Revival, a design trend that began in the 1890s, inspired by a nostalgia for an imagined American past before industrialization, immigration and urbanization with their accompanying problems. Quilts were an important part of the pseudo-colonial decor, and magazines and pattern companies sold many patterns by fabricating colonial pedigrees for designs and styles that were in reality only a few decades old.

The Household Magazine, around 1911, showed two traditional applique designs, suggesting up-to-date color schemes for reproductions of the old blocks which were "dark green, dark red and a rich orange yellow . . . Although dark colors were used in the original, lighter colors make a beautiful combination". Most magazines and pattern companies were content to modernize traditional designs with new fabrics and colors, but a few needlework editors continued the crusade to uplift quiltmaking by integrating current design ideas influenced by Art Nouveau, the Arts and Crafts movement and the Art Needlework movement, which advocated professional designs for needlework and crafts. Marie Webster of *The Ladies Home Journal* designed and sold patterns for quilts with a modern look. Her innovations were a pastel color scheme that made use of the new shades possible with improved synthetic dyes, an overall design with strong borders recalling the medallion format that had died out before the Civil War, and a more literal, flowing applique style that owed much to Art Nouveau. Webster's floral applique patterns were easily recognizable as poppies, irises and sunflowers, a signficant change from the stylized roses of the nineteenth-century applique artist.

The magazine designers were the first to develop patterns specifically for children's quilts. Quilts scaled to crib-size were no novelty but images such as nursery rhyme characters, animals and toys, designed to appeal to children began appearing in print with more frequency. Webster showed a quilt featuring an applique version of Sunbonnet Sue in 1912, but the idea did not trickle down to the quiltmaking public until the late 1920s. Webster's Sunbonnet Sue and a number of her other designs were collected in her 1915 book *Quilts: Their Story and How to Make Them*, the first book on quiltmaking and quilt history (65).

A look at the surviving quilts from the first quarter of the century indicates that few quiltmakers were ready to abandon the scrap look or dark, inexpensive calicoes for the color-coordinated pastel color scheme with purchased yardage advocated by Webster and others. The new styles were expensive and they required a higher standard of handwork—two changes the average quiltmaker did not accept until the mid 1920s.

Quilts from 1925 to 1950

The pastel quilts from the mid-twentieth century are among the first styles a novice quilt collector learns to recognize. People commonly refer to the Wedding Rings and Dresden Plates and other characteristic quilts of the time as "Depression Quilts", but the fashion for light clear colors, representational applique and a scrap look combined with a plain white cotton developed before the 1929 stock market crash and the economic crisis of the thirties, during the mid-twenties when American life was undergoing a different set of social changes. Women who bobbed their hair and shortened their skirts were apparently ready to take up quiltmaking as long as the look was modern. Rose Kretsinger, a lawyer's wife in Emporia, Kansas, was typical of her middle-class peers in that she taught herself to make quilts in the mid-twenties when she wanted a colonial-looking quilt to cover an antique bed. In a woman's magazine, she found an appliqued tulip design in the decidedly modern color scheme of orange, black and green on a white background. She was so pleased with the results that she began a 20-year quiltmaking career that won her local and national recognition for her updated versions of nineteenth-century applique designs.

Women like Kretsinger, who was about 40 years old when she began making quilts, often had some traditional grounding in the craft. Many had learned as children but had rejected quiltmaking in the years after the turn of the century. With a continuing emphasis on the colonial look in decoration, stylish women in the 1920s turned to quiltmaking, but their work looked nothing like their mothers' dark, functional quilts. Styles that must have seemed old-fashioned (the Log Cabin and the Crazy Quilt and other foundation patch-

The cover of one of Grandma Dexter's pattern pamphlets captures the colonial decorating ideal of the 1930s, a *Grandmother's Flower Garden* quilt on a maple bed surrounded by rag rugs. Author's collection.

work, tied comforters and red and white color schemes) were replaced by new designs (the Double Wedding Ring, appliquéd butterflies and variations on the Sunbonnet Sue figure like the Colonial Lady and Overall Bill). Older designs, such as the hexagon mosaic (renamed Grandmother's Flower Garden) and the Japanese fan (renamed Grandmother's Fan), were recycled into fad patterns. Nearly every pattern company offered variations of the realistic floral designs pioneered by Marie Webster. Outline embroidery designs continued to be popular and were embroidered in the new shades of cotton thread. Companies sold pre-stamped blocks or transfers for quilts featuring state birds and flowers or juvenile themes of animals and nursery characters.

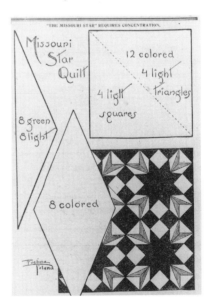

Erma June was posed on her *Sunbonnet Sue* quilt in a photo postcard dated 1931. The appliquéd figure is usually seen in profile with a huge hat hiding her face. The black button hole stitching around the applique is typical of the 1925–1950 period. Author's collection.

The Kansas City Star was one of the few periodicals to offer a full-size pattern in its weekly quilt column, which printed 1,068 patterns between 1928 and 1961. Author's collection.

30

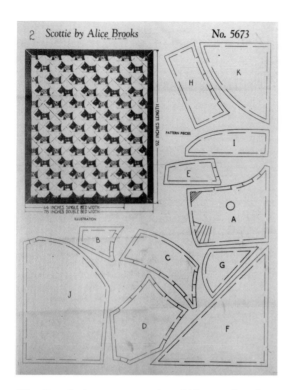

Alice Brooks is one name under which a needlecraft syndicate has sold patterns since the early '30s. Quilters could order the *Scottie* (dated 1936) and hundreds of other full-size designs by sending a dime to their local papers, which forwarded the orders to the New York company.

Contemporary events worked their way into patterns offered by periodicals and pattern houses. Lindbergh's 1927 flight across the Atlantic inspired designers to draft patterns for pieced and appliqued airplanes for years. The Roosevelt presidency was commemorated with a Roosevelt Rose, eagle designs symbolizing the National Recovery Act and a multitude of Scotty dogs—a decorating fad after Roosevelt's speech about his ''little dog Fala''.

Magazines and newspapers responded to the widening quilt market by increasing their quilt-making features. By 1934 more than 400 newspapers included a quilt pattern column, according to publicity from Stearns and Foster, a leading batting manufacturer. The *Kansas City Star*, *Capper's Weekly*, the *Rural New Yorker*, the *Oklahoma Farmer-Stockman* and the *Dakota Farmer* were a few of the dozens of periodicals that ran a pattern feature originated by a staff member in the late twenties. To meet the ever-growing demand, syndicated pattern columns replaced most of the unique columns in the thirties. Personalized under names that combined colonial breeding and down-home folksiness, columns written by Aunt Martha, Grandmother Clark, Hope Winslow and Nancy Cabot were advertisements in thin disguise for the pattern syndicates that further homogenized the national style in the thirties.

Although a colonial reference was an important selling point, the designers who worked for the pattern companies also looked to contemporary trends like Art Deco and comic strip graphics for inspiration, producing the curious blend of professional design and traditional folk art that has characterized commercial quilt patterns since.

Copywriters liked to recall quiltmaking's long and glorious history (which they often exaggerated as longer and more glorious than it actually was), but they also occasionally advised modern seamstresses to avoid design pitfalls of the past. Emma S. Tyrrell, writing in *Wallace's Farmer* in 1929, suggested readers make charm quilts with a more controlled color scheme than those of the nineteenth century. ''I would like a quilt made from this design with the center of each block white; that would give uniform patches of white over the quilt and form a pretty contrast to the figured fabrics'' (66).

Quiltmakers and designers made the most of the new cottons that appeared in the twenties. New dyes and new technology for printing them enabled fabric mills to offer inexpensive cottons printed in the whole spectrum of colors. The simple geometrics and sparse florals of the past forty years were replaced by splashy prints covered with layers of stylized flowers. Art deco zigzags, plaids and stripes coexisted in the same fabric with tulips, daisies and pansies. Pinpointing the year when quilts changed from the dark calicoes to the modern pastel look is impossible, but a change is noticeable during the mid-twenties in the fabric offered in the Sears catalogs. The 1924 catalog pictured 17 prints in the Dolly Madison line (a cotton for clothing that was also probably used in quilts). Twelve were single-color dark prints; five were multicolor brighter prints. In 1926 the line had fourteen prints; four were single color; ten were multicolor. In 1928 only one of the twenty was single color. In 1922 the colors offered in another line of cotton were rather dark: black, navy, cadet (a gray-blue), white, claret (wine), gray, red, blue and tan. In 1927 the navy, tan and cadet blue were still available, but brighter shades such as tangerine, pink, French blue, green and heliotrope had replaced the others. These changes in brightness and number of colors per print reflect the changes we see in quilts in these years, with 1925 marking a mid-point in the transition between the two styles.

31

Judges at the 1933 Century of Progress quilt contest display the prize-winning quilt, pieced and stuffed by Mattie Black, quilted by an unknown quilter and entered by Margaret Rogers Caden. Behind them are the runners up. Although the contest rules encouraged innovative designs commemorating the Chicago World's Fair, the judges obviously preferred traditional designs and eye-catching quilting.

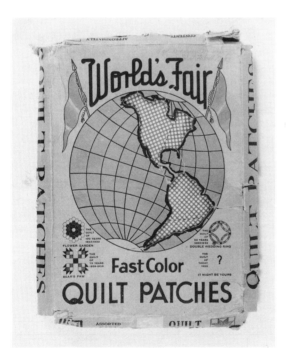

During the scrap quilt craze of the '30s several companies sold cotton scraps; this never-used box was ordered through the Sears catalog for 25 cents. Courtesy of Helen Berger.

The new well-to-do quiltmakers of the twenties and thirties often had the leisure time to spend on the handwork that applique, embroidery and fine quilting required. Less affluent women, especially during the Depression, had no choice but to spend their time at home, time they often filled by doing inexpensive, time-consuming needlework. As a result, quality in quiltmaking took a turn for the better. Quilt contests sponsored by department stores, newspapers and magazines inspired a whole generation of quiltmakers to new competitive heights. A Sears, Roebuck and Company contest at the 1933 Chicago World's Fair drew nearly 25,000 entrants, a gauge of quiltmaking's popularity at the time (67). Contests during the current revival of interest and competitiveness in quiltmaking have not yet attracted 10,000 contestants (68).

The middle class vogue for quilting developed despite the fact that quilts continued to serve as bedding, hobby and livelihood for the poor rural families made even poorer by the Depression. Women who could afford neither the patterns nor the fabric for iris medallion designs and fan quilts of cotton sateen adapted some of the new patterns and color schemes to their tied comforters and quilts pieced of sewing scraps and recycled feed sacks.

Cotton fabric bags were nothing new (white sugar sacking fabric is apparent on mid- to late-nineteenth century quilts), but it wasn't until the 1930s that manufacturers began using printed fabrics for feed sacks. Wartime fabric rationing in the early 1940s encouraged use of feed sacks for clothing and curtains as well as quilts. The fabric restrictions contributed ultimately to the end of the quiltmaking craze. Also, women's entrance into the work force left them little time for sewing; wartime paper shortages put pattern companies out of business and reduced the number of quiltmaking features in the press. In the late forties and fifties, tastemakers found little room for quiltmaking in their home design and hobby pages, a trend that would continue until the beginnings of the current revival in the 1970s.

The social context of quiltmaking underwent fewer changes than the styles during the 1925-1950 period. Women still made friendship quilts for which periodicals printed appropriate patterns, both new and antique. Ruby McKim, writing in 1929, in the *Kansas City Star*, offered an "Album Pattern . . . a real old-timer". She suggested setting the signed blocks with alternate white squares and warned, "Be sure that the names on each block run in the same direction".

32

While her husband was fighting in World War II, an unknown woman spent the time making the baby quilt she shows in this photo dated 1942. Collection of Larry Schwarm.

Some women of the period favored outline embroidered designs for their friendship quilts. These multi-colored pastel designs worked on white cotton followed in the mid-nineteenth century sampler album tradition, wherein each maker contributed a different block. Twentieth-century album quiltmakers often obtained their designs by purchasing pre-stamped blocks or iron-on design transfers. Fewer signature quilts from this era were fundraisers, although there were still seamstresses willing to embroider hundreds of names on a quilt for a good cause. Groups who met for recreation also made signature quilts; many friendship quilts from this period owe their origins to Sunday school classes, charitable organizations and social groups with names like Busy Fingers or the Jolly Quilters.

Women making tops during these years often "hired the quilting out" to groups or individuals. Of fourteen contestants answering a questionnaire in the 1970s and '80s about their 1933 Century of Progress entries, five indicated that the quilting had been done by a different seamstress. Typical of the division of labor is the making of Rose Tekippe's entry. In 1982 Ada Tekippe Schlick re-

Morning Glory quilt, made by Iffie Espey Arnold (1870–1945) in Emporia, Kansas. Estimated date: 1930–1945. Appliqued and quilted. Cotton. Collection: Helen F. Spencer Museum of Art, the University of Kansas. Gift of Iras A. Armour.

Iffie Espey Arnold was a friend of Rose Kretsinger whose applique and quilting designs inspired the quiltmakers of Emporia. The feather quilting is a Kretsinger design and she is said to have originated the *Morning Glory* and *Trellis* pattern (although original designs in the age of the printed pattern are rare). This quilt is single-bed size (65 1/2 × 80 inches), one of a pair.

called her family and friends in Fort Atkinson, Iowa, cooperating on a New York Beauty. Sister Rose pieced the top (from a design found on a Mountain Mist batting wrapper). Ada marked the quilting designs with a hard lead No. 2 pencil that would rub off after the stitching was done. Mother Anna's quilting group, the Twelve Faithful Quilters (one of two she belonged to), did the quilting in the Tekippe home. The batting was Dixie Queen brand, bought in the larger town of Decorah, fifteen miles away. The thread, Stiles Waxed, was ordered from New York. Like the batting, it was chosen for quality; fine materials allowed smaller stitches. The quilters worked so closely together "no difference can be seen . . . in any of the stitches. They all averaged ten to twelve stitches to the inch, which is very fine quilting" (69). The quilt won Rose a $25 prize as one of thirty national finalists.

The Twelve Faithful Quilters obviously held themselves to high standards. A number of the

Quilting did not die out in rural America after World War II, although few new patterns or styles evolved until the 1970s. Here women in Vinland, Kansas, show off a variety of their quilts at the Grange Fair in the late 1940s.

masterpiece quilts from the era were quilted by such professionals. They often charged for their services by the yard of quilting thread used, extra for densely quilted pieces.

As the quilting fad of the '20s and '30s faded, quality quilting and quiltmaking became rarer. The formula looks propagated by the pattern companies and the magazines survived. Rose Kretsinger, writing in the early '30s had criticized the trend: "Women are depending more upon the printed pattern sheet to save time and labor. These having been used time and again often become very tiresome" (70). Her low opinion of the fad quilts was not shared by many quiltmakers, who went on producing Double Wedding Ring, Dresden Plate, Grandmother's Flower Garden and Sunbonnet Sue quilts. It wasn't until the 1970s, around the time of the nation's Bicentennial, that new styles, new looks and a new emphasis on creativity and craftsmanship brought quiltmaking out of its mid-twentieth century doldrums.

CLUES IN FIBER AND FABRIC

Of the many clues to date in a quilt, the two most important are fabric and style. Knowledge of fabric includes an understanding of fiber, textile construction, dye and printing processes and the changes in them over the years. Textiles are so important it will take the next three chapters to do them justice.

Until this century, textiles were obtained from four natural sources—silk and wool derived from animals, or linen and cotton derived from plants. From these four major fibers, textile manufacters produced hundreds of fabrics, many of which were made into quilts.

Fashion, technology, politics and necessity have all affected the rise and fall of different types of cloth. Fabrics that the colonists knew well, such as corduroy and denim, are just as familiar to us today. Other fabrics mentioned in their European orders or newspaper advertisements are no longer in use. Their quaint names, like hum-hum, cherryderry and calimanco, have been passed on, but in some cases only the names have been passed on; we have no idea what type of cloth they describe. Many names have changed meaning as well. Textile terms that mean one type of fabric to us may have meant something completely different one hundred or even fifty years ago. Today a calico is a cotton printed with a small scale figure; the word once meant any cotton—printed, plain or white. Chintz once meant any printed cloth, usually with a glaze. Today we buy either plain or printed chintz; but both with a surface glaze, which is what makes a fabric a chintz to us.

Spinning and Weaving

Before it can be woven into cloth, fiber obtained from the cocoon of the silkworm, the fleece of the sheep, the boll of the cotton or the stem of the flax plant must be processed and spun into yarn using a hand spinning wheel or a factory machine. It is woven by interlacing the warp (the threads that run the length of the fabric) with the weft or filler (the threads that run across the fabric). Quality is dependent upon both the yarn and the weave, including the strength, weight and twist of the yarn, the number of plies in the yarn, and the compactness of the weave. Compactness is measured by thread count, a higher number of threads per inch indicating a more compact, more durable, higher quality fabric. To measure thread count, one determines the number of warp and weft threads in a square inch of fabric. Tobacco cloth, a cotton used to shade tobacco plants (and one that occasionally is used in quilts), has a low thread count of 20. Fine percale sheeting has a thread count of 200. The standard plain weave cotton, the kind typically seen in quilts, has a thread count from around 50 to 75.

There are three basic weaving patterns, plain, satin and twill, from which all others are derived. The myriad fabrics we find in old quilts are variations on these fundamental weaves. The type of weave is not often a clue to date, since the basic weaves are common in all time periods, but a few combinations of fiber and weave were popular at certain times and can be indicators of dates.

PLAIN WEAVE

In plain weave, the most common, each of the filling yarns passes successively under and over warp yarn so that rows alternate. An equal number of warp and filler threads show in an alternating pattern. Plain weave is also called taffeta or tabby weave. Because plain weave is so common in all fibers, it is not a good clue to age.

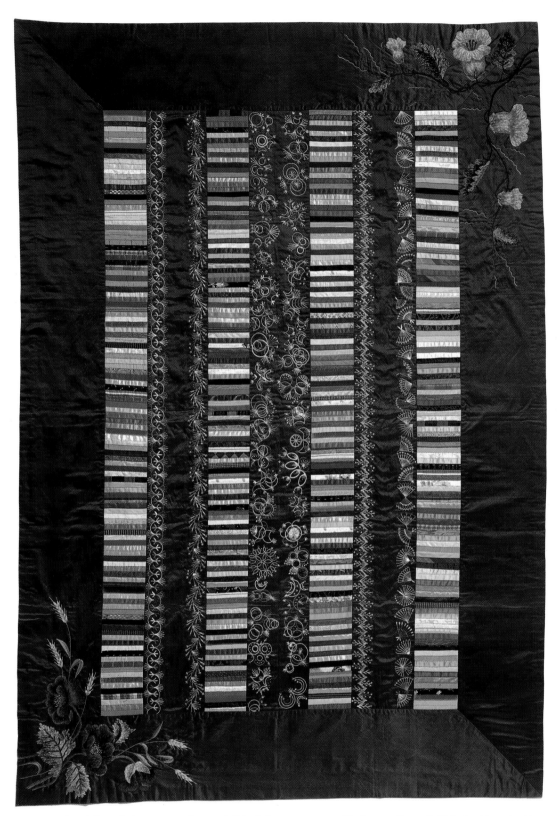

Roman Stripe quilt made by Lucy Weeks Kendall in Oakland, California. Estimated date: 1880–1900. Pieced, embroidered and tied. Silk. Collection: Joyce Gross.

Silk show quilts embellished with embroidery were popular during the last half of the nineteenth century when silk was widely available.

TWILL WEAVE

In a twill weave the regular under-over pattern is varied to produce diagonal lines on the face of the cloth. The filler yarn may go under one and over two warp threads. Familiar twill patterns include gabardine and denim. Many wool quilts include twill weaves and the weave itself is rarely a clue.

One distinctive fabric that points to a specific date is a twill weave cotton called cretonne. It is unglazed, has a large print and was popular for furnishings (curtains and upholstery) from about 1880 through 1920. It appears in quilt and comforter backings, and sometimes turns up in scrap quilts from that era.

SATIN WEAVE

In a satin weave more filling threads float on the surface of the fabric; in the repeat each filler yarn passes over many yarns in an irregular pattern that produces a surface sheen. In a warp-face satin the process is the same, but the warp yarn is the surface yarn. Because textile terms are not absolute, there is some confusion as to the difference between satin and sateen; some references make the distinction that a satin is a warp-faced satin weave and sateen is a filler-faced satin (1), but others do not distinguish (2). In the vernacular, satin generally refers to silk or silky-looking synthetics and sateen to cotton fabrics. For the purposes of this book I will use the vernacular distinction and call cotton fabric *sateen* and silk or silky fabric *satin*.

A lustrous top surface is a good clue to a satin weave fabric; the back is usually dull. Often the lustrous look has been enhanced by finishes like glazing or polishing.

Cotton sateens in solid pastel colors are a strong clue to a 1925-1950 date. Though cotton sateen in prints and plains was manufactured earlier, and was included in nineteenth-century scrap quilts, quiltmakers during the second quarter of the twentieth century began a fashion for making quilts entirely of sateen. Satin of synthetic fabrics was also popular for whole cloth quilts and tied comforters during this era. Puffy satin coverlets from the second quarter of the twentieth century were both manufactured items and a home quilted craft.

Finishing

Glazes are applied to plain and twill fabrics as well as to satins. To glaze or calender a fabric, the cloth is passed between rollers or calenders that produce a shiny surface through heat and pressure. Glazed effects are also produced by adding substances like wax, egg white or resins. The glaze, whether mechanical or chemical, often fades with laundering, although some finishes are more durable than others.

Calendered wool was popular for the top fabric in whole-cloth and pieced wool quilts dating from the last half of the eighteenth century through the 1840s. This fine-woven, shiny wool is an excellent clue to that era.

Calendering also produces surface effects like moire and water marked fabrics. Other finishes are the stiffening we see in taffetas and the napping in flannel. Napped fabrics are combed with wire to raise the surface fibers and make them warmer or more durable. Cotton flannel was a distinctive quilt backing fabric in the last quarter of the nineteenth century and first quarter of this one. Plaid and striped flannels back many wool quilts from that era.

Pile Weaves

To make fabrics with a pile, like velvet or corduroy, an extra yarn is added during weaving. It projects from the foundation weave and is cut evenly to form the soft surface. Velvets formerly were woven of silk and/or cotton fibers; today they are generally of synthetics.

Pile weaves are a good clue to the 1875-1925 era when velvets, corduroys and plushes were combined with brocades, taffetas and satins in Crazy Quilts and other types of show quilts. These quilts are commonly described as being of silks, velvets and satins. To be accurate the description should be "silk velvets and satins", since the fiber is silk and the fabrics are velvets and satins.

Homespun and Homewoven Fabric in Quilts

The term "homespun" is often used to describe the fabric in quilts from the colonial era through

37

the recent past. The colonists grew flax to make linen and raised sheep for wool; they spun the fiber at home and then wove it into clothing, bedding and household linens. By the 1800s farm families were self-sufficient at manufacturing their own household textiles from these fibers (3). However, town and city dwellers and the upper class, who seem to have produced most of the quilts that survive from this era, more likely purchased their fabrics from importers. Inventories, import orders and newspaper advertisements describing fabrics testify to the lively international fabric trade with the colonies. Neither the written material nor the fabric in these quilts gives much support to the theory that most early quilts were of homespun fabrics.

A comment on the prevalence of imported fabric was the mid-eighteenth century movement advocating homespun as a symbol of colonial pride. Anti-British Americans boycotted all imports, including fabric, which were funneled by law through English ports no matter where they were manufactured. Anna Green Winslow noted in her diary in February, 1771: "As I am, as we say, a Daughter of Liberty, I chuse to wear as much of our own manufactory as possible" (4). Colonial historian Alice Morse Earl quoted an undated pre-Revolutionary article in the *Boston Newsletter* reporting on some of Anna's sister Daughters of Liberty. "A number of thirty-three respectable ladies of the town met at sunrise with their wheels to spend the day at the house of the Rev'd Jedidiah Jewell in the laudable design of a spinning match. At an hour before sunset, the ladies then appearing neatly dressed, principally in homespun, a polite and generous repast of American production was set for their entertainment"(5). The men in Harvard University's 1768 and Brown University's 1769 graduating classes made it a point to dress for commencement in homespun, a symbolic gesture that indicates homespun was a novelty, at least among the upper classes.

The homespun fabric worn during the awakenings of independence that led to the Revolution was probably woven of wool or linen or a combination of the two. Silk and cotton, being harder to cultivate and to spin into yarn, were far less frequently spun at home.

Home-produced wool and linen did make their way into American quilts. Late-eighteenth and early-nineteenth-century glazed wool quilts (usually called linsey-woolsey quilts) often had backs of homespun and woven fabric (6). Nineteenth-century linsey quilts and other utility wool quilts have been passed down with reliable family stories of homespun linen, wool and combination fabrics. One clue to homespun wool is the ply of the yarn, or the number of wool threads in the twist. Single-ply wool yarn may be homespun; double-ply is probably mill spun yarn (which could, once purchased, be woven at home) (7).

Many family stories describe the cotton backings of quilts as homespun, but there is not enough evidence of home spinning and weaving of cotton on a scale to support the tales. By the 1830s when cotton was becoming the most common fiber for quilts, homespun fabric of any type was increasingly rare in settled communities. Most of the backings called homespun cotton today are in reality a factory-produced, natural-colored, coarsely-woven cotton cloth, spun and woven on machines, but to lower standards than the finer and more expensive factory-produced cottons in the quilt's top. Early nineteenth-century American cotton mills specialized in producing a coarse cloth, and it may be that the cloth on the back of a quilt is American made, while the top is of finer, imported cottons.

Homespun cotton is largely an American myth, and the facts are difficult to separate from the myth at this point. Home spinning unfortunately has been confused with home weaving. Home weaving of cotton was far more common than home spinning. After the development of the cotton spinning industry, many home weavers purchased cotton yarn for home weaving. There is much evidence that home woven cotton was produced from factory spun yarn. In an 1817 how-to book on home cloth production, the chapter on preparing and dyeing cotton begins, "The yarn is commonly received from factories in five pound bundles" (8). An 1819 newspaper article outlining the rules for the Hillsborough County (New Hampshire) Fair invites weavers to bring their home manufactured cloth for competition, and reminds them that it "must not have been wove or the yarn of which it is made, spun at a manufactory, except the cotton yarn . . . which may be factory yarn" (9). Account books of mid-nineteenth coverlet manufacturers indicate that the clients often brought in their own hand spun wool yarn, while the weaver supplied factory spun cotton yarn for the combination fiber coverlets (10).

Although cotton spinning at home was not common, exceptions occurred. In the southeast where cotton grew easily, self-sufficient plantations manufactured fabric from field to clothing. John Lawson, who traveled through North Carolina in 1760, noted that the women "made a great deal of cloth of their own cotton, wool and flax" (11). In 1786 Thomas Jefferson wrote that

Captioned "Primitive Cotton Factory in Alabama", this photograph illustrates the steps in cotton production from the raw cotton in the basket on the left through woven fabric. The woman seated in the chair is carding the cotton with combs. The younger woman appears to be spinning the cotton onto the spindle of her walking wheel (more commonly used for wool and linen). The child winds the yarn onto a reel, and the woman at the loom weaves the fabric. The two different shades of yarn may indicate they are preparing cloth of both cotton and wool, or the darker fabric may be dyed cotton. Smithsonian Institution Negative 22760.

Americans in the four southernmost states wore a homespun cotton, "as well manufactured as the calicoes of Europe" (12).

During the Civil War a Union embargo on manufactured cloth from Europe and the northern states created a black market in the south where calico sold for $25, $50 and $100 per yard (13). In some areas daughters of the confederacy were forced to swear an oath of allegiance to the Union before they could purchase cloth, a moral dilemma each had to solve in her own way; the patriotic solution was homespun, some of it likely cotton (14). In cotton-producing frontier areas like Texas, factory cloth, cheap in the industrialized east by the 1840s, was so difficult and expensive to obtain that pioneer housewives grew, spun and wove their own cotton fabric.

Two tests apply to any tale of homespun cotton. Was the quilt made in a cotton-growing area? Was factory-spun cotton so unavailable that the maker had to invest her time in hand spinning cotton? Only if both answers are yes, is the fabric possibly true homespun.

Discriminating homespun yarn from factory spun yarn or homewoven fabric from manufactured cloth is difficult. The crudity of the cloth is not always a clue. Many home weavers took great pride in the excellence of their craft; their product would be well-made, elegant and evenly woven. On the other hand, factories produced cheap, imperfect, quickly-made cloth for utility purposes such as quilt backing.

The width of the fabric is not a reliable clue either. The eighteenth- and nineteenth-century hand looms produced cloth 60, 45, 30, and 27 inches wide(15). Manufactured cloth was often of the same width; cotton cloth sold by Sears, Roebuck and Company from 1895 to 1900 came in widths of 25, 27, 29, 3l, 32, 36, 40, 42, 45, 54, 68, 80, 81, 88, 90, 96 and 104 inches.

Because handwoven cottons spanned the entire nineteenth century and may have continued into the twentieth in rural areas (where quilts were also likely to have been made), and because they are difficult to detect, it is probably not worth the effort to try to discriminate between hand and factory woven cottons for dating purposes.

Determining Fiber Content

Some knowledge of fiber content is useful in dating. Linen was less common after 1850, so its presence in a quilt is a significant clue to an early date. Cotton thread for sewing and quilting was rare before 1800; thread in an eighteenth-century quilt would most likely be of linen or wool. To properly study early quilts it is often imperative to be able to discriminate cotton from linen.

Knowledge of fiber can also be useful on a practical level. Wool fabric requires different storage from cotton and linen because of its susceptibility to moth damage. Before wet cleaning any quilt, one should be sure about the fiber content in the top, the backing and the batting. Enough antique cotton quilts had wool batting to make it worth the time to make sure the batting won't shrink.

Visual experience with different weaves and yarns helps to identify fibers. When accuracy is important, more technical methods like microscopic examination, chemical solubility tests and the burning test are called for. Yarn fibers examined under a microscope differ significantly. Textile scientists also dissolve yarn in chemicals and observe the reactions that indicate different fibers and dyes. The most accessible test, requiring no special equipment, is the burning test, in which a swatch or raveled yarns from the fabric are consumed by fire. The ash and burning pattern differ for each fiber. See page 41 for a chart of the properties of various fibers revealed by burning. Raveling a thread from an old quilt is usually possible and gaining experience with burning is easy. Just remember to hold the thread with tweezers and

move it slowly into the match flame; some fibers can go up very quickly and burn your fingers.

BURNING TESTS

Cut a thread, a yarn or a small swatch of fabric (threads or yarn are usually the only option in quilts). Hold it in a tweezers and move it slowly towards a small flame such as a candle. Observe the way the yarn acts as it approaches the flame, as it burns in the flame and after removal from the flame. Notice the odor as it burns and the ash that remains. Burn only half of your sample. If you suspect a mixed fabric with different warp and weft, test both lengthwise and crosswise yarns. (See chart on opposite page.)

The burning test is most useful in discriminating between cellulosic fibers (from plants—cotton, rayon and linen) and protein fibers (from animals—silk and wool). It is of little use in distinguishing cotton or rayon from linen, since they burn in a similar fashion. Microscopic examination is usually necessary.

For more information about microscopic, chemical solubility, and burning tests for fabric see a textile science book such as *Textiles* by Hollen, Sadler and Langford (16). A simple microscope and experience with different fibers will refine your skills in fiber identification. Ask a friend who teaches science or home economics to get you started.

For most dating purposes an educated guess based on the look and the feel of the fabric is sufficient. To help you train your hand and eye, go to fabric shops; ignore the fiber content signs and labels until after you've handled and examined any material and made a guess. Then check the label for feedback on your accuracy. You will find yourself improving your fiber identification skills with practice.

Silk

Silk is derived from the cocoon of the silk worm. It has always been a luxury fiber, valued for its long fiber (a filament that extends 1000 to 1300 yards), its strength and its lustrous look. It takes dyes well; including the desirable deep, vivid colors. Pure, unadulterated silk is strong and rather resistant to deterioration, although it is

BURNING TESTS

Fiber	Approaching the Flame	In the Flame	After Removal from Flame	Odor	Ash After the Flame
Silk	Fuses; curls away from flame, smolders	Burns slowly; Sizzles and sputters	Stops burning	Burning hair	Round shiny, brittle, black beads
Wool	Fuses; curls away from flame, smolders	Burns slowly; Sizzles and sputters	Stops burning	Burning hair	Irregularly-shaped, brittle, black ash
Linen	Scorches; does not fuse or shrink	Burns quickly	Continues to burn with afterglow	Burning paper	Light gray, feathery ash
Cotton	Scorches; does not fuse or shrink	Burns quickly	Continues to burn with afterglow	Burning paper	Light gray, feathery ash
Rayon	Scorches; ignites	Burns quickly	Continues to burn	Burning paper	Light gray, feathery ash
Nylon	Fuses; shrinks from flame	Burns quickly; melts	Stops burning	Celery	Round gray beads, not brittle
Polyester	Fuses; shrinks from flame	Burns slowly; melts	Stops burning	Sweet	Hard, round black beads

This table has been adapted from burning tests in several textile science books, among them Hollen, Norma; Jane Sadler and Ann Langford, *Textiles* (5th Edition). McMillan, New York, 1979.

more susceptible to damage by sunlight than other natural fibers. Certain dyes, particularly brown and black, can cause tendering or rotting of the fabric. Silk fabric is often weighted with metal salts deposited on the fiber to improve its feel and appearance. Late nineteenth-century fabric manufacturers found methods of doubling the weight of silk fabric, to the delight of Victorian ladies who loved the rustle that weighted silk added to their dresses. Weighted silks deteriorate and break due to the abrasion of the metal salts; unfortunately they were popular for the late-Victorian Crazy Quilts and Log Cabins that we find today in such bad shape.

Silk was combined with other fibers. Combination of fibers in a fabric can sometimes be detected by characteristic patterns of wear, with the silk warp deteriorating faster than a cotton or wool weft. In a cotton-silk combination fabric, the silk sometimes disappears, leaving nothing but cotton weft yarns.

Silk fiber has generally always been imported to America. While the textile industries were developing, entrepreneurs hoped to raise silk worms on mulberry trees in the U.S., but the northern climate was too cold for mulberry trees and the southern states found cotton more profitable (17). By the 1830s the age-old conflict between a labor-intensive industry and the cheaper price of imports all but finished off the infant U.S. silk culture (18). At the end of the nineteenth-century, America became an important silk weaving country with factories weaving silk yarn imported from China.

Imported silk fabric, generally from China or France, was used in whole-cloth quilts during the colonial years. Although no examples from the seventeenth century survive, descriptions of silk quilts in wills and inventories exist. In 1689, Jane Jocy willed her "silken quilt" (19). In 1744, Dorothy Stevens willed "a cradle quilt, silk on one side calico on the other" (20). In 1753, Elizabeth

Coates Paschel willed her "silk bed quilt" (21). The cradle quilt and bedquilt we can assume were bedding; the other silk quilts may have been quilted petticoats which were fashionable in wool and silk in the eighteenth century.

The oldest date-inscribed American bedquilts found in the literature are silk whole-cloth quilts, dated 1746 and 1761 (see page 14). The oldest dated patchwork quilt on the American continent (1726), the *McCord Quilt*, has a border of silk brocade framing silk patches among scraps of cotton and linen (see page 14). The quilt is believed to have been made in England, but it is typical of the later eighteenth-century patchwork quilts made in America (22). The medallion format, the fields of simple patchwork and the mixing of scraps of different fiber content were common design traits. Fabrics were too scarce to allow patchworkers to choose fabrics all of one fiber. Silk was imported and expensive in the colonies and the young United States, but so were the other fabrics included in quilts. The concept that a seamstress should segregate her fabrics into cotton for a cotton quilt and silk for a silk quilt did not develop until the nineteenth century when fabric became more plentiful.

As cotton became commonplace and thus inexpensive, in the second quarter of the nineteenth century, all-cotton patchwork quilts became the dominant style, and silk quilts and those incorporating more than one fiber became increasingly rare. Silk, in turn, became more available in the mid-nineteenth century with the expansion of Chinese trade and a silk show-quilt style developed parallel to the calico cotton quilt style. These mid-nineteenth century silk quilts tended to resemble English quilts—mosaics made of shapes like hexagons, rather than of block-style patterns. Silk quilts were often pieced English-style over paper templates, rather than with American-style running stitch seams. They reflected the influence of ladies' magazines that recommended English-style patchwork and silk fabric as the only elegant quilts. In 1859, English author Mrs. Pullan characterized cotton patchwork as unworthy of "either candle or gas light" (23). In 1882 Englishwomen Caulfeild and Saward described "silk . . . patchwork (as) suitable for cushions, hand screens, fire screens, glove and handkerchief cases and pincushions; cloth patchwork for carriage rugs, couvrepieds, and poor people's quilts. . ." (24). American Florence Hartley defended American-style cotton quilts in the *Ladies Hand Book of Fancy and Ornamental Work*. "We think the real old patchwork of bits of calico infinitely prettier

At the turn of the century, a father and child relax in Victorian style with potted plants in the yard, a silk puff patchwork pillow on the porch and a velvet crazy-patch pillow in the grass. Author's collection.

than bits of silk sewed together for parlor ornaments" (25).

Through the second half of the century, silk quilts and parlor ornaments became increasingly popular in America as the influence of the magazines widened and the price of silk dropped. By 1900 American mills produced 66% of the world's silk fabric (26), and it sometimes seems to us that two-thirds of that wound up in American Crazy Quilts. Historian Rachel Maines points out that the silk Crazy Quilt fad that gripped the country in the 1880s was directly related to the mass-produced domestic silks (27).

Soon after the turn of the century the silk quilt fad died. Crazy Quilts and their cousins, the Fans and Log Cabins, were more likely to be made of wools or wools combined with silks. By the mid-1920s silk quilts were again unusual. Maines attributes the end of the craze for silk quilts to the Chinese Civil War in the early twentieth century when silk yarn exports dwindled and the price of silk here relative to other fabrics increased.

Since silk waxed and waned with fashion and availability, the presence of silk in a quilt is a good clue to date. The majority of the silk quilts we come across were made in the last quarter of the nineteenth century. More unusual are mid-nineteenth century silk quilts, and even rarer, eighteenth- and early-nineteenth-century silk quilts. Discriminating whether a silk quilt is early or later means looking at color scheme, weight, style and pattern. Earlier silk quilts have a lighter color scheme; later silk quilts are darker with black a popular color. Earlier silks are lighter in weight;

Needlecraft magazine still offered a half pound of silk scraps in 1928 as a premium for soliciting subscriptions. A good deal of the silk in late nineteenth-century and early twentieth- century quilts was factory cutaways rather than home-sewing scraps. Author's collection.

late-Victorian weighted silks are heavier, even to the eye, and the later weighted silks have an unfortunate tendency to deteriorate. Style and pattern differ significantly. Early silk quilts will be of simple patchwork, usually organized in a medallion format. Mid-nineteenth century quilts are commonly mosaic patterns with hexagons the most popular design. Late nineteenth-century silk quilts are often pieced on a foundation with Crazy Quilts, Log Cabins, string quilts and Fans typical.

Silk quilts are typically embellished with embroidery, which also changed over the years. Late Victorian quilts have two distinctive embroidery styles not found in earlier quilts—outline embroidery with no shading in the design and seam lines covered with fancy linear patterns like featherstitching.

Wool

Wool is the fiber from the fleece of an animal, usually a sheep, although relatives like Cashmere goats and South American vicuñas produce luxurious wools. Wool is prized for its durability, flexibility and warmth. It also takes dye well, compared to cotton and linen that are more resistant to natural dyes.

Two hundred, one hundred and even fifty years ago wool appeared in dozens of weaves and fabrics that are no longer produced in the age of synthetics and standardization. We occasionally come across old quilts with wool fabrics like calimanco, a glazed satin-weave wool, that remind us how limited our current view of wool is. Today we can hardly imagine wearing wool in the summer or as a wedding dress or a petticoat.

Raising sheep, spinning wool yarn and weaving wool fabric were American home crafts and cottage industries during colonial days, although much fine wool was imported from Europe (28), a fact revealed by the surviving eighteenth- and early nineteenth-century wool quilts, which generally include imported wool fabric. England effectively discouraged colonial wool production by forbidding the export of wool beyond the boundaries of any individual colony (29). What was produced here was of low quality because the colonists did not systematically breed sheep for their fleece. In his journal, Peter Kalm, a Swedish visitor, commented on wool production in Phila-

Log Cabin spread, Barn Raising Set. Maker unknown. Made in Lewisburg, Pennsylvania. Estimated date: 1875–1900. Pieced. Collection: Smithsonian Institution, Negative # 76–2663.
Log Cabin designs were one of the few patterns that crossed over from silk show quilts to everyday calico quilts to wool comforters. There are 5500 silk "logs" in this one.

delphia around 1750, "You'll meet with excellent masters in all trades and many things are made here fully as well as in England. Yet no manufactures especially for making fine wool cloth are established. Perhaps the reason is that it can be got with so little difficulty from England and that the breed of sheep which is brought over degenerates in process of time and affords but a coarse wool" (30).

Post-Revolutionary efforts at developing a self-sufficient wool industry in the new United States came to a sad end in 1793 when, the story goes, the first pair of high-quality Spanish Merino sheep imported to Boston as breeding stock were acci-

Whole-cloth glazed wool quilt, made by Esther Wheat in Conway, Massachusetts. Estimated date: 1775–1840. Quilted. Wool. Collection: Smithsonian Institution, Negative # 73–5251.

Glazed wool was an excellent fabric for showing off fancy quilting. The surface sheen, designed to imitate more expensive silk, reflected the light beautifully.

dentally eaten (31). Within a few decades, however, descendants of luckier Merino sheep and successfully imported Saxony breeds were producing an adequate grade of wool.

Although the first American woolen mill, established in 1788, preceded the first cotton mill, the wool industry soon lagged behind. The typical early nineteenth-century wool shop had difficulty obtaining yarn for their few looms. Without spinning factories, weaving factories could not grow (32). Factory production began to accelerate around 1830 and matured during the Civil War,

which encouraged huge growth in both textile production and clothing manufacture for wool uniforms. After the war the wool industry converted to producing fabric for civilian clothing. As the readymade clothing industry developed, home production of wool cloth and clothing declined.

The nineteenth-century American wool industry never achieved the success of American cotton manufacture because cotton's popularity outpaced wool's. In 1800 wool accounted for 78% of the world's fabric production, cotton only 4%. By 1900, wool had dropped to 14% of the world's

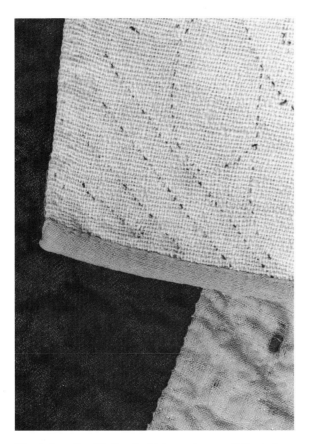

Wool pieced quilt (detail). Maker unknown. Estimated date: 1775–1840. Pieced and quilted. Wool. Collection: Elizabeth M. Watkins Community Museum.

The detail shows several different wool fabrics in a single quilt. The center of the quilt, the dark fabric, may have been a quilted petticoat. The fabric is a navy blue twill weave, unglazed and probably imported from England. The coarse weave in the upper right corner is part of the backing—a tan wool in plain weave that may be homespun and home woven.

production, and cotton had risen to 76% (33).

Wool quilts reflected the availability and diversity of the fabric available to American women. The earliest surviving wool quilts are primarily of imported fabric, in the style commonly called the linsey-woolsey quilt, a name that incorrectly implies a combination linen and wool fiber. Experts who examine these late eighteenth- and early nineteenth-century quilts have determined that the tops are woven of both wool warp and wool weft. If there is any linen in the quilts it is in the backs, which are occasionally a combination fabric (34). Because the top of the quilt is wool, a better name to describe the style is whole-cloth wool quilts. Popular from about 1775 through 1840, whole-cloth wool quilts are closely related to the fashion for quilted petticoats, worn in the United States during the seventeenth century (35). Some whole-cloth wool quilts are evidently

reworked petticoats, made of out-of-fashion clothing too valuable to be discarded.

The whole-cloth wool quilt was a distinctive style, using distinctive fabrics, but wool also appeared in early scrap patchwork quilts made entirely of pieces of both homespun and imported wool or of wool pieces combined with linen, cotton and silk patches. Wool was not as common as other fibers in the combination quilts, probably because of its incompatible, heavier weight. *Anna Tuel's Marriage Quilt* is an exception to the rule. It is dated 1785, and in it Anna's mother combined two separate styles. She pieced linens, silks and cottons in a central patchwork field and bordered it with a glazed wool quilted in a feather pattern.

Once the craze for calico quilts began in the l840s, wool fabric faded in importance. Not a single wool quilt appeared among the 339 quilts in the database dated between 1840 and 1865, although there are undated wool quilts as diverse as mosaics, album quilts and applique floral vases attributed to those years. When a mid-nineteenth century quiltmaker decided to use wool, it seemed more a mattter of personal whim than fashion. After the Civil War, with the rise of inexpensive domestic wool, a new style developed for wool pieced quilts in the Log Cabin pattern and its variations like the Pineapple. These designs were constructed on a foundation and were as likely to be tied together as quilted. Wool Log Cabin quilts usually date from about 1865 to 1920.

It is not clear whether the style for tied quilts freed the quiltmaker to use heavier wools since she was no longer required to quilt them, or whether the abundance of inexpensive wools inspired an increase in tied quilts. In the last quarter of the nineteenth-century, far more heavy wools were used in a variety of pieced patterns. One typical turn-of-the century wool style was the Brickwork comforter made of rectangles, which were often precut suiting samples. Tied wool comforters usually date from the 1880s through the 1950s with the decades around 1910 being a prime time for the style. Wool utility quilts and comforters have almost disappeared with the post-World War II rise of synthetic fabrics—today's utility quilt is a polyester doubleknit comforter.

Crazy Quilts, which developed in the early 1880s as extravaganzas of embroidered silk, changed character very quickly as quiltmakers began minimizing the embroidery and substituting practical wool scraps for the elegant silk patches. A generalization: A wool Crazy Quilt is likely to date from 1890 through the 1920s; an all-silk Crazy Quilt is more likely to be from 1880 to 1900.

Another distinctive wool style is the Amish

Pieced quilt. Made by the mother of Anna Tuel. Inscribed in applique: 1785. Pieced, appliqued and quilted. Wool, cotton, linen and silk. Collection of the Wadsworth Atheneum, Hartford, Connecticut. Gift of William L. Warren in memory of Florence Paull Berger.

The artist appliqued the words, "Anna Tuel her bedquilt given to her by her mother in the year Au 23 1785", in red wool in the center of this quilt that combines a number of techniques, styles and fabrics. The bright pink wool border is typical of the glazed wool whole-cloth quilts of the times; an unusual frame for a design pieced of silks, cottons and linens.

quilt. Amish quiltmakers used patterns and color schemes different from mainstream quiltmakers, but they continued to do fancy quilting on their wool quilts (made of relatively fine wools), while mainstream quiltmakers moved to heavier wools and tied their end-of-the-century coverlets. The quilted wool Amish quilts date from around 1880 through 1940.

Linen

Linen is made from the fibers in the stem of flax, a blue-flowered plant, easy to cultivate in many climates. Today linen is a luxury fabric, valued because of its crisp and irregular "natural" look. It is long-wearing, becoming softer and more beautiful with washing. Twice as strong as cotton, linen is still used to stitch shoe soles (36).

Linen, like other cellulose fibers derived from plants, is more resistant to dyes than protein fibers like wool and silk. Therefore it is often seen as a natural tan or white fabric, bleached rather than dyed. Another disadavantage is its quality of wrinkling easily.

Linen production is labor intensive; home production from seed to spun fiber took colonists 16 to 18 months (37). Wool and linen were the two homegrown, homespun and homewoven fibers from which they produced their clothing, bedding and household furnishing fabrics (still called linens, although made of other fibers). As factory-manufactured cotton became abundant in the first quarter of the nineteenth century, home linen production disappeared. Factory production of linen in the U.S. never developed to any degree, so linen in American quilts after 1850 is uncommon and, thus, a useful clue, especially to corroborate an early date. Discriminating between cotton and linen takes a practiced eye, and microscopic examination is probably the only way to be sure, since linen and cotton burn similarly and look quite a bit alike. To the eye, linen appears stiffer or crisper, and its luster differs from cotton's. Linen feels cold and smooth like cotton, but it has a more leathery feel. It is usually found as a white, plain cloth, but textile printers printed linen with the same designs as cottons, and printed linens are found in many pre-1830 quilts.

Before the development of the American cotton spinning industry in the 1790s, the short fibers of American grown cotton made it difficult to spin by hand and too weak to serve as warp threads. Americans who wove cotton would have used a warp of linen and a weft of cotton (38). English manufacturers were restricted by law to printing only a combination linen and cotton fabric, known as fustian. This information might seem useful to confirm a pre-1790 provenance for a quilt, with the argument being that a quilt with all cotton fabric in it could not have been made prior to 1790. However, some all-cotton fabric was imported both legally (plain white cotton was exempt from many of the English import acts) and illegally. Therefore, the presence of pure cotton fabric without a linen warp does not automatically negate an eighteenth-century date.

One of the earliest references to a quilt with linen in it is a 1759 order from George Washington

Unfinished bedcover made by Ann Taylor (1774-?) in Spotsylvania, Virginia. Inscribed in cross stitch: 1798. Pieced, appliqued and embroidered. Cotton and linen (embroidery thread is silk; construction thread is cotton). Collection: The Daughters of the American Revolution Museum, Washington, D.C. Loan of Anna Taliaferro Livingstone.

Ann Taylor's husband John was lost at sea in 1798; she embroidered a memorial to him and their family in the center of this medallion quilt. The fabrics are block-printed and hand painted (penciled) cottons and linens. The dog-tooth border that frames the central medallion is cut from a printed fabric estimated to date from 1795–1805. It may have been printed especially for quilts; there are tiny dotted lines along the edge that could be imitation quilting stitches. At least one other quilt from the era survives with the same border fabric.

who asked his London upholsterer for a 99 inch whole-cloth quilt of "Chintz Bleu Plate Cotton" backed with "Scotch Linnen" (39). The combination he ordered is not unusual; a patchwork quilt solely of linen is rare. Typically, quiltmakers combined cotton, linen and mixed cotton and linen fabrics in their early scrap patchwork and cut-out chintz coverlets. Mid-nineteenth-century quiltmakers who used linen might applique a design of figured cotton calico on a white linen background or incorporate an old but still serviceable linen sheet as the back to an all-cotton patchwork top.

At the end of the nineteenth-century the influential magazines promoted a quilting technique called "etching on linen" in which the quiltmaker used embroidery (usually stitched with red cotton thread) to outline pictures on a white background. The finished product might be a dresser scarf, a pillow cover or a block for a quilt. The dresser scarves may have been embroidered on linen, but the majority of the outline embroidered quilts are of cotton despite the dictates of the magazines. The average quiltmaker used an inexpensive white cotton, and many recycled sugar or flour sacking as background fabric for the embroidery.

Linsey and Linsey-woolsey Fabric

The term linsey-woolsey currently is used in this country to designate fabric with a linen warp and a wool weft. This combination fabric was common in eighteenth- and early nineteenth-century household furnishings such as bedhangings and blankets (40).

As with other textile terms, linsey-woolsey has been used to describe different things at different times. With regard to the composition of cloth, it seems most likely that in common American usage linsey or linsey-woolsey meant a combination of linen warp and wool weft when linen was in common use. When cotton became more available than linen in the second quarter of the nineteenth century, the term probably came to mean a combination of cotton warp and wool weft (41). In England, Caulfeild and Saward, in their 1882 *Dictionary of Needlework*, defined linsey as "a coarse mixed material of wool and flax" named after the town of Linsey in Suffolk (England) where it was first manufactured. They distinguished "woolsey" as a mixture of wool and cotton. They also mention, however, that the two names were sometimes used together, as "linsey-woolsey" to mean any combination of the fibers (42).

Confusion has been compounded because the terms "lincey" and "linsey" and "linsey-woolsey" also have been used to describe types of quilts. There are many historical references to "lincey quilts" or "linsey quilts". A 1780 Maryland inventory mentions a "new Linsey quilt country-made" (43), and an 1869 diary entry by Nancy Holman describes a "lincey quilt" (44). What type or types of quilts people meant in these references is difficult to determine today. Historian Merikay Waldvogel suggests that references from the middle of the nineteenth century are to a country or utility type of quilt, pieced of simple patterns, quilted plainly and made of coarse cloth combining wool and cotton, a conclusion drawn from the discovery in the Quilts of Tennessee project of several mid- to late-nineteenth-century examples of "linsey quilts" with these characteristics (45).

As discussed elsewhere, wool whole-cloth quilts are often mistakenly called "linsey-woolsey quilts". The Tennessee "linsey quilts" noted by Waldvogel are quite different from the earlier wool whole-cloth quilts, which were made of a fine wool fabric, often glazed or of a satin weave, and elegantly quilted.

Determining whether an antique quilt with at least some wool in the fiber content is of the plain linsey type or the fancy whole-cloth wool type is not difficult. Style characteristics, especially quilting, differ markedly between the types.

You can quickly learn to see the difference between tops made of cloth woven from one fiber (as used in wool whole-cloth quilts) and cloth woven from a combination of fibers (as used in the linsey quilts described by Waldvogel). Because wool accepts dye more easily than cotton and linen do, the same dye will not yield the same shade of color in the protein and cellulose yarns. Thus, a mixed fabric will have warp and weft of different shades, even if both were processed in the same dye bath. An even more striking contrast between warp and weft can be seen in mixed fabrics where the cellulose yarn has not been dyed. The differences in color are obvious whether the fabric is unpatterned or woven in a plaid or a stripe. Plaids, stripes and checks are common patterns for mixed cloth because they make a virtue of the color differences in warp and weft.

Determining whether the warp of a mixed fabric is cotton or linen is useful for dating (linen would likely be earlier), but requires detailed scrutiny. For general identification purposes it is necessary only to distinguish between an all-wool fabric and a mixed fabric.

Cotton

Cotton is a vegetable or cellulosic fiber that grows around the seeds in the bolls of the cotton plant. For thousands of years cotton has been cultivated for its fiber, which is valued for its comfort, washability and versatility. When compared to protein fibers like silk and wool, cotton is more resistant to dyes; another of its drawbacks is its tendency to yellow and become brittle when exposed to light, a problem all too apparent in old quilts.

Cotton will grow in sub-tropical climates around the world; differences in soil and weather produce different qualities of cotton. Plants that produce the longest staple or fiber (cotton staples range from 1/2 inch to 1 3/8 inches), the whitest and finest fiber are valued as the best cotton. Asiatic cottons, for example, produce coarse, short fibers, far less desirable than the long, fine, high-lustre fibers of Egyptian cotton.

Christopher Columbus discovered Sea Island cotton growing in the West Indies. Colonists transplanted seeds to Florida and other Southern colonies where the plants grew but with a characteristic short staple that made American cotton inferior to the near eastern varieties used by Europeans and Indians in textile production. It was not a profitable crop until late-eighteenth-century technical developments, especially Eli Whitney's 1793 cotton gin and Samuel Slater's first American cotton spinning mill in 1798, led to factory-spun cotton that was strong and of a consistent quality. The cotton spinning mills generated the yarn for an American cotton weaving industry,

established in 1814 when the first cotton cloth spun and woven on machines was produced in Massachusetts.

The technical advances in cotton production—the cotton gin for cleaning cotton, the spinning machines and the power loom—actually started America's industrial revolution. They led to significant changes in family and national life as the country moved from an agricultural to an industrial economy in New England and deeper into a slave economy in the agricultural south. The industrialization of cotton production also revolutionized the American quilt as cotton decreased in price in comparison to wages. Whereas the average seventeenth- and eighteenth-century American might have only a single change of clothes, nineteenth-century Americans could afford the luxury of fabric purchased specifically to make a quilt.

Abigail Adams wrote of paying $6 per yard for muslin imported from India in 1798. (46) In 1832, American calico was 37 1/2 cents a yard (47) and it dropped to around 12 cents by 1843 (48). By

Princess Feather quilt, made by Christina Hays Malcom (ca. 1820-ca. 1880) in Grant County, Indiana. Inscribed in the quilting: May 6, 1873. Appliqued and quilted. Cotton. Collection: Helen F. Spencer Museum of Art, the University of Kansas. Gift of Iva James.

Christina Malcom combined four colored cottons (a plain yellow-orange, two shades of double pink and a

green calico) on a plain white background in this *Princess Feather* quilt made for her son Jonathan. His niece donated twelve of Christina's cotton quilts to the Spencer Museum. All were made in the decades right after the Civil War when cotton calico was plentiful, well-made and inexpensive.

1872, calico at 4 cents a yard was so cheap that merchants in San Antonio used it as a substitute for brown wrapping paper (49). Factors that initially lowered the price of cotton fabric were mass production (as more yards were produced each yard dropped in price) and better technology (reducing the cost of labor per yard). Towards the end of the century, corner cutting by manufacturers maintained the low price. Calicoes with a low thread count, a limited range of colors and fewer details in the prints were the staple prints bought for everyday clothing and everyday quilts. These fabrics, which Sears, Roebuck and Company sold for 5 to 10 cents a yard in 1900, were probably similar to those that Mable Tuke Priestman had in mind when she complained in 1910 that the "old-time prints were certainly much more beautiful than those of today . . . The materials worked into these [antique] quilts bear little resemblance to the cheap aniline-dyed calicoes of today" (50).

One shortcut relied on by manufacturers in England and America was heavy sizing to give thin fabric more body. In 1882 Caulfeild and Saward warned that "cheap sorts (of calico) are dressed with a coating of lime and china clay to detect which a corner should be rubbed together in the hands wherein it will fall off in a powder" (51). Heavily sized and coated cotton fabrics are often apparent in unwashed quilts and unfinished tops and blocks from the 1875 to 1925 era.

Because cotton has been so popular in quilts, a knowledge of details such as print style and how colors have changed over the decades is useful both in identification and dating. Therefore, separate chapters are devoted to Clues in Color and Dyes (Chapter 4) and Clues in Cotton Prints (Chapter 5).

One general clue about cotton that can be useful in dating early quilts: although cotton fabric in a quilt is possible before 1800, the quilts from that era are more likely to contain combination cotton and linen fabrics and scraps of linen and silk as well as cotton. An all-cotton quilt is thus a strong clue to a date after 1800.

COTTON SEWING THREAD

A thorough examination of a quilt with a possible pre-1850 date should include a look at the thread. Thread fiber identification is particularly important for quilts made prior to 1800 or so, as any quilt made before 1800 more likely has been constructed with thread of silk, wool or linen than of cotton.

Cotton thread, which we take for granted today, was not commercially manufactured until about 1794 when, the story is told, Hannah Wilkinson Slater, wife of Rhode Island cotton mill owner Samuel Slater, realized that the cotton yarn he was spinning to weave into cloth could be adapted for hand sewing. The Slaters and their distributors began selling cotton thread in hanks somewhere near the turn of the century (52).

A few years later in Scotland, James and Patrick Clark, forced to do without silk heddle string for their looms because of a French trade embargo during the Napoleonic wars, substituted cotton and arrived at the same idea as Hannah Slater. In Paisley, Scotland in 1812, the Clarks built the first factory for production of cotton thread. Like the Slaters they sold the thread in hanks; it was three-ply or three-cord thread, three separate yarns twisted together to supply the strength needed for hand sewing. The Clark family is also credited with the development of thread on spools; initially the spools cost an extra halfpenny and could be returned for a refund (53).

The story of the development of a cotton thread industry is sometimes told with the implication that Hannah Slater invented cotton thread. But hand spinners can produce a thin cotton yarn suitable for hand sewing easier than they can produce a thicker yarn suitable for weaving. Surely hand spinners in the cotton growing colonies and states of the eighteenth century could produce cotton thread for sewing, long before the Slaters or the Clarks were selling it. Ann Taylor pieced a quilt top dated 1798 (pictured on page 47) with cotton thread. Since she lived in Virginia where she may have had access to cotton, she probably spun her own thread. A quilter living in a colder climate would have been far more likely to use thread of another fiber.

The invention of the sewing machine in the mid-1840s created a problem for cotton thread manufacturers; their three-ply thread was not strong enough to withstand the stress of machine sewing. The initial solution, developed in the late 1840s, was six-ply thread, six separate yarns twisted to provide twice as much strength. But the first six-ply thread was not the perfect solution to the sewing machine problem. In the 1860s the Clark company opened a factory in New Jersey to manufacture a different type of six-ply or six-cord thread they called "Our New Thread" (Clark's O.N.T. spool cotton). The six yarns were twisted into three sets of two, and then the three branches were twisted (see page 51), resulting in a more satisfactory thread that could be used for hand or machine sewing, and one soon adopted

Three Different Thread Constructions:
a ''Three-Ply Thread''
b ''Six-ply Thread (six separate yarns)''
c ''Six-ply Thread (three twists of two yarns)''

by other manufacturers like the J. and P. Coats Company, who later merged with Clark.

The history of thread manufacture is relevant to quilt dating because thread construction can settle date conflicts but only in terms of the earliest date a quilt might have been made. The different types of threads have co-existed; today manufacturers make both three-ply and six-ply (three twists of two yarns) thread. Finding a three-ply thread in a quilt therefore does not prove that it was made before the invention of six-ply thread. Six-ply thread is a more useful clue: the presence of a simple six-ply thread means a quilt could not have been made before the mid-1840s, and the more complex six-ply (three twists of two threads) signals a date after 1860.

Cotton Thread as a Clue to Date	
Thread	*Era*
Any manufactured cotton thread	After 1800
Three-ply thread	After 1800
Six-ply thread (six separate yarns)	After 1840
Six-ply thread (three twists of two yarns)	After 1860

To examine thread, find a protruding end; determine which direction the thread is twisted and twist it the other way. You should be able to count the yarns with a magnifying glass (a useful tool for all kinds of detectives). To determine whether thread in an early quilt is cotton or another fiber, you will need to examine a clipped piece with a microscope or have someone do it for you. If possible, examine thread samples from all stages of the quilt's construction—the patchwork, the setting, the borders, the backing and the binding.

Clark's O.N.T. Spool Cotton was a six-ply thread known originally as ''Our New Thread''. Trade card from author's collection.

Rayon and Synthetic Fibers

Because silk traditionally was both desirable and expensive, textile manufacturers hoped for centuries to find an alchemist's formula for an artificial silk. Rayon is one of the first successes. It is technically a synthetic fiber, but since the fabric is made of regenerated cellulose—the organic carbohydrate that is found in vegetation like cotton, which is about 96% cellulose—rayon is usually not classified as a synthetic fiber. The cellulose fibers are turned into liquid form, forced through holes called spinnerets and hardened by a variety of methods. Rayon, originally called artificial silk, was discovered in 1885, and the first commercial production began about 1890. The name rayon was adopted in 1924. Textile manufacturers experimented with rayon in the first decades of the twentieth century with varying degrees of success, so one can expect to find rayon in the scrap quilts and fancy quilts made anytime in this century.

Rayon's main advantage is its cheapness, since it is made of wood pulp and waste cotton. Another advantage is its silk-like sheen and luster. Its disadvantages are many; washability and resistance to wrinkling are poor, and early rayon was inconsistent in quality. Anyone who has washed a rayon dress with disastrous results will appreciate quiltmakers' reluctance to use rayon in quilts.

Determining if a fiber is rayon is difficult as it can imitate other fibers. Being cellulose, it burns like cotton; more technical tests are usually required.

Acetate is another form of rayon designed to imitate silk. Commercial production of acetate dates from 1919; it is common in twentieth century Crazy Quilts, scrap quilts, and utility quilts.

Rayon and acetate satins were popular for tied comforters and whole-cloth quilts in the mid-twentieth century. Magazines in the 1920s and 30s, such as *Needlecraft*, offered patterns for "puffs"—whole-cloth quilts made of satin, crepe de chine or taffeta, woven from silk, rayon or acetate. One brand name for a rayon satin is "silkoline", which Marshall Field and Company advertised in 1925 as an "artificial silk that was desirable for covering cotton or wool comforters". In 1927 Sears sold "Comforter Silkoline", advertised for "coverlets, comforters, crib comforters and carriage robes".

Rayon was commonplace enough as a quilting material in the early thirties that Rose Kretsinger warned against using it in her chapter on quilting in *The Romance of the Patchwork Quilt in America*: "I make mention of the modern quilted boudoir accessories, cushions, etc. which are so familiar to all of us and may be purchased as stamped and ready to work products in all department stores. They are in colored rayon, made to affect a satin elegance, when in reality they are quite unenduring, materially, artistically and in workmanship" (54). She was correct; the style did not endure. It fell from favor in the 1950s, so it is a good clue to the 1925-1950 era.

Nylons and polyester fabrics are not based on cellulose as rayon is; they are woven of synthesized fibers manufactured from long-chain molecules called polymers. Nylon was introduced around 1940; its first use was in knit stockings, and after World War II, it began appearing in woven fabrics that wound up in quilts.

In 1946 the DuPont Company purchased the rights to manufacture polyester in the United

Rose quilt, made by Mrs. S.J. Freeman in Chicago, Illinois. Date attributed by maker: 1933. Appliqued, embroidered, gathered and quilted. Rayon satin. Collection: Franklin D. Roosevelt Library, Hyde Park, New York.

Mrs. Freeman entered her rayon satin quilt in the contest at the 1933 Chicago World's Fair, where it (like tens of thousands of others) did not win a prize. A few years later she sent it to President Roosevelt as a birthday gift.

Gathered applique was sometimes used in mid-nineteenth century album quilts and late-nineteenth century Crazy Quilts, but three-dimensional decorative techniques were so rarely used that they are not a clue to date.

States. Their trade name fabric, Dacron, was first produced in 1953; Eastman Kodak followed in 1958 with their trade name Kodel. By 1977, 23 companies were manufacturing different brands of polyester fabric (55).

Woven polyester fabrics and polyester/cotton blends began appearing in quilts in the 1950s. Polyester batting also dates from the 1950s but did not become widespread until after 1960. The Mountain Mist division of Stearns and Foster, one of the largest manufacturers of quilt batting, began selling a polyester batting in 1963 (56).

Synthetic fabrics have a distinctive look and feel that makes them easy to single out, but visually discriminating blends of cotton and polyester from 100% cotton fabric takes practice. A burning test is helpful; burnt synthetics and blends have a distinctive acrid smell (familiar to anyone who has ironed a polyester shirt at a "cotton" setting), and they melt rather than turn to ash as natural fibers do.

Because synthetic fabrics and batting do not appear in quilts made before 1950 they are out of the scope of this book, but they do appear as repairs in older quilts and have been used as setting, backing and batting in recently quilted pieces. Being able to identify synthetic fibers and fabrics is therefore a useful skill for accurate dating of antique quilts.

Batting & Filler

Quilts are generally made of three layers, the top and the backing plus the filler between, which varies in thickness. The most common filler is batting, a fluffy layer of non-woven fiber. Batting is also called a batt, and in England it is called wadding. English quilts with a filler (a type less common there than here) are called wadded quilts.

Before the introduction of polyester batting around 1960, cotton was the most common batting, with wool another option. Wool and cotton batting in themselves are not clues to date; early quilts were filled with both. The seventeenth-century Indian chintz quilts had cotton batting; the English wool bedquilts in those years were filled with wool (57), and both fibers are still used for quilt batting. The first commercial cotton batting was produced in 1846 by the Stearns and Foster company who are in business today selling both cotton and polyester batting under the name Mountain Mist (58).

Wool batting is found inside wool quilts and comforters, but it was occasionally used inside cotton, silk and combination fabric quilts. Some wool batts inside otherwise washable cotton quilts have shrunk dramatically, resulting in a significantly smaller quilt with a puckered top. These shrunken quilts are sometimes described as a style of "gathered" quilt, but many puckers in an otherwise conventional quilt style probably indicates a wool batt washed in hot water and not a novelty piecing technique.

There are few hints as to the date of a quilt batting. One observation is that quiltmakers working in the last quarter of the nineteenth century and the first quarter of the twentieth were more likely to use a very thick cotton batt than quilters working earlier or later. Turn-of-the-century are often quite thick, but this clue is very weak, at best only circumstantial evidence that needs lots of other support.

There is some discussion in the quilt literature about cotton seeds in the batting being a useful clue to date. In her 1929 book, Ruth Finley gave a formula for dating quilts by counting the number of seeds per square inch, based on conclusions about the invention of the cotton gin and a comparison of ginned cotton to hand cleaned cotton (59). Most of her information about quilts was gathered near her New York home, and her understanding of southern quilts, hand carded batts and cotton seeds in general was limited. Unfortunately, her formula for determining a date was only wishful thinking. Many novice collectors are quick to point out any seeds visible in a batting when the quilt is held up to the light. The conventional wisdom is that visible seeds mean a quilt is rather old; some neophytes believe that seeds mean the quilt dates from before the invention of the cotton gin in the 1790s.

Such notions are based on three misconceptions. The first is that the spots visible inside a quilt are actually cotton seeds. Cotton seeds are about the size of navy beans, much larger than the dark specks apparent inside quilts. What is visible is cotton refuse, fragments from the hulls, stems and other dark parts of the plant.

The second misconception is that cotton cleaned by machine is refuse-free. Commercially produced batting was available in all grades. An ad from the 1897 Sears catalog, a century after the invention of the cotton gin gives an idea of the variety available. "Our bats are patent folded and are not simply a wad of cotton to be repicked and put into the quilt in bunches; each batt is nicely papered, is folded and will open up to the same thickness. 36 inches wide and 7 feet long.

    8 cents per roll—fair quality
    9 cents per roll—good quality
    12 1/2 cents per roll—fine quality
    15 cents per roll—clean white"

Sears also sold "Snow white cotton batting . . . used for medical purposes, baby quilts, etc. Extra long staple, no specks. Per roll 25 cents".

Each of the batts weighed 16 ounces, so the differences in quality were probably due to whiteness and cleanliness. From the catalog description it is apparent that the 8 cent per yard batting was neither snow white nor speck-free. It is also apparent that competitors' battings might be nothing more than "wads of cotton to be repicked and put into the quilt in bunches". It is likely that the more inexpensive batting was used in many of the thick utility quilts and comforters of those years. When such quilts are held up to the light the 8 cent or even the 15 cent batting might contain quite a few brown spots.

The third misconception is that once the cotton gin was invented all batting thereafter was ginned by machine. Quiltmakers continued to clean cotton by hand. As late as 1937, Kentucky quilters were described as carding their own wool and cotton batts (60), and even today women who raise cotton and sheep continue to make their own batts, although the practice is less common than it was 50 or 100 years ago. Pecolia Warner, a Mississippi quiltmaker, described in a 1982 interview beating cotton with a switch into padding for quilts (61). Many of the inaccurate family stories about homespun cotton backing may have originated as stories about home-produced batting, because it was far, far more common than homespun cotton.

In summary: specks in the batting are a better clue to an inexpensive batting than to a date.

Quiltmakers used filler other than batting for their quilts. They commonly used woven blankets, sometimes worn quilts. Exceptionally poor or exceptionally frugal quiltmakers recycled clothing as filler. Paper inside a quilt is probably a remnant of a construction technique not a filler. Seamstresses who used the paper template or foundation piecing methods worked over paper generally removed the paper before the quilt's layers were assembled. Some left the paper inside, however, possibly for added warmth or a crisp look.

The presence of a polyester batt under an old quilt top is reliable evidence that the top was quilted after 1960 and the introduction of the polyester batt. To determine if an invisible batting is polyester, rely on the look and the feel of the quilt. Polyester has a distinctive loft that looks puffier than cotton. Polyester springs back after being compressed and has a slippery feel if the quilt is rubbed between two fingers. Polyester batting, because it is of a continuous synthetic filament, requires less quilting than short-staple cotton that balls up after washing. If the quilting lines are more than three inches apart the batting may be polyester.

4.

CLUES IN COLOR AND DYES

Because fabric colors have changed through the decades due to fashion, economics and improvements in technology, color is a major clue to the date of a quilt. Learning about color from a book is difficult because verbal descriptions are always inadequate and photographs rarely capture true color. I have tried to describe the colors well enough so that the next time you come across a chrome orange or a chocolate brown you will recognize it, recall its name and file the shade in your visual memory.

The most significant change in the coloring of fabrics was the development of synthetic dyes. For centuries people all over the world have used dyes from natural sources, primarily plants. When the colonists settled America they dyed their imported fabrics and their homespun linens and wools with imported vegetable dyes and a few home grown varieties. America's textile manufacturing industry developed around the time of the Revolution, using age-old dye technology. During the first decades of the nineteenth century experiments by European dye chemists resulted in new mineral dyes like Prussian blue and antimony orange. These brighter colors soon appeared in America's fabrics and quilts.

In 1856 William Henry Perkin, an English chemist looking for artificial quinine to fight malaria, invented the first synthetic dyes when he discovered that the coal tar derivatives he had splashed on his clothing produced purple spots that would not wash out. The synthetic dyes (also called aniline dyes) that followed his serendipitous discovery added many new colors to the palette of late nineteenth-century quiltmakers, although synthetic dyes brought new problems as well as new shades. Early synthetic dyes tended to fade to dun-colored brown rather than fading true to a paler, more subdued version of the original color as most vegetable dyes do. Despite their unreliability, synthetic dyes gradually took over the market because they were more predictable for the dyer, cheaper and easier to standardize and

use. Synthetic dyes were used for both commercially colored fabrics and home dyeing.

Until the first World War, synthetic dyes were mainly imported from Germany, which held internationally honored patents. During the war German factories turned to munitions production and British ships stopped what German trade there was. Forced to do without the German synthetic dyes, American fabric manufacturers faced ruin, until enterprising American chemical companies developed their own formulas. After the armistice, the German patents were awarded to American chemical companies as the spoils of war (1). A healthy postwar American dye industry produced colorfast fabrics in a variety of inexpensive shades for all types of fabrics; the only limits were the taste of the times.

Types of Dyes

Dyes can be classified in many ways. They are natural or synthetic. The natural dyes can be animal (made from insects or mollusks), vegetable or mineral. Dyes are also classified by whether they dye fabric directly or require a mordant. Turmeric (the yellow in curry powder) is a direct natural dye that produces a clear yellow on cotton. Direct dyes are also called substantive dyes.

Most natural dyes are mordant dyes, also called adjective dyes. They require a mordant and a coloring agent to produce a fast color. Mordant dyes thus have two components. An example: logwood as a coloring agent combined with nitrate of iron as a mordant produces black. When mordanted with tin, logwood produces a shade of purple. Many natural dyes will color fabric a multitude of shades, depending on the fiber, the mordant, the intensity of the dyebath, the length of time the fabric is in the bath, etc. Madder, a

Larry Schwarm

Flying Geese, unfinished quilt top. Maker unknown. Estimated date: 1825–1850. Pieced. Cotton. Collection: Pam Johnson.

The triangular "geese" are a wonderful flock of mid-century prints. Note the printed plaid, the madder-style prints of red-orange and brown, the yellow-orange (probably chrome orange) prints, the printed ginghams, the two rainbow prints (one graded from purple to gold, the other from Prussian blue to green) and the prints of chrome orange on indigo blue. The setting strips are a printed plaid with the characteristic cloudy green found in many mid-century quilts.

56

common vegetable dye, can color cotton various shades of red, brown, black, orange or lavender depending on the mordant.

No dye is completely colorfast, but some are more resistant to light and washing than others. Color loss occurs in washing (bleeding), from light (fading), from abrasion (crocking), and through shifting to other areas (migration) (2). We see examples of all types of color loss in antique and new quilts. Color is described as either fast or fugitive. Some dyes, like Turkey red, have a reputation for being quite fast; others, like turmeric, are quite fugitive.

Today we expect our dyes to be colorfast, and we are always surprised to find they fade (except in the case of blue jeans which are expected to). Today's synthetic dyes are more colorfast than some natural dyes and most early synthetic dyes. Earlier generations expected their dyes to be fugitive; redyeing was everyday household work. A faded shirt or apron was no disaster; it could easily be redyed. A faded quilt, if not a disaster, was certainly a disappointment. We can imagine that quiltmakers looked to reliable dyes for quilts they hoped to pass on to future generations.

Dyes can actually harm cloth, especially cotton and silk. Certain dyes, particularly those with tin and iron mordants, can tender or rot the fiber (3). There is much evidence of tendered fabric in old quilts; brown and black cottons and silks are notorious for deteriorating. Sometimes we find the brown figure completely rotted away, leaving small holes in the colored background.

When we are looking at the colors in quilts it is important to recall that dyes interact with fibers in different ways; wool and silk take dye differently from cotton and linen, so some colors obtainable in silks and wools were not feasible in cottons until late in the nineteenth to mid-twentieth century. Purple is a good example of a color that was far easier to obtain in the animal fibers (wool and silk), than in the vegetable fibers (cotton and linen). Nineteenth-century purple cottons (even after the discovery of synthetic mauvine, as Perkin called his new purple dye) were dull and quite fugitive.

HOME DYEING VS. FACTORY DYEING

The vast majority—if not all—of America's printed fabric was factory manufactured, since printing fabric was never a widely practiced home craft in this country. Plain fabrics, however, could be dyed at home, and many of the plain fabrics we find in nineteenth-century quilts were home dyed. Whether dyed at home or in the factory, fiber can be dyed at three different stages in its manufacture—before yarn spinning, in the yarn stage, or in the piece after the yarn is woven into cloth. Yarn-dyed fabric can be woven into plains, or into patterned fabric like stripes, checks or ginghams. Yarn dyeing was a routine home craft when home weaving was common before the Civil War. It is still a standard technique with commercial fabric manufacturers. Many of the stripes, checks and chambrays we buy today were dyed in the yarn and then woven. Because yarn-dyed checks, stripes and ginghams have been produced so widely over such a long period of time they are poor clues to a specific date.

Piece dyeing was practiced extensively at home through the nineteenth century, and even through the 1950s in rural areas. Many living quiltmakers recall dyeing inexpensive fabrics like recycled white sugar sacks for quilts. Piece dyeing with natural dyes persisted at home after most manufacturers switched to synthetics. Home dyeing using synthetic dyes began about the last quarter of the nineteenth century and still goes on wherever Rit dyes or similar packaged dyes are sold.

Dyers, whether housewives or professional textile dye specialists, followed recipes for natural dyes. These recipes were passed on like biscuit recipes in families, published in farm magazines and home advice columns and printed in dye books available to new brides and apprentice dyers. Some were simple; others required real skill and experience. The materials necessary for natural dyes—the plant leaves, nuts and roots could be gathered in the woods, cultivated in the garden or purchased. Indigo, the staple natural blue dye, was the only American commercial dye crop of any consequence. Southern ports, especially Charleston, exported many tons of indigo. Madder, important for reds and browns, was raised commercially in America on a smaller scale (4). Most of the other dyes were imported, like turmeric or logwood, or gathered, like walnut hulls and black oak bark.

In 1863 packaged natural dyes came on the market. Housewives could buy packets with mixed ground coloring agent and mordant. Soon after, synthetic dyes were packaged for sale, and by 1880 synthetic dyes in packets were available across the country (5).

It is difficult to determine if a fabric was dyed by a home dyer or a textile manufacturer since they used the same dyes. Dyeing is a skill; com-

Larry Schwarm

Synthetic dyes in packages have been marketed since the last quarter of the nineteenth century.
Although easy to use, many of the early examples were not particularly color fast. Trade card from author's collection.

mercially produced cottons were sometimes quite ineptly dyed, and home dyers were sometimes very good at their craft. So be cautious about attributing all fugitive or crudely dyed fabrics to home dyers. Many of the blotchy, fading fabrics we see in old quilts were probably factory-dyed.

It is also difficult to determine the dye that colored the fabric. One cannot say with certainty that a blue is from indigo or a black from logwood without chemical tests. However, there are some characteristic shades of color and patterns of wear that do provide evidence for an educated guess about a specific dye.

The changes in dye technology and in fashion affected the shades of fabric available and the way quilts looked. Some colors like wine-red and gray-blue were popular for a relatively short period of time, and they are far better clues than the old staples like Turkey red or navy blue that are as likely to be in a quilt made in 1840 as one dated 1920.

A single color in isolation provides some information, but fashionable combinations of colors—color schemes—are more useful in as-

signing dates. Look for familiar color schemes in the fabric, like the combination of shades known as the "madder style"—a coppery red, a purplish brown, and a black in a print. Madder-style prints are a clue to the last half of the nineteenth century. Learn to recognize color schemes in quilts, like the bright red, green and white quilts that were popular from 1840 through 1900.

To familiarize you with the way dyes and color changed in quilts we will look at six colors (green, red, blue, yellow, orange and purple) and three neutrals (brown, black and white), focusing on the shades and dyes that are the strong clues to dating, and a bit on the technology, economics and politics that affected the way quilts have looked.

Clues in Green Fabric

Green fabrics offer many clues to the quilt detective. Although green is the predominant color in nature, there is no single vegetable dye that produces a fast green. Using vegetable dyes a dyer must first dye the piece yellow and then overdye it blue to make it green. Dyers can also use vegetable dyes to color yarn blue and then yellow (or vice versa) to make green, and weave the green yarn into stripes, checks and other woven patterns. But before the advent of synthetic dyes a fabric designer who wanted green figures in his prints, had trouble. Since green is so important to flowered fabric, resourceful textile manufacturers came up with solutions. One method was to print the leaf or stem blue and then print yellow over it (or vice versa) in a process called overprinting. Another method was handpainting or stenciling the second color atop the first in what was called penciling. Ideally, overprinting or penciling would produce a cleanly registered green leaf, but often the blues and yellows did not overlap perfectly, so a trace of yellow outlined the leaf on one side, a trace of blue on the other. In some cases, the manufacturer didn't even try for registration, printing a blob of blue atop a blob of yellow with haphazard results.

Even if registration were excellent, the two dyes may have had different degrees of fastness. If the blue faded before the yellow, yellow leaves were left. If the reverse happened, the leaves and stems faded to blue.

Much of the literature about fabric, dyes and quilts describes a "single-step" or "solid" green, a simpler process for producing greens from veg-

58

etable dyes in a one-stage process, that is usually attributed to the years between 1810 and 1820. Jim Liles, a dyer and dye historian, is skeptical about the existence of such a green, which he notes involved a "secret mordant" that was never disclosed. More likely the solid green was a mordant printing process in which a blue dye was mixed with a mordant for the yellow. The yellow was applied in the second step, but because yellow remained only in the mordanted areas, registration was better than in the penciling or other overprinting processes. Differential fading still occurred, however, resulting in stems and leaves with bluish or yellowish casts.

The mineral dyes that were developed during the first half of the nineteenth century continued to make use of overprinting. Some mineral greens were so fast that differential fading was less of a problem than with vegetable greens or combination vegetable/mineral greens. However, many mineral greens were cloudy, chalky and lifeless when compared to the vegetable or combination greens, and chalky greens are a good clue to a mid-nineteenth century fabric.

The only true solid greens (applied in a single step) came from synthetic dyes, which were listed in dye manuals only after 1875, according to Liles (6). Liles's research upsets a commonly held theory (held by me until he convinced me otherwise) that any quilt with a single-step green in it must have been made after 1815 or so. That clue appeared useful, a comfortable idea to hold on to, but it has two problems. The first is that the date must be moved up to about 1860—after the invention of synthetic dyes. (The new rule: any quilt with a single-step green in it must have been made after 1860 or so). The second problem renders the clue virtually useless; if registration and color fastness were good, as in the mordant-printed, two-step mineral greens, it is difficult for us to determine how many steps the printer used. It takes real skill to be able to discriminate a single-step green.

One concludes that a fast green print with good registration is hardly a clue. The dye could be a skillfully applied vegetable, mineral or synthetic green that has not faded. Fast green prints, whether chintz or calico are, for the novice dater, a really weak clue to a long period of time—nineteenth century or later.

Knowledge of the processes and problems with greens is nevertheless useful because the presence of a cotton print with obvious overprinted or penciled green (marked by telltale signs of poor registration or differential fading) is a good clue that the fabric was printed before 1860 or so. Remember that the end of the antebellum period,

Larry Schwarm

Unfinished quilt top. Maker unknown. Estimated date : 1825–1850. Pieced. Cotton. Collection: Pam Johnson.

The leaves and stems in the floral chintzes along the left edge are obviously not single-step greens. In one the yellow dye has faded, leaving blue leaves and blue streaks on the flowers. In the other both blue and yellow are fast, but the poor registration is a sign of overprinting or penciling. The green leaves and stems in the striped fabric appear to be a single-step green but may be a mordant printed compound green. Note the white halos around the flowers to make registration easier.

1860, is a rather arbitrary cutoff point for overprinting and penciling of prints. And overdyeing of plain fabrics, as we shall see, continued even longer.

Green calicoes with tiny figures are very common, so common for so long that they are also of very little use in themselves in assigning a date narrower than "second quarter of the nineteenth century or later". Until the 1980s, when the company that printed them finally stopped, we could buy green calicoes that were almost perfect copies of nineteenth-century fabrics; detecting the difference between a green cotton with a tiny black flower printed in 1870, 1930 or 1970 takes much practice.

59

Unfinished friendship quilt top. Made by members of the Crow and Bird families in Killeen and Burnett, Texas. Inscribed in embroidery: 1953 (blocks possibly set together later). Pieced and embroidered. Cotton. Collection of the author.

Very few quilts were dated in the 1950s, an era when postwar values discounted handwork and antiques. This traditional friendship quilt uses a jumble of fabrics. The multicolored, splashy, crowded prints are good clues to a mid-twentieth century date. The yellow cowboy print used in the squares in the sashing is an object or conversational print typical of the 1950s when Roy Rogers and Dale Evans were juvenile heroes. The green calico in the top left-hand block is of the type found in quilts from the mid-nineteenth century through the present, a fabric that offers little help to the novice quilt dater.

Overdyeing (first blue and then yellow or vice versa) was used to create plain fabrics by both professional and home dyers for decades after the advent of the single-step synthetic green dyes. We see overdyed greens in cotton quilts made until the last quarter of the nineteenth century; they are sometimes easy to spot because one color or the other has bled out, leaving streaks or blotches in combinations of blue, yellow and green. The vivid yellow-green seen in many applique quilts from 1840 through 1890 is probably an overdyed green that has lost some of its blue. We read of a mid-nineteenth-century green called apple green or Victoria green (named after a favorite color of the young queen (7), which may be the yellow-green so popular in quilts; but it is likely that there was not quite so much yellow in the fabric on the bolt.

Basket of Fruit and Flowers (detail). Summer spread. Signed in ink: J.A. Caspar (?), made in Pennsylvania. Estimated date: 1840−1880. Applique, reverse applique and embroidery. Cotton. Collection of the author.

The yellow-orange in the basket of pineapples is probably chrome orange. The plain red in the strawberries is probably Turkey red, and the green appears to be a compound dye, possibly a Prussian blue and a faster yellow. Alkaline laundry soaps damage Prussian blue; the splotches may have been caused by an unusually harsh wash. Most compound dyes do not differentially fade in so obvious a manner.

A number of nineteenth-century floral quilts have blue appliqued stems and leaves. We cannot tell at this time whether the maker started out with a green fabric, but we can guess that a number of those blue leaves were once green.

Overdyed greens appear both as plains and as the background in calico prints. The overdyeing is most apparent if one of the dyes is fading in blots rather than evenly across the surface. Like most vegetable dyes, they fade true, to paler, muted versions of green, blue or yellow rather than to a brown. The overdyed greens seem to have been most common in quilts in the 1840-1875 period.

A combination mineral/vegetable dye produced Chrome green, the even, dark green (much like the green in window shades and awnings) that was used in many mid- to late-nineteenth-century quilts. Chrome green was an Indigo or Prussian blue overdyed with chrome yellow, that appears in quilts after 1840 or so. It had a reputation for fastness, and the many red, white and green quilts surviving from the 1840s through the end of the nineteenth century attest today to its durability.

Larry Schwarm

Set of blocks in the *Disk* or *Flower Basket* pattern. Maker unknown. Estimated date: 1880–1920. Pieced. Cotton. Collection of Heidi St. Royal.

These blocks vividly illustrate how synthetic dyes fade. The baskets probably were once green with red and yellow diamonds. They may have been part of a cotton comforter cover, which was used, washed and taken apart (possibly because the setting squares or sashing had begun to disintegrate). The salvaged blocks were stacked and set aside for decades where the one on top absorbed the most light and faded the most. The fact that those in the middle faded more than those on the bottom illustrates that light does pass through fabric, so checking the seams of a brown piece of cotton for signs of its original color is not reliable. The seams are also likely to fade.

Synthetic greens appeared around 1875 (8). The synthetics were often fugitive; like most synthetics, they did not fade true but took on a distinctly brownish cast when exposed to light and washing. We often come across red, white and tan applique quilts in which the tan was once another shade. Clues to the original shade lie in the once-matching thread (it may not have faded as much as the fabric) and the fabric visible inside seams or on back sides of applique where light has not done as much damage.

Some believe the red, white and tan quilt to be a distinct end-of-the-century fashion, but an intentional red, white and tan quilt is likely to be rarer than those that have faded. I personally have created two such quilts by using antique green fabrics before I realized how fugitive they are. My block for the Douglas County, Kansas Bicentennial quilt—so green in 1976—is now the same dun-colored brown we see in these old quilts. Occasionally I do see a red, white and tan quilt that was intentionally designed in the color scheme, but most are copies of older quilts, with the copier unaware that the tan in the model was once green.

Late nineteenth-century greens and early twentieth-century greens could also fade away completely, leaving ghostly white leaves and stems among the still-bright flowers.

Synthetic greens, both plain and print, faded to brown, tan or white throughout the last quarter of the nineteenth-century and well into the twentieth, but one can generalize that green fabric fading to brown is a good clue to an 1875 to 1900 date (although some greens with a definite mid-nineteenth century origin also take on a brownish cast). As the unreliable synthetic green dyes took over the market at the end of the nineteenth century, it seems likely that quilters lost their faith in green cottons and stopped using them. Green is not a common color in quilts from the 1890-1925 era.

Knowledge of green's characteristic fading is not only useful in assigning dates; it is also valuable information for the quilt collector since some late nineteenth century quilts and tops in mint condition (never used, never washed) are going to fade dramatically when washed or hung on a well-lit wall.

61

Water Lily quilt, made by Dr. Jeannette Dean Throckmorton (1883–1965) in Iowa. Dates inscribed in embroidery: 1946, 1946. Appliqued, stuffed and quilted. Cotton. Collection of Jean Martin.

Dr. Jeannette Throckmorton obtained her pattern from the manufacturers of Mountain Mist batting, who offered patterns as premiums in their batting until recently. The Nile green background, pastel plain cotton sateens, scalloped edge and lifelike water lilies characterize it as a quilt of the 1925–50 era. Her stuffed-work dragonflies are a revival of the nineteenth-century technique. Unlike many other well-known applique artists of the 1930s, she did her own quilting.

A useful clue for dating quilts is the slightly gray, or slightly bluish pastel green that was the rage in quilts in the 1925-1950 era. Sears, Roebuck and Co. called the shade "Nile green" in their 1927 catalog, echoing the same name used in an 1884 art needlework catalog (9). In 1929, Ruth Finley called it colonial green and mentioned that it was popular for interior woodwork (10), a legacy in the name kitchen green, which is popular today along with institutional green. The shade became available again in the 1980s; for years it was impossible to find in cottons, frustrating many would-be repairers of Depression-era quilts.

Nile green occasionally turns up in nineteenth-century scrap quilts, but its presence as a print or a plain cotton and especially as a dominant color is strong evidence that the quilt is from the late 1920s or '30s, when the pastel green meandered among the bouquets in countless applique pansies, dahlias and Grandmother's Flower Garden quilts.

Clues In Red Fabrics

There are several shades of red and pink cottons that are among the easiest colors to learn to spot. Turkey red, cinnamon red-orange, wine and a bright pink are all recognizable to novice detectives and were popular enough at times to be useful.

Turkey red is unusual because the name for the color has passed down to us with the quilts. Since it is so colorfast, many of the old quilts are still the same shade of red they were when their makers demanded Turkey red. The name comes not from the bird, but from the old European idea that any eastern Mediterranean country was part of Turkey. Dyemasters in that area knew how to dye cotton a fast red in a process that was unknown to Europeans until the mid-eighteenth century. The dyestuff was madder root. Europeans were familiar with madder, but only the Eastern dyers knew how to get a fast, vibrant red from it. The process took 13 to 20 steps and many months. One step involved boiling the yardage in an oil mordant, explaining why the much desired shade was sometimes called "oil-boiled calico".

In the 1750s the secret of Turkey red dyeing was leaked to the European continent where French and English mills began producing Turkey red plain and print cottons. Because the process was so complex true Turkey red dyeing (using natural materials) was never carried out on a commercial level in the United States (11). In 1868 the synthesis of alizarin, the coloring agent in madder, simplified the Turkey red process somewhat and American mills began producing the cotton. Turkey red dyeing with natural materials or the alizarin process was so complex that mills specialized in that type of cotton, sometimes selling the plain red yardage to other mills that created prints by overdyeing a dark figure or by applying other colors after using chemicals to discharge areas of the red dye.

Casual observation cannot distinguish Turkey red from later fast red dyes, but the appearance of a red that has retained its brightness is a clue that the quilt was made after Turkey red fabrics became commonplace in the 1830s and '40s. One clue to Turkey red cotton is a characteristic pattern of wear. Because the dyeing process is so hard on cotton fiber, Turkey red prints and plains often do not wear as well as the other fabrics in a quilt. The fabric seems to wear thin from abrasion on the surface becoming lighter in the high relief areas of the quilt. The color remains dark and the fabric stays intact in the low places near quilting and seams. Because the dye colors the outside of

Larry Schwarm

Feathered Star quilt made by Sarah Maria Grizzel (1853–1914) in Barton County, Kansas. Estimated date: 1880–1900. Pieced, embroidered and quilted. Cotton. Collection: Mrs. W. Elden Harwood.

The red fabric and embroidery thread were probably dyed using the Turkey red method. Turkey red outline embroidery is a good clue to a date between 1880 and 1925. Turkey red plain cotton is not so specific. It is seen in quilts from the 1830s through the 1930s, as are the green calicoes.

each yarn, the interior, undyed shaft of the yarn begins to show with wear. As Turkey red wears, it becomes streaked with white rather than fading to a uniform pink or brown.

Turkey red, in plains and prints, became a staple in clothing and quilts during the second quarter of the nineteenth century and lasted until the end. The plain red is not a particularly useful clue if one wants to narrow the date of a quilt to something beyond "nineteeth or early twentieth century", but bright red prints are more helpful. The first Turkey red calicoes with tiny cones, flowers and geometrics appeared at the beginning of the nineteenth century (12), when they occasionally were used in scrap quilts. It wasn't until about 1840 that they became the characteristic fabric for quilts, especially applique quilts. Turkey red calicoes from the mid-nineteenth century are printed with black, yellow, blue and green figures—some of which have rotted away due to tendering from

Larry Schwarm

Double Wrench comforter. Maker unknown. Estimated date: 1900–1925. Pieced and tied. Cotton and wool. Collection of the author.

The setting strips are of the type of fabric advertised in the 1907 Sears catalog as "red ground oil-boiled comforter calico at 6 cents. Comes in red grounds with combinations of black in scroll and oriental medium and large sized designs." Both Sears and Montgomery Ward called these red, black and white prints robe prints; and quiltmakers used them for whole-cloth tied comforters, for quilt backs and in scrap quilts.

The block was first published in *Farm and Fireside* magazine in 1884 as *Double Wrench.* It now has 41 published names, more than any other design.

Note the brown fabric that is deteriorating along the edges of the photograph. Only one thread is rotting; apparently warp and weft were of different fibers.

the dyes and from the chemicals used in the discharge process. Most, if not all, of these multicolored calicoes are European imports. They are a clue to a general 1840-1900 date, with the quilt more likely to be from the first thirty years of the era than the last thirty.

There is a second distinctive red print found in quilts from about 1875 through 1925, when American mills produced an inexpensive black on red ground. Common subject matter in small scale prints were sporty objects like horseshoes, anchors and tennis rackets. In larger scale prints, paisley cones and florals were typical. Both Montgomery Ward and Sears sold large-scale red and black prints that they called robe prints. The catalogs frequently mentioned their suitability for quilts and comforters. Sears also referred to its red and black prints, small and large scale, as Garibaldi Cloth, a probable reference to the Italian hero

whose followers wore red shirts. Garibaldi Prints, Robe Prints or black on red prints, are strong clues to the 1875 to 1925 era, when both the large-scale and small-scale versions were popular for quilt backing, sashing, for whole-cloth tied comforters and for patches in scrap quilts.

Turkey red remained popular after synthetic dyes became the norm towards the end of the century. Authentic Turkey red cottons still required an old-fashioned, multi-stage dyeing process (somewhat simplified by this time) and so were often priced considerably higher than other fabrics sold for clothing and quilts. From the 1875-76 Montgomery Ward catalog quiltmakers could order red prints for 9 1/2 cents per yard or "Turkey Red prints (in oil colors)" for 27 1/2 cents. The reliability of the true Turkey red fabric was apparently worth nearly three times the price. The difference in price between red and true Turkey red fabric fluctuated over the following thirty or forty years, but Turkey red was always at a premium.

Quilters who recall the times remember that World War I had a strong impact on the availability of red fabrics and the subsequent decline in the popularity of red quilts because the Turkey red fabric and many of the synthetic red dyes were imported. (The British embargo on German goods, which began in 1914, meant fast reds became scarce.) Examination of the Sears catalogs from those decades lends some support to this theory, although a hard and fast end to the availability of Turkey reds is not apparent. Inexpensive plain cottons in red were harder to find during the War years, and in those years even the usually pink-colored index pages in the catalogs changed. (The pages were colored brown for the duration or were a fugitive pink that has since faded). However, there is little pattern to the unavailability of red prints and plains; red prints were available throughout the war; red plains began disappearing in 1910, years before the War.

Because Turkey red fabrics cost more than other reds and had a better reputation, the name was sometimes used to misrepresent synthetic red dyes. Housewives could buy packaged dyes labeled Turkey red but authentic Turkey red is a process rather than a dye-stuff. Regardless of what the packet said, it contained a less reliable dye such as Congo Red, which produced a bright red that soon faded to brown or pink. The misrepresentation of fugitive dyes may explain why surviving quilts from the era have reds ranging from pink to brown to white. A faded red dress might be quickly and inexpensively redyed with another package of Congo Red, but a faded red and white

Turkey red is a dyeing process, not a coloring agent, so a packet of Turkey red dye is impossible. The packet probably contains a synthetic dye that will fade quickly. Author's Collection.

Devil's Claws quilt. Maker unknown. Estimated date: 1890–1925 (quilted later). Pieced and quilted. Cotton. Collection of the author.

The pinkish-tan shade was probably once a bright red, dyed with a fugitive synthetic dye like that sold in the packet shown on page 58. The wonderful name, *Devil's Claws*, was printed in the Ladies' Art Company catalog, which may have been the quiltmaker's pattern source.

quilt remained faded.

The presence of a faded synthetic red is a good clue to a date from about 1875 through 1925. Red, as noted above, could fade to pink or brown and sometimes completely to white. The pinks usually have a telltale brownish cast. Clues like red thread and some residual color left in the seams can help determine if a tan and white quilt was once red and white.

Helpful to dating quilts is a second shade of red, a cinnamon red, called madder red. Its orange

tinge makes it easy to differentiate from Turkey red which has a bluish cast. Both reds were originally dyed with the root of the madder plant as a coloring agent, so both are technically forms of madder red, but common parlance classifies madder red as various shades of red ranging from red-brown through cinnamon orange and Turkey red as a bright, slightly bluish red.

Madder red is found in chintzes and calico cottons as well as in wool, silk, linen and combination prints. Cotton calico prints "in the madder style", as color combinations based on the cinnamon red were called, were especially popular in the last half of the nineteenth century. The various shades of red-orange were often combined with a dark, purplish brown. Black, light purple and light blue were common accent colors in the print.

The color scheme is reminiscent of paisley shawls; some of the wools found in the wool quilts at the end of the century may actually have been cut from the shawls that were part of every fashionable woman's wardrobe. Many of the figures in the prints were derived from the shawl designs of oriental cones and pears that we call paisleys; geometrics, florals and stripes were also very popular in the red-orange color scheme.

Most of the figures and grounds in madder-style prints were printed with different mordants and passed through the madder dye bath a single time, although some accent colors may have required a second run. After the development of synthetic dyes the color scheme remained popular so all fabric dyed in the madder style is not necessarily dyed with madder dyes. In the mid 1880s the Cocheco Printworks ceased claiming that their madder style fabrics were "Warranted Full Madder", an indication that they had turned to synthetic dyes to produce the color combination.

Madder-style prints are seen in patchwork quilts from the beginning of patchwork through the nineteenth century. Subtle clues like the fineness of detail in the print and print content indicate a narrower range of date, so it is a good idea to pay attention to madder prints, as skill in discriminating the earlier from the later examples is useful.

Even novices should have little problem distinguishing between the cinnamon madder red with an orange cast and a brighter, synthetic red with an orange cast that is typical of the mid- to late-twentieth century. The more recent reds tend to be a tomato color, rather than the rusty reds of madder red or the cherry reds of Turkey red. Anyone hoping to match a nineteenth-century Turkey red cotton with the fabrics available today learns quickly that it is difficult to find a bright red without an orange tone to it.

In summary, the significant variations in the shades of true red are the bluish-red that is likely to be Turkey red, the cinnamon or rusty red that is likely to be a madder red, and the bright tomato red with an orange cast that is a twentieth-century synthetic dye (and a good indicator of a post 1925 date).

At the turn of the century a dark, wine-colored red became quite popular in cotton prints. The Sears catalog called it claret or wine; sample cards from the Simpson Mills described it as madeira. Today we might call it burgundy, reflecting the change in our tastes in wine. The wine-colored fabric was probably colored with a synthetic dye, but one that was fast, as we see it unfaded in so many quilts from the 1890-1925 era. The fabric was cheap, printed economically with a white or black figure on a wine ground. (Third colors that increase production costs are not typical). This somber, purplish red is an excellent clue to the 1890-1925 period.

The pastel version of red is common throughout the history of cotton quilts. Some of the pinks we see in old quilts, of course, were originally meant to be red, and the subtle shade is all that remains of a bright red that did not stand the tests of washing and sunlight. Soft pastel pink prints are found in early scrap quilts and the shade was extremely popular in the 1925 to 1950 era; so most pink prints are not particularly useful.

One pink calico is a distinctive clue to a wide span of time. Look for a tiny pink figure, printed in thousands of variations throughout the nineteenth century, usually in two shades of pink, a double pink. If much of the white background shows through, the pink is pale; if a darker shade of pink is dominant, the resulting color is very bright, the color of Pepto Bismol or bubblegum. There are many references to a number of descriptive names for the brilliant pink calicoes: Merrimack pink (because the mills in the Merrimack valley of New England printed it for so long) (13), and seaweed. Today's authors call it stawberry pink (14) and bubblegum pink (15). Charlotte Jane Whitehill (1866-1964) referred to the shade as Norwegian pink in an 1880 quilt she donated to the Denver Art Museum (16). Other names that people recall are Portuguese pink and slave pink. It is probable that names with an ethnic or racial reference are slurs that refer to the brilliance of the color and the fact that new immigrants or the poor were more likely to wear brighter colors than the mainstream or middle class population. The wide variety of names for

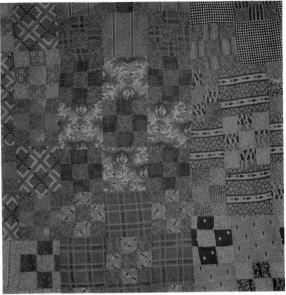

Fragment of a Nine Patch quilt top, possibly from a comforter cover. Maker unknown. Estimated date: 1875–1900. Pieced. Cotton. Collection of the author.

Chocolate browns and double pinks were a popular late-nineteenth-century color combination. The variety of prints available in these colors seems infinite. In the center nine-patch is a print in a madder-style color scheme, featuring eagles and a portrait of Lafayette, French hero of the Revolutionary War. Like most Revolutionary War commemorations in quilts, this one was pieced long after the event. The fabric was printed for the Centennial in 1876.

pink calico may be similar to today's Polish jokes, in which the butt of the joke changes from community to community reflecting regional ethnic prejudices (17).

Period references to pink calico include the name "rose" in dye and cotton printing books (18) and "old rose" and "rose pink" in the popular press. "Piecing the Quilt," a poem published in 1888 described "rose pink squares" (19). The Cocheco Printworks in 1886 referred to swatches of the pink on sample cards as double pink, and the technical author Persoz described it as *rose double* in French in 1846 (20). Double pink seems an appropriate name because it describes the two intensities of pink on the white ground (although there are sometimes three shades of pink in these calicoes). Double pink calico is an indicator of a very long period; the fabrics are common in scrap quilts throughout the nineteenth century and up to World War II. Pinpointing a narrower time period relies on rather subjective clues. It does seem that quilters of the 1875-1900 era (when other shades were becoming increasingly unreliable) used more of the double pink than earlier quilters, possibly because of its fastness. Whether it was function or fashion— or both—a bright pink color scheme in a quilt is a clue to a last quarter of the nineteenth century date.

Another distinctive pink appeared in the 1925-1950 era when plain pink cottons, sometimes in a cotton sateen weave, were combined with pale green and other pastels in the quilts typical of the twentieth century. *The Ladies Home Journal* was showing pastel pink and green applique quilts in the early teens under the design leadership of Marie Webster, who also showed some in her 1915 book, *Quilts: Their Story and How to Make Them*, but they did not become a real fad until the mid 1920s (21). A pale pink plain cotton is thus an indicator of a post-1925 date (especially if it forms a good part of the quilt's color scheme).

Clues in Blue Fabrics

There are distinctive blues helpful to beginners dating quilts, but indigo blue is too common to be one of them. Indigo is a vegetable dye, one of the oldest dyes known to civilization. Indigo is also the name of a shade of blue, a dark or blackish or navy blue—the color of a new pair of blue jeans (some of which are still dyed with indigo blue). Indigo dye could produce other shades and intensities of blue, and other dyes could produce that distinctive shade, but we associate the navy color with the dye.

Indigo is unusally colorfast in all fibers, so weavers and quiltmakers relied on it. Dark blue plains and printed calicoes appear in quilts throughout the nineteenth century and into the twentieth. Because of the complexities of the dyeing process, most manufacturers printed indigo with a simple reserve technique, resulting in a white figure on a navy ground. Pinpointing the era of a navy blue print requires a sophisticated examination of characteristics like fineness of detail and content of print.

Other blues are more indicative of specific eras. A vibrant blue was popular in mid-nineteenth century cottons. It may be a Prussian blue dye, introduced in the United States in 1832, also called Lafayette blue after the Revolutionary War hero who had recently revisited the United States (22). Other names for the vibrant blue are Napoleon's blue and Berlin blue (23). Lafayette blue appeared in plain cottons and in prints; it is common in florals, chintz-scale pillar prints and rainbow prints where the background is shaded from light to dark. This blue was often printed with a

Larry Schwarm

Feathered Star quilt. Maker unknown. Inscribed in the quilting: F.M. (?) October, 1838. Pieced and quilted. Cotton. Collection: Pat Hughes.

Blue and white calicoes have been favorites of quilters since the eighteenth century. The figure here is a small white dot and the ground is navy blue (probably dyed with indigo). Because of their long-term popularity, navy blue and white prints are of little use in assigning a date.

The quiltmaker's haphazard approach to symmetry in the feathers of her stars might be explained by some quiltmakers as a deliberate and superstitious avoidance of perfection. The truth is that mid-nineteenth century quiltmakers had inconsistent standards. Colors were shuffled and points turned every which way. There is no evidence of a folk tradition for avoiding perfection in quilts that can be traced further back than the 1930s.

drab tan; it was also combined with other colors with electric results. Lafayette blue is a good clue to a date between 1830 and 1860.

Light blues are usually not good clues. One exception is a light, vibrant blue-violet popular as a shirting print in the 1870s, '80s and '90s. It is so vivid it appears to be a twentieth-century addition, but the checks, florals or geometrics printed in this blue-violet on a white ground are a definite clue to the last three decades of the nineteenth.

At the turn of the century a grayed blue enjoyed widespread popularity for everyday clothing

A neatly sorted collection of turn-of-the-century swatches exemplifies the common color choices in inexpensive cottons between 1890 and 1925. On the left—black mourning prints; top center—black ground prints with bright figures; bottom center—navy blue and white prints; top right—maroon ground with white figures; bottom right—gray blue or cadet blue. Collection of the author.

and quilts. We associate the color with women's wrappers or Mother Hubbards, and it was commonly used for aprons, blouses (or waists, as they were called) and children's clothes. The light or medium gray blue was generally printed with a small white figure, dot or stripe, and it looked like a faded version of the standard indigo or navy blue. In some cases, what we see today in quilts is actually a faded navy blue, but the lighter shade was also widely manufactured; it was called cadet blue in the turn-of-the-century Sears catalogs. (Cadet blue is defined in the 1934 *Webster's Dictionary* as "a color blue in hue and of low saturation and medium brilliance"). A catalog of cottons from the American Printing Company, published around 1905, called the shade Calcutta blue. Its popularity during the 1890-1925 era makes cadet blue or Calcutta blue a strong clue to that era.

In the mid-1920s clearer, truer light blues became available and cadet blue and navy blue fell from fashion. The 1932 Sears catalog sold the clear pastel colors we associate with quilts of the Depression era, but they also continued to offer a few gray-blues and some other sedate, darker colors "for the older generation" who resisted change in clothing (and quilts). It is probable that cadet blue and navy blue prints will be found in quilts made through the 1930s and '40s.

A note about another nineteenth-century blue dye may explain why so many quilts that are otherwise exclusively blue and white have some pieces of pinkish fabric disrupting the regularity of the design. Not a deliberate color change caused by the maker's superstitions, the grayed pinkish or lavender fabric was most likely blue at one time. Logwood dyes produced a blue that initially resembled indigo but quickly faded to a pinkish or purplish shade (24).

Clues in Yellow and Orange Fabrics

Yellow calicoes, like green calicoes, are hard for the novice to date because they were produced over such a long period of time, from the mid-nineteenth century through the 1980s. The most distinctive yellow found in quilts is a garish, intense yellow-orange that was popular after 1840, especially as an accent in red and green quilts. It is much like the shade we call safety yellow, the color the highway department uses to paint yellow lines. Some people classify the color as yellow; some as orange, and the shades we see in quilts vary in the spectrum between yellow and orange. The most commonly used names, antimony orange and chrome orange, refer to the dyes used to produce it. Fast nineteenth-century yellow-orange fabrics were probably dyed with one or the other of two mineral dyes, antimony orange (discovered in 1817) and chrome orange (produced commercially in the U.S. in the 1840s) (25). The striking color is a good clue to a mid-nineteenth century or later origin.

Plain chrome orange has a tendency to lose color by crocking (rubbing off). Collectors should exercise extra care in folding quilts with yellow-orange plain cottons, checking for signs of crocking onto other colors and other quilts. Some of the plain yellow-oranges tend to turn brown, and the brown often crocks or migrates to other areas. (The applique quilt dated 1858 pictured on page 142 has this problem.) It is prudent to fold acid-free tissue between the folds of yellow-orange fabric to prevent the migration of the dye.

The color appeared in plain cotton and in prints. Yellow-orange was printed in fine lines on a white ground, which the eye reads as a pastel—but not a pale yellow, more like a butterscotch. Period names may be reflected in an 1851 fashion note from *Godey's*: "There is an intense yellow, not disagreeable in small spots or stripes upon a white ground, called by the French 'California'. It was 'bouton d'or' (gold button), and is exactly the color of the double gilt buttons worn upon dresses some seasons ago" (26). The butterscotch yellow print is a good clue to the 1840-1890 era.

Bright yellow-orange also appeared as a figure on a navy blue ground (probably indigo dye) in quilts throughout the nineteenth century, and into the first decade of the twentieth. The yellow on navy cotton is a strong clue to a long era, and therefore not useful in narrowing the date for a quilt unless one can learn to discriminate the subtleties of design and printing technique that dis-

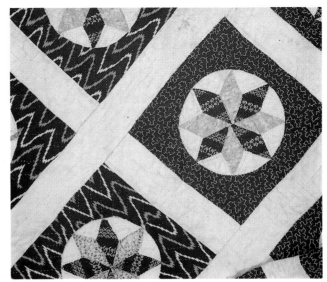

Larry Schwarm

Star of LeMoyne quilt (detail). Maker unknown. Estimated date: 1840–1875. Pieced and quilted. Cotton. Collection of the author.

The combination of a navy blue ground (probably indigo blue dye) with a yellow-orange figure (probably chrome orange dye) was used in prints from the 1830s through the 1920s.

tinguish such a print produced in the second quarter from one produced in the last quarter of the nineteenth century. If you are looking at scrap quilts from these eras, take the time to pick out the yellow and blue prints and make a mental file for later reference.

Quilters also used a true orange plain cotton, as noted earlier, in their nineteenth century quilts, again probably derived from chrome. This version of chrome orange, not quite as popular as the yellow-orange fabric, indicates an 1840-1900 date.

Yellow plain cottons and yellow ground calicoes were common accents in red and green quilts in the mid- to late-nineteenth century. The lemon yellow was probably dyed with chrome yellow or black oak bark, one of the fade-resistant vegetable dyes.

The burnt orange, madder style color scheme was so popular in scrap quilts like Charm Quilts, Log Cabins and other pieced designs, that collectors come across it often and learn quickly to rely on it as a clue to a mid- to late-nineteenth-century date. It fell out of favor with quiltmakers around the turn of the century. Orange cottons did not appear as a color scheme again until 1925 when synthetic dyes made bright oranges and all shades of pale orange possible. Tangerine, melon, and peach became popular enough in both prints and plains to be reliable clues to the 1925-1950 era.

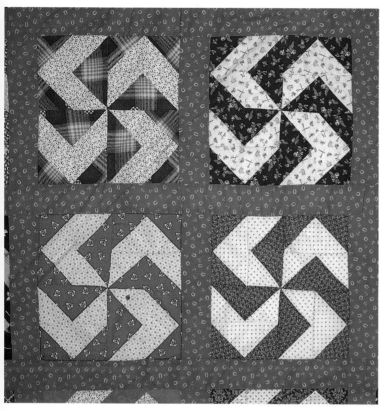

Larry Schwarm

Dutchman's Puzzle or **Dutchman's Wheel** (detail), unfinished quilt top made by Doris Wheeler. Estimated date: 1890–1920. Pieced. Cotton. Collection: Pam Johnson.

This typical turn-of-the-century dark quilt includes white shirting fabrics and a few sporting prints with horseshoes and horse's heads. The cadet blue and white fabrics are good clues to the time period. The purple calico, which was never bright, is fading to brown, the fate of many pre-World War I purple cottons. The pattern appeared in the Ladies' Art Company catalog as *Dutchman's Puzzle* in 1889; in the *Ohio Farmer* in 1894 as *The Wheel*; and again in the *Ohio Farmer* in 1898 as *Dutchman's Wheel*.

Clues in Purple Fabrics

A fast, vibrant purple was a difficult color to obtain in cotton with natural dyes. Overdyeing blue and red to produce purple was more successful with silks and woolens than with cotton. Although the first synthetic dye, discovered in 1856 was mauvine, a shade of purple, it was also more useful with the protein fibers than with cotton.

The story of the discovery of purple dye is told in some references on dating quilts with the implication that a purple cotton was impossible before the mid-1850s. There are too many purple cotton quilts inscribed with mid-nineteenth century dates to support this implication, and too

much evidence of purple cottons in dyebooks and written references of the era. The purples were a dull lavender, rather than a strong purple, and they were apt to fade to brown or pink. Collectors who find purple cotton quilts from any nineteenth- century time period should excercise caution. The quilt may still be purple because it has not yet been exposed to enough light or washing to fade it.

Twentieth-century synthetic purple dyes produced both a stronger purple and a true, clear lavender, colors that became very popular in quilts after World War I. Plain and print purples in shades of lilac and raspberry, orchid and lavender are good clues to an origin in the second quarter of this century or later. While light purple does appear in quilts from the 1900-1925 era (especially in plaids), it didn't really catch on until after 1925.

Larry Schwarm

Double Wedding Ring quilt (detail). Maker unknown. Pieced and quilted. Cotton. Collection: Elizabeth M. Watkins Community Museum.

The *Double Wedding Ring* was a favorite pattern for displaying the variety of multicolor prints made possible with improved synthetic dyes.

Clues in Brown Fabrics

Brown is common in nineteenth-century quilts for several reasons. It was a relatively easy color to obtain with vegetable dyes and therefore was popular with both professional and home dyers. Min-

Odd Fellows quilt (detail). Inscribed in ink on the reverse: Dorothy (?) Walker, January, 1876. Pieced and quilted. Private collection.

The madder-style brown prints were in fashion for dresses and scrapbag quilts of the 1860s, '70s and '80s. Some of the browns in this scrap quilt are a dark, purplish chocolate. Others are warmer, ranging to red-orange.

eral and synthetic dyes also produced many shades of brown and the color was fashionable in clothing throughout the nineteenth century. We see a lot more brown in quilts than the makers intended, however. Fabrics originally dyed brighter shades have turned brown over time due to fading from washing and light.

The easiest generalization to make about brown as a clue is that it dates a quilt before the twentieth century. Few quiltmakers in the years 1900 to 1950 chose brown for a color scheme. Certain shades of brown can be a more specific clue to narrower eras, although distinguishing among the various shades takes practice. A list of the browns mentioned in nineteenth-century dyebooks indicates how common and diverse they were. In wool, silk, cotton or linen one could have London Brown, Spanish Brown, Smoke Brown, Liver Brown, Light and Dark Snuff Brown, Bat Wing Brown, Slate Brown, Dove or Lead Brown, Ash Brown, Drab Brown, Dark Forest Brown, Mode Cuir, Stone Drab, Buff, Chocolate, Bismarck Brown, Manganese Bronze, Dark Cinnamon or British Mud.

Among nineteenth-century browns, one of the easiest to recognize is a dark purplish-brown, often combined with coppery red and burnt orange in madder-style prints. This deep, rich brown is consistently called chocolate in dye books and swatch books, and the shade is similar to the color on today's can of Hershey's chocolate syrup or the wrapper on a Hershey bar. It was also called puce, a name derived from the French word for flea (the etymological connection between insect and fashion is obscure, although fleas *are* brown). Chocolate brown was originally obtained from natural madder dye; by the end of the nineteenth century the shade was copied with synthetic dyes. Chocolate brown, simple for the dyemaster to obtain and popular with the women who wore calico dresses, was used in quilts throughout the eighteenth and nineteenth centuries.

A light tan with a somewhat greenish cast is easy to recognize as it was commonly printed with the bright Lafayette or Prussian Blue. Look for the combination of blue and tan cottons. The print content included everything from pillars to plaids. Stripes and rainbow backgrounds were also common in this color scheme. A tan/bright blue color scheme in a cotton print signifies an 1830-1860 date.

A similar shade of khaki tan with a greenish cast was popular combined with red and white figures in cotton prints. It was probably printed with a manganese mineral dye and the color combination was known as the Manganese Bronze Style. Manganese Bronzes were printed from 1850 to 1910 or so (27) and are especially common in quilts at the end of that period.

Besides being popular with calico printers, brown was a common home-dyed color since natural browns could be obtained from plentiful American plants like black walnut or butternut hulls. Resourceful housewives used other materials at hand to produce browns. Tea, for example, colors fabric in a range of brown shades. Today's quilters use it to overdye their cottons to tone them down, not a new idea. A few of the cottons in the Baltimore Album quilts were tea dyed (28). Home dyers in the southern states used the distinctive red dirt of the region with its high iron content to dye cottons in shades similar to the color of a clay flower pot. Bresenhan and Puentes quote a Texas woman who recalled mud-dyeing fabric by burying it until it was the desired shade of terra-cotta (29). Plain terra cotta cottons in quilts from South Carolina to the Southwest may have been mud-dyed.

Synthetic dyes were also used to produce browns in the latter half of the nineteenth century.

Larry Schwarm

String quilt. Maker unknown. Estimated date: 1900–1925. Pieced using the foundation method and quilted. Cotton. Collection of the author.

What happened here? Did the maker begin with two different red fabrics—one a genuine non-fading Turkey red and one a fugitive imitation that faded? Or did she intend to alternate red setting squares with tan? Red could—and often did—fade to tan. Green and blue (and nearly any other color) might also wind up tan with enough exposure to light or hot water.

Bismarck brown was a popular early synthetic brown. The swatch books show a cafe-au-lait shade with a touch of pink. Like other nineteenth-century synthetic dyes Bismarck brown was liable to fade.

Determining if a brown fabric in a quilt was always brown is not easy. Be suspicious. Look at the patchwork design; brown leaves and stems in a floral applique were possibly green when new. Brown grapes and roses are likely to have looked fresher once. Look for evidence of the original color in the sewing and quilting thread and in the seams where the fabric may have been protected from light (but do recall that light filters through the weave). The browns left after fading are distinctive; they tend to be pale and dun-colored, rather than the rich, warm shades of deliberate browns. Some very uninspired brown shades, it must be said, were also deliberately included in quilts, so the quiltmaker's intent is not always easy to judge.

In the decades at the end of the nineteenth century when synthetic dyes became the standard, fabric fading worsened. Shades likely to fade to brown were green, purple, blue and red. Red sometimes faded to a salmon shade of tan; blues and purple to khaki. Faded dun-colored browns found today are likely to date from the end of the last century or the early years of this one.

Collectors know that the browns in their quilts are likely to be the first to deteriorate. Disintegrating browns were probably dyed with madder mordanted with iron, which will tender fabric (30). One often finds a print colored in madder shades in which the reds and oranges have outlasted the browns that had required more of the abrasive iron mordant.

Brown's loss of popularity after 1900 may have been a reaction to the earlier rage for brown-looking charm quilts, Log Cabins and scrap quilts, or they may have been following the wider fashion for clothing. Dianne Fagan Affleck, curator at the Museum of American Textile History, noted a distinct change in the swatch books of the 1890s when the previously ubiquitous brown prints gave way to black (31). Although the turn-of-the-century quiltmaker could still buy inexpensive brown prints, she didn't often use them, preferring instead a black, gray or blue look. It wasn't until the 1960s that brown again became fashionable in quilts, so fashionable that future quilt detectives will have no trouble spotting the brown quilts from the 1970s and '80s.

Clues in Black Fabrics

Before the 1860s black played only a minor role in quilts as the color of the figure in prints (very popular in Turkey red calicoes). Black did not really appear as a color on its own until the Civil War era. In the last half of the nineteenth century, it was a fashion necessity in Victorian clothing and equally important in silk quilt styles where it dominated Crazy Quilts, Log Cabins and Fan designs. By the end of the century black was also common in cotton and wool quilts.

Throughout most of the nineteenth century, black came from natural dyes, many of which required mordants that injured fabrics. Silk was especially prone to tendering from black dyes, but cotton also was affected.

Fagan Affleck quotes an 1886 letter from Cocheco's distributor complaining that customers returned fabric due to "rusty blacks" (32), a

Larry Schwarm

Log Cabin quilt. Maker unknown. Estimated date: 1890–1920. Pieced using the foundation method and tied. Wool, silk and cotton. Collection: Larry Schwarm.

Black highlights the rich red wools in this Log Cabin quilt. Black wools were common in the tied wool comforters made from about 1880 through the 1930s.

common problem with natural black dyes (33). Cocheco and other mills developed reliable black dyes in the '90s, and a profusion of black cottons appeared. Those that were pieced into quilts from that time seem to be quite fast.

Black ground cotton prints are strong clues to the 1890-1925 era. One distinctive print features bright, multicolored figures. The vibrant colors, magenta purple, yellow-green, pink, and gold, are electrified by the contrast with the black background. Quiltmakers often used these prints, which look very modern to our eyes today, in their early twentieth-century scrap quilts.

Another easy-to-recognize print that is a strong clue to date is a shirting cotton with fine black lines or tiny figures on a white ground. The lines and figures are so small and so close together that the eye reads the print as gray. The prints were known by several names. Fabric historian Florence Pettit recorded the name Shaker Grays although she notes that there is no record that the Shakers actually wore them (34). A catalog from the American Printing Company mill listed them as Silver Grays. The Sears, Marshall Field and Montgomery Ward catalogs called them Mourning Prints. Montgomery Ward in the 1889–1990 catalog advertised Half Mourning Prints, "very suitable for elderly ladies not in mourning". Quilt-

Larry Schwarm

Variable Star (variation), unfinished quilt top (detail). Maker unknown. Inscribed in pencil: November 24, 1900. Pieced. Cotton. Collection: Muriel Pech Owen.

White shirting prints contrast with the maroon, black and blue cottons in the standard turn-of-the-century color scheme. The black on white prints were called silver gray or mourning prints. The black ground print with bright figures (here—pink, but also done in gold, chartreuse, purple or blue) has no period name. The bright on black ground prints are, like black and white mourning prints, a good clue to the 1890–1925 era.

This quilt top, which may have seen service as a comforter cover (the fading is a clue to some use), is dated in mirror writing on the maroon block in the upper right hand corner. When the top is held to a mirror the penciled inscription can be read: "Nov 24 1900. Joined it and ists (sic) showering down rain."

makers found them so suitable for quilts that they are a strong clue to an 1890–1925 date.

Gray cottons in which the gray is a single-step color (printed as gray rather than as black-on-white) do appear in earlier quilts but are most typical of the end of the 1925-1950 era. Gray grounds for multicolor prints were popular after 1940 or so.

Black as a fashionable color for quilts had a limited life; by the late 1920s when the pastel look took over, black must have seemed old-fashioned. It is a color scheme to look for, in both individual fabrics and overall look of a quilt. In cotton quilts, black indicates an 1890-1925 origin. In silk quilts

it indicates a date between 1860 and 1910 roughly. In wool quilts it seems to have been most popular from 1880 through 1925.

Exceptions are the quilts of the Amish. Like mainstream quilters in the 1880s, the Amish relied heavily on black for their color schemes but, unlike mainstream quilters, they continued to use black through 1950. A few Amish communities still use black and some are reviving its use for sale to outsiders whose appreciation for the older black quilts continues to grow. Novice fans of Amish quilts may come across wool quilts with a black color scheme and assume they are Amish, and thus very collectable. Because mainstream quilters very often included black in their wool quilts and comforters, it is unwise to assign an Amish provenance to any black wool quilt without corroborating family history.

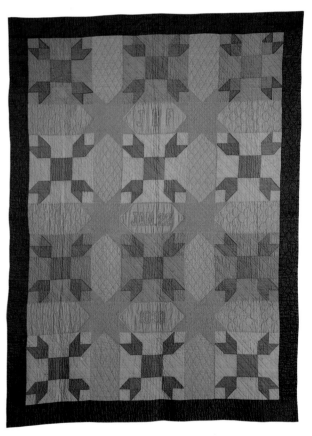

Rabbit Paw quilt. Made by an unknown Amish woman, possibly in Indiana. Inscribed in embroidery: JDF Jan 22, 1930. Pieced and quilted. Cotton. Collection: Esprit.

The Amish often used plain black cottons in their quilts, something mainstream quiltmakers rarely did until the recent rage for Amish quilts inspired copies of their color schemes. The Amish did not often use mainstream names for their designs. The Ladies' Art Company catalog called the pattern *4X Star*, not nearly as appealing as the Amish name *Rabbit Paw*.

Clues in White Fabrics

Natural fibers must be bleached to produce a true, bright white. The original bleaching method, still used for fine linens, was exposure to sunlight; cottons and linens were spread out on the grass and left for weeks or months in direct sun between periodic dampenings and washings that aided the process known as "grass bleaching" (35). Some references and much oral history attribute the bleaching effect to interaction between the chlorine in the grass and the sun's rays, but it is more likely that it was the sun alone that whitened the fabric (36). Grass bleaching was used as a home bleaching method through the 1930s and '40s, when it was relatively effective in removing the lettering from flour and sugar sacks for recycling into quilts.

Chlorine, the first chemical bleach, discovered in 1774, shortened and simplified the bleaching process (37). It is still important in fabric manufacturing and home laundry. All bleaching methods, including chlorine, sun bleaching and acids like lemon juice and buttermilk, weaken fibers, a fact that should inspire quilt collectors to exercise great care in trying to whiten old quilts.

White cottons, linens and silks are so common in quilts they are of little use in dating. Plain white or off-white fabrics have been the standard for the background of applique quilts, and they were commonly used as background in pieced designs too. One relatively short-lived fashion for white prints as background is a strong clue to dating, however. Between 1870 and 1925 quilters were fond of white shirting fabrics for pieced quilts. The standard shirting prints featured small, isolated figures on a white or off-white ground. Typical offerings in the decade between 1874 and 1884 were the Allen Print Works' line of shirtings in one of four colors on white: black, a dull red, a chocolate brown and a bright, blue-violet. Content was diverse: geometrics, florals and stripes.

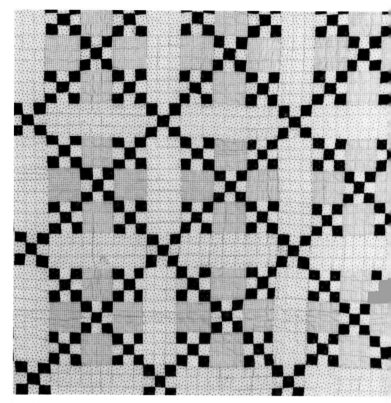

Double Nine Patch or **Irish Chain** quilt (detail) made by Harriett Theetge James (1865–1929) in Chanute, Kansas. Estimated date: 1900–1925. Pieced and quilted. Cotton. Collection: Spencer Museum of Art. Gift of Iva James.
   Navy blue and white quilts are difficult to date because blue and white calicoes were printed over such a long period of time. The white fabrics—shirting prints—help narrow the date; quiltmakers favored white shirting prints between 1875 and 1925.

The most memorable are the object or conversational prints featuring pictures of cats' faces, horses' heads, needles, horseshoes, tennis rackets, pincushions or thumb tacks. Around 1925 the fashion for shirting prints in quilts disappeared and plain white cottons again became the standard background fabric for pieced designs.

75

Larry Schwarm

Vestibule or **Morning Star** (detail), unfinished quilt top. Maker unknown. Estimated date: 1900–1925. Pieced. Cotton. Collection of the author.

The quality registration, small area of repeat and continuous print characterize these cottons as roller-prints. The quiltmaker had distinctive taste; most working in the first decades of this century used more subdued colors.

CLUES IN COTTON PRINTS

Printing Techniques

The surface design on cotton is often a significant clue to a fabric's date of origin and to the date of the quilt. Print style has varied according to taste over the centuries, but much of taste has been shaped by technology in the printing industry, so a knowledge of printed fabric requires a familiarity with the mechanics of printing as well as the history of social and political trends that have shaped fabric and quilt design.

There are many ways to obtain a design on a piece of fabric; the most direct is by painting it on free hand, a technique found in the fabrics in early quilts. Hand painting dyes on fabric was common work for women and children at the end of the eighteenth century. In Carlisle, England, more than 1000 were employed at penciling designs in textile factories (1).

Fabric manufacturers can also dye fabric in patterns. One method is by tie-dyeing, bunching fabric together in pleats and tucks before dyeing. Tie-dyeing, popular recently as a home craft in the United States, has a long tradition in Japan. Another dyeing technique is ikat in which the warp and/or weft threads are dyed in patterns before the cloth is woven. Although dye-patterned fabric is found in American quilts (especially in nineteenth-century silks) the technique is not significant.

The most common method of designing the surface is to print a pattern using a repetitive technique. Today most fabrics are printed by roller-printing technique. It can produce thousands of yards of patterned fabric by passing the cloth through presses that have copper rollers on which the pattern is impressed. The roller-printing or cylinder-printing method is only two hundred years old. Earlier fabric printers pressed color into their cloth using wooden blocks or copper plates.

BLOCK PRINTING

Printing yardage with wood blocks was a time consuming process in which the textile worker applied dye or mordant to the raised surface of the block and pressed the block onto the fabric, applying the colorant and moving the block

"The Calico Printer" is using wood blocks (tapped with a mallet) to decorate the yardage. The engraving was published in 1807 in *The Book of Trades.* Smithsonian Institution Negative 55511.

around on the material. As he applied the chemicals to the block and pressed it down, he was careful to line up or register one printed area with the next. If more than one color was desired, a different block with the chemicals for a second, third or fourth color was printed. Additional colors made registration more difficult because the edges of the successive colors had to match the edges of the preceding. To guide the printer with registration, metal wires in the corner of the block printed dots or registration marks.

Block printing on fabric is not as direct as those of us familiar with block printing on paper would imagine. Applying dye is more complex than paints and inks; most natural dyes require a mordant, so the printer might print a mordant, such as a metal oxide, on the cloth and then pass the whole cloth through the coloring agent. Only the mordanted areas would take the color.

The process of obtaining fast color prints using block printing or free-hand painting was so complex that for centuries Europeans could only wonder how the printers of India achieved their colorful, fast chintzes and calicoes. During the last quarter of the seventeenth century, English and French textile manufacturers discovered their secrets and began turning out their own versions of block printed cottons and linens. The first records of English cotton printing dates from 1676-77 (2). Block printing was carried out in Europe and America during the eighteenth and first part of the nineteenth century and ceased in the 1830s when the roller press replaced it.

PLATE PRINTING

Significant to the development of roller printing was the invention by a mid-eighteenth-century Irish printer named Frances Nixon of the copperplate printing process. He etched or incised designs into a plate, then applied a dye or mordant over the entire plate. The plate was wiped off, leaving the dye or mordant in the fine grooves to be picked up by fabric pressed into the grooves. Far greater detail could be obtained since lines etched into copper were finer than lines cut into wood. Flowers and birds could be rendered with biological exactness and the detail possible added new subject matter like portraits and landscapes to the designer's repertoire.

Because of the extremely detailed motifs registration was difficult. Plate prints were therefore monochromatic, typically a blue, a pinkish red or a brown on a white background. Only a single English printer, J. and M. Ware, was known to have produced multicolor plate prints (3). Most printers who wanted a multicolor cotton combined printing techniques. A piece of fabric might have a finely detailed copperplate background behind a simple floral design in another color that was applied with a wood block. Leaves and foliage might be applied by hand with a brush.

One well-documented firm famous for plate printing was Christophe-Phillipe Oberkampf's printworks in the French town of Jouy, which began using the process around fifteen years after its discovery. Copperplate prints are sometimes known as *Toiles De Jouy* (fabric from Jouy), whether they were printed there or not. The name implies that most copperplate prints are of French origin, but plate printworks are known to have existed in Ireland, England, Switzerland and Holland too.

ROLLER PRINTING

In 1783 a Scotsman named Thomas Bell realized that the copperplate could be curved around a roller, an invention that enabled printers to decorate a continuous roll of fabric. Bell's process gradually came to dominate the western textile printing industry. At Jouy a single new roller machine replaced 42 block printers (4). The roller printers not only saved labor; they also allowed a new diversity of design. Initially, as with the plate prints, registration was such a problem that only monochromatic fabrics could be printed. Secondary colors might be painted in, applied with small wood blocks, or obtained by combining wood and metal rollers.

Textile historians give conflicting dates as to when printers learned to print more than one color by roller. Stuart Robinson in *A History of Printed Textiles* credits Bell with the ability to print six colors by roller in 1785 (5). Within a century printers could roller print eight colors on both sides of the fabric in the same process, and today printers can print up to sixteen colors on both sides (in a technique known as duplex printing). Today's printers use essentially the same techniques as their nineteenth-century counterparts, and in some cases the very same rollers, which are replated and etched with new designs.

DISCRIMINATING PRINTING TECHNIQUES

The ability to discriminate between block, plate and roller printed fabric is useful in dating quilts

Copper-plate printed fabric. "Offrande a L'Amour" ("Offering to Love"). Pattern designed by Jean-Baptiste Huet (1745–1811) and printed at Oberkampf Manufactory in Jouy, France ca. 1804. Collection: Helen F. Spencer Museum of Art, the University of Kansas. Gift of the Cooper-Union Museum of Art.

A true toile-de-Jouy, this plate print was designed by one of Oberkampf's foremost artists. The single color on white, fine line detail, classical pastoral scenes, and large area of design repeat are typical of copper-plate prints which appear in quilts from about 1750 to 1850.

since the presence of a block or plate printed cotton is a clue to a pre-1850 origin, and the presence of a multicolored roller printed calico means the quilt in question could not date from before 1800 or so. Important clues to printing technique are print style and detail. Plate prints, as described above, have great detail in the drawing; they are almost always one color. The subject matter was a scene—possibly a fair, a country landscape, a scene from a novel or an historic event such as William Penn signing a treaty with the Indians. Finely detailed florals and trees were also popular images.

Early roller printers imitated the look of plate prints, however, and it takes a trained eye to decide if a pink and white pastoral scene is a plate print from the 1790s or a roller print copy from the 1820s. The length of the repeat (the unit of design that is printed over and over again) is a clue if there is enough of the fabric in question in the quilt's border or back to measure. Because copperplates were about 33 to 45 inches square, the repeat could be up to 45 inches. Rollers were 15 or 16 inches in diameter and could be repeated no larger than that. A repeat larger than 16 inches is thus a clue to a plate print. Whether it is a true plate print or roller printed copy, a finely detailed, monochromatic print on a white ground strongly suggests a pre-1840 origin.

Wood block prints were usually not so finely detailed as plate or roller prints. The wood block designs generally were not rendered in lines or dots, but in areas of color, sometimes in blobs of color. By the end of the eighteenth century, however, printers were inserting small pins into the blocks to obtain a "picotage" or pin-dot texture and inlaying metal wires to obtain fine lines.

Since wood block prints disappeared in the west in the mid-nineteenth century, they are not often found. Block printing is still used in India and other parts of the world, and the India print bedspreads popular for American decorating in the 1960s are usually made with the wood block technique. A trip to an import store to examine the India print spreads will give you some experience with wood block prints. Note that some of the edges of the color areas may not be sharp. Note also the smears, smudges and bubbles where the dye is not inked smoothly and check out how the different colored images register.

Good clues to a wood block print are the registration marks; printers often hid these dots in the pattern, and one must look carefully to find them. Another clue to a block or plate printed fabric is an awkward gap where a strip of background shows with no printed pattern. Roller prints appear to be continuous across the length of the fabric, so look for gaps that are a sign of an earlier printing technique. Many wood block printers did excellent work, and were not guilty of poor registration or gaps in the color area, but if you come across these signs in an old fabric they may very likely point to a wood block print and a pre-1850 quilt. For more information on distinguishing between printing techniques, see Gillian Moss's *Printed Textiles 1760-1860*, the catalog for a 1987 exhibit at the Cooper-Hewitt Museum (6).

ROLLER PRINTING METHODS

Rollers can apply pattern to cloth in many ways. It is rarely obvious to the casual observer how a printer obtained the design on a piece of cloth, but knowledge of the four major methods used in roller printing can help you discriminate nineteenth and twentieth centuries cotton prints.

Direct Printing

The simplest method is direct printing on a white fabric. The dye is applied to a roller etched with a design, a horseshoe print, for example. The roller is wiped; the color remains in the low spots—in the horseshoe design—and is pressed into the fabric as it passes by. Using this method the printer can get a colored horseshoe on a white ground or a white horseshoe on a colored ground (by printing the ground and not the figure).

The procedure can become more complex as more colors are directly printed atop one another. A second opaque color can be directly printed atop the first one (the printer could add black details and an outline to the horseshoe) or a second color could be printed in the white areas reserved for it (resulting in a colored horseshoe on a colored ground).

Discharge Printing

Another way to obtain a white print on a colored ground is through discharge printing in which cloth is dyed in the piece and then a discharge agent (for example, a bleach) is selectively applied by a roller. The color is destroyed in the figures—in our example, the horseshoes. The bleach is thoroughly washed out and the result is a white horseshoe print on a colored ground. More colors can be added by direct printing.

Discharge printing was first used in the United States in 1806; thereafter it became a very common printing technique (7). One clue to the process

is a figure that wears out before the background does, an indication that a harsh bleaching agent or one that wasn't thoroughly removed has caused differential rotting of the fabric.

Mordant Printing

Many dyes require a mordanting agent, a substance that fixes the dye into the cloth. For centuries calico printers have taken advantage of this fact to produce different shades in a fabric that passes through the dye bath only once. Madder, as described in the preceding chapter, is an excellent example of a dye that can be mordant printed. The rollers, rather than printing the coloring agent, print figures of mordant. A second mordant is applied with a second roller, a third and a fourth, and when the single coloring agent is applied four colors appear on the fabric. A typical madder-style print color scheme includes red-orange, chocolate brown, black and lavender, all printed with different mordants. Greens can also be printed using a mordant printing method. In one process the first step involves printing a figure of indigo blue dye mixed with an alum mordant (the mordant for the second dye). After the second dyebath (yellow) the figures become a well-registered green.

Resist Printing

In resist printing, a resist agent, such as wax or a chemical paste, is applied to the fabric in a pattern. When the fabric goes through the dye bath, no chemicals can pass through the resist. Later the resist is removed through heat or another chemical process, leaving undyed areas in a colored ground. Indigo was commonly used in the resist process, to produce a white figure on a blue dyed background. Resist is an old technique and can be combined with other techniques to produce a multi-colored fabric.

Combination Techniques

Printers are not limited to one method in roller printing. By 1815 they were able to combine mordant printing with discharge printing, applying a mordant for the second color at the same time they discharged the first color. After a second dye bath, the results were a perfectly aligned colored figure in a ground of a second color, a technique probably used for many of the multicolored Turkey red calicoes we see in old quilts. Resist and mordant dyeing techniques could also be combined in a similar manner, and these technological developments enabled nineteenth century manufacturers to produce prints of several colors neatly registered in adjacent small areas, the kinds of prints that are so characteristic of the American calico quilt.

CHARACTERISTICS OF COTTON PRINTS

Number of Colors

A single color print requiring only one roller application and one dye bath is generally cheaper to produce than a multicolor print. Because late nineteenth-century quilters tended to use inexpensive fabrics in their quilts, we find many single color prints in quilts from the 1890-1925 era when the textile printers were cutting costs by cutting quality. The presence of many single color prints in a quilt is a clue to this era.

In general, the rule is that the more colors in a print the more likely it was made before 1875 or after 1925. When counting colors and considering the complexity of a fabric's printing operation, one must remember that mordant printed madder style prints with shades of red, brown and lavender in the same print, and double pinks (multiple shades of pink due to different mordant strengths and line density) remained popular over many decades because they were cheap to print.

Registration

The quality of the color registration in a cotton print is obvious. When printing a red flower with a green stem on a yellow background, a printer must leave white space for the figures in the ground, and then print the flower and stem exactly where the space has been reserved. If he doesn't, a color overlap will appear on one side of the figure and a white gap on the other. The red flower and green stem must also meet exactly with no overlap or gaps. If they don't, the registration is off.

Printers working with natural dyes and block prints had many registration difficulties. Designers minimized such difficulties by outlining figures with heavy black lines that covered overlaps or gaps, so a heavy black outline around a figure is a good clue to a pre-1850 date. Printers also avoided poor registration by leaving white halos

around the design elements. Look for rather awkward white halos separating colored figures from colored grounds; they are good clues to a pre-1850 origin.

As printers perfected the roller printing techniques described above, registration improved. A quilt with many well registered multicolored prints is likely to be from 1840 to 1890 when registration was at its best.

The introduction of synthetic dyes required new printing techniques to permit precise registration. Around the turn of the century, printers of inexpensive fabrics avoided registration by reducing the number of colors; after World War I they returned to using the white halo to separate multicolored areas. Twentieth-century manufacturers showed more skill in incorporating halos into their designs than had earlier printers, but the halos are apparent. Halos are thus a clue to a pre-1850 or 1925-1950 print.

SCALE IN PRINTS

Quiltmakers since the 1840s have shown a decided preference for small-scale, figured cottons that we today call calico. By that time, cotton was inexpensive enough to allow a quiltmaker the luxury of buying fabric specifically for a quilt and of choosing fabric from the scraps left over from dressmaking or home decorating . Calico became such a favorite fabric that the scale of a print in a quilt can be a clue to its date. A quilt that is made up of only calicoes and plain cottons is likely to date from 1840 or later. A quilt of chintz or of mixed calicoes and chintzes is likely to date from 1865 or earlier. Of 127 eighteenth or nineteenth-century date-inscribed quilts in our sample, characterized as of chintz or of mixed-scale fabrics, 98.5% were made before 1865. Only two chintz-scale quilts (1.5%) were made in the years between 1865 and 1900. One occasionally sees chintz-scale quilts made in end-of-the-century cretonnes, but they are unusual.

In the 1920s and '30s, larger-scale florals became more popular again for quilts, but the differences in color scheme between pre-Civil War large-scale prints and post-World War I large scale prints are so pronounced that there should be little confusion between them.

CHINTZ

The word chintz derives from the Hindu language; it may mean variegated or colored (chint) or spotted (chitta). Since sixteenth century English traders first brought chintz back from India, the word has consistently meant a printed fabric. To the Englishwoman, Mrs. Trollope, traveling in America in 1828, chintz meant "the material of a curtain" (8). A stricter definition of chintz defines it as a large-scale print, suitable for furnishings like drapery and upholstery, with a glaze (which is liable to wash out with use).

The first chintz imports were remarkable in their color brightness and fastness, but they were printed to Indian taste with dark colored backgrounds and light colored patterns. A letter survives in which an importer advises the "painter" to cease using "sad red grounds which are not so well accepted here" (9). The English preferred a white ground with colored prints and they liked florals and trees with a touch of the Oriental; the importers sent botanical drawings and designs they wished the printers to adapt. The Indian printers were glad to comply, changing their colors and designs to please the export trade.

Indian chintzes were printed as yardage and as finished bed covers known as palampores. The palampores were also quilted and sent to Europe as whole-cloth quilts stuffed with cotton batting. The chintzes produced for the European trade were exceedingly popular, prompting English and French textile manufacturers to learn the secrets of chintz and calico printing. By the end of the seventeenth century they were able to turn out their own cheaper versions of the Indiennes, as the Indian textiles were called. The Europeans did not have the color versatility of the eastern dyemasters, as previously stated, but they did produce colorful fast prints that were well received in Europe and the American colonies. The competition alarmed the better established English and French textile producers of silk and wools. To protect the English textile industry, Parliament in 1700 forbade the importing and wearing of imported print cottons, silks and linens. The trade protection only stimulated the English printing industry, further threatening the wool and silk weavers and causing Parliament, in 1721, to prohibit the sale or use of English printed cottons (woven elsewhere but imported to England for printing). Thanks to a loophole in the new law, English printers continued to print linens, and in 1736 they were permitted to print fabric with linen warp and cotton weft. The trade restrictions continued until 1774 when English printers were again permitted to print cotton but required to weave three blue threads into the selvages of the cotton made for export. This law, repealed in 1811, is of great use to those who study antique textiles, as the presence of three blue threads in the selvage of a cotton print means the fabric is English, made during that 37-year period. The fact is of some importance to those hoping to date quilts, but selvages too rarely appear on quilts. It is always worth checking the edges of borders and the backs of early quilts to see if the blue selvage threads are there, indicating English manufacture between 1774 and 1811.

Despite the laws, chintzes continued to be popular for bedding, furnishings and clothing in both America and England; the laws only forced the price up on an already expensive product. In 1776 American Peyton Randolph's inventory valued "1 Chintz Bedcover" at £3; his marble table was worth only £2 (10).

The English reliance on trade restrictions to support their native industries extended to the American colonists, whom they desired to maintain as consumers of English goods rather than as competitors. At various times during British rule the colonists were encouraged or forbidden to produce certain textiles by law with prohibitions being more frequent than encouragements. American importation of any tools or machinery for factory textile production was forbidden, and even the English export of plans for such items to America was prohibited. Many Americans, realizing a break with England was approaching, felt that America must become self-sufficient in manufacturing. Skilled textile workers from England were encouraged to immigrate, and several made the move. The earliest reference to American cotton printing goes back to 1712 when George Leason and Thomas Webber, "lately arriv'd here from England", advertised in a Boston newspaper that they printed "all sorts of linnens" (11). The best documented eighteenth-century American printer is John Hewson who established a Philadelphia printworks in 1774. Like Samuel Slater, who established the first American cotton spinning mill, Hewson arrived with his knowledge of textile techniques and machinery in his head, a head so valuable that the British put a price on it. To them the export of such information was treason.

Examples of Hewson's prints survive in quilts made during the last quarter of the eighteenth century and the first quarter of the nineteenth centuries. As the American chintz industry developed in the first years of the nineteenth century, Americans continued to import chintzes; many of the chintzes we find in our quilts were from England, France and India as well as the infant American factories. An excellent catalog of dozens of chintzes likely to be found in pre-1850 quilts Florence Montgomery's out-of-print *Printed Textiles* (12).

Nine Patch quilt, maker unknown. Estimated date: 1825–1850. Pieced and quilted. Cotton. Collection: Smithsonian Institution, Negative # 73–4284.

The combination of large-scale chintz prints and smaller-scale dress prints is a good clue to a pre-Civil War quilt.

Although printers occasionally catered to quiltmakers (Hewson and others in America and England produced prints specifically for the centers of quilts), the major use for chintz has always been other furnishings. When quiltmakers stopped using chintz around 1860 manufacturers continued to produce it, so even though we don't see it often in post Civil War quilts it was available. An individual quiltmaker might choose to use it, or quilters in a region might maintain a style for chintz borders as they did in South Carolina after quilters in other regions had turned to calico and plains.

One way to determine the date of a piece of chintz is by its content and style. The differences across the decades in florals, the most common content, are subtle, but other subject matter can offer a more substantial clue.

Whole-cloth quilt made of an Indian palampore, maker unknown. Estimated date: Palampore—1775–1800; quilted—mid-nineteenth century or later. Cotton. Quilted. Collection: Smithsonian Institution, Negative # 61037.

The single piece of cotton in this quilt is a palampore, a word derived from the Persian and Hindi languages meaning bedcover. Palampores generally featured trees and floral patterns. They were imported as spreads or as finished quilts, but this one was apparently quilted later.

Many of the design conventions in early applique quilts are derived from palampores. In both we see a light background, a central design, floral borders and the image of the flowering tree.

Trees

The tree-of-life design, popular in chintzes made before 1850, features a serpentine, blooming tree, usually bearing a wide variety of flowers and fruits, and growing from a hillock or small mound, or sometimes out of a basket. The image is an amalgam from various cultures. Sources have been traced to Chinese, Persian and Indian designs

(13). English traders encouraged Indian textile printers to adapt the flowering tree for their bedcovers or palampores, and it remained popular from the last quarter of the seventeenth century through the mid-nineteenth. Based on the evidence of the quilts left to examine, American quiltmakers were fond of cutting the tree-of-life designs out of the palampores and appliqueing them to their spreads or quilts. They also created their own flowering tree designs.

Other variations of tree designs called arborescent patterns, were popular subjects for chintzes after 1740. Gnarled branches laden with full-blown peonies and exotic birds combined Oriental exoticism and English gardens. One particularly good clue to date is a palm-tree and game bird design, also called palm tree and pheasants, that was popular in the first half of the nineteenth century. Many versions of tropical palms and long-tailed pheasants were printed in block and roller printed methods through the 1830s (14). Palms were so popular they appeared in settings as incongruous as English villages. So look for palm trees; they are good clues to an early nineteenth-century quilt.

Floral Baskets and Vases

In addition to the tree-of-life, the other major motif that appeared in the center of medallion-type cut-out chintz quilts was a floral vase or basket. Hewson's print works produced a vase of flowers on a coverlet fabric that was so popular that at least seven quilts featuring the print and two complete spreads survive. The dates inscribed on the quilts with Hewson vases are 1807 and 1848, but the fabric was probably printed as early as the 1790s (15).

Trophy of Arms or Hunt Cornucopia

A wood block print that appears in many chintz quilts featured the tools of the classical soldier or hunter—a quiver of arrows, a shield, a bow and a hunter's horn amid a bouquet of flowers. This "Trophy of Arms" fabric is thought to have been produced especially for quiltmakers. Florence Montgomery in *Printed Textiles* dates it as about 1815 (16).

Pillar Prints

Architectural columns hung with flowers were a classically inspired motif that appeared in wood

Whole-cloth cotton quilt (detail). Maker unknown. Estimated date: fabric–eighteenth century; quilting–nineteenth century. Cotton. Quilted. Collection: Smithsonian Institution, Negative # 76–2680.

The fabric in the top of this quilt is believed to be Indian and much older than the fabric on the back; it may be that the top cotton was used as bed hangings before being made into a quilt. Arborescent patterns (tree limbs) with exotic birds were common motifs for block prints in the eighteenth and early nineteenth century.

Eight Point Star with Hewson square. Quilt made by Elizabeth Hart (ca. 1829-?) in Bucks County, Pennsylvania. Inscribed in ink: 1848. Pieced and quilted. Cotton. Collection: Helen F. Spencer Museum of Art, the University of Kansas.

Elizabeth Hart's quilt is a transition between two styles. The Hewson square in the central medallion is typical of early nineteenth-century chintz quilts. The star blocks are typical of the calico block style that developed mid-century.

The center block, printed by John Hewson of Philadelphia, America's most sophisticated early printer, pictures an urn surrounded by birds and butterflies. This print is thought to have been produced for quiltmakers between 1790 and 1810, years before Elizabeth Hart's birth. The Turkey red calicoes were popular in the 1840s when the quilt was made.

Chintz quilt, made by a member of the William Allston family, near Charleston, South Carolina. Estimated date: 1820−1840. Appliqued, pieced and quilted. Cotton. Collection: Smithsonian Institution, Negative # 45821-A.

The center panel, the Hunt Cornucopia, appears in several quilts from the first half of the nineteenth century. Two additional panels have been cut in half to form the corners in the central medallion. The outer borders are chintz strips; the inner border is appliqued.

block chintzes from about 1800, and on roller printed chintzes after 1825. Pillar prints faded in popularity with printers in the mid 1830s, but quiltmakers continued to use them through the 1840s and into the 1850s.

Rainbow Prints

The roller press encouraged printers to experiment with a type of design called rainbow prints. By gradually shading the colors on the roller, they

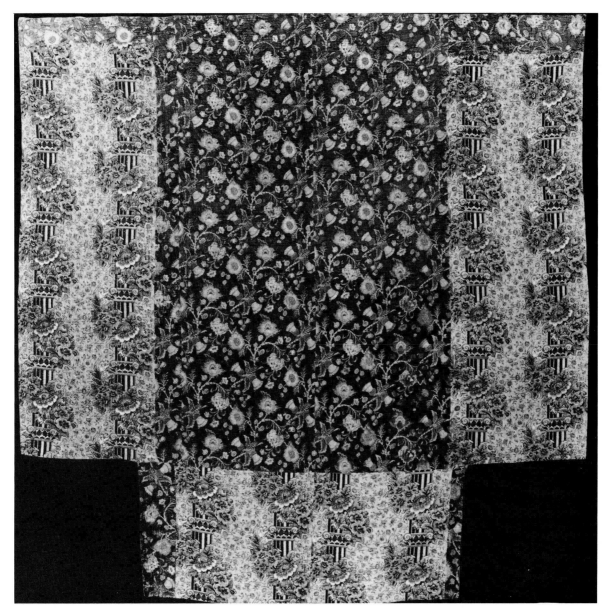

Chintz quilt. Maker unknown. Estimated date: 1800–1840. Pieced and quilted. Collection: Helen F. Spencer Museum of Art, the University of Kansas. The William Bridges Thayer Memorial.

The fabric in the outside border is a pillar print with fluted columns and capitals visible behind the garlands of flowers.

could obtain a rainbow of different colors or of different intensities of a single color, which could wash smoothly from one color to the next or vary with ripples and zigzag effects. The term rainbow appeared in an 1826 reference to wallpapers, which were also printed in the rainbow style (17), and an 1846 reference to fabric (18). Other names for the style are fondu prints, from the French word meaning to melt or dissolve, and ombre, French for shaded or tinted (19).

Rainbow shading was used in both the backgrounds and the figured areas of cotton prints.

Found in many colors, it was exceptionally popular in varying intensities of a bright blue, and also in a khaki tan. Rainbow grounds were fashionable behind stripes and in plaids, as well as behind figured prints like florals and scrolls. Mid-nineteenth-century quiltmakers used them in their sets and borders, their pieced designs and in applique. The skillful artists who made the mid-nineteenth century Baltimore Album Quilts used the shaded colors to suggest the texture of baskets, watermelon rinds and eagle feathers and the roundness of architectural columns in their pictorial applique.

Chips and Whetstones or Mariner's Compass. Detail of a quilt made by Susanna Richards Mosely, in Pembroke, Kentucky. Estimated date: 1825-1850. Pieced and quilted. Cotton. Collection: Helen F. Spencer Museum of Art, the University of Kansas.

Susanna Mosely combined sprigged calicoes with stripes, rainbow prints and other large scale fabrics in her scrap quilt. The north/south points on the compass may appear faded, but actually the fabric is a rainbow print, deliberately printed to melt from one shade to another. Note the triple line quilting, for which she used light thread in the blocks and dark thread in the striped sashing.

The rainbow printing technique was also used with wood blocks in the 1820s, but it became more common as roller printing advanced. A general date span for quilts with rainbow prints is 1820 to 1860.

Commemorative Chintzes

During the last quarter of the eighteenth century the detail made possible by the copperplate printing process encouraged a variety of patriotic and commemorative prints. Many of the prints designed to appeal to the American spirit of independence were printed in Europe. The development of the patchwork quilt during these years meant that some of the few surviving examples of these early commemorative prints are preserved in quilts.

Cotton or cotton/linen yardage featuring war hero George Washington posed in classical settings were exported to America as early as 1785. (20). William Penn's Treaty with The Indians was another popular subject. The plate process was particularly suited to such designs, but English,

French and American printers also printed commemoratives using the wood block and roller processes. Commemoratives appeared as yardage, handkerchiefs and as pieces of fabric intended to be sewn into quilts. Quilt centers in celebration of George III's Golden Jubilee in 1809 and Princess Charlotte's marriage in 1816 were intended for English quiltmakers, while a handkerchief that marked The Death of General Washington in 1799 was sold to Americans.

Later commemoratives used by quiltmakers include Hard Cider and Log Cabin yardage from the 1840 presidential election. William Henry Harrison, whose campaign image came from his hard-drinking western roots, characterized his opponent Martin Van Buren as an effete, wine-sipping patrician. Fabric mills printed Harrison campaign cottons picturing cider barrels in the yard of the cabin home.

Political bandanas featuring many late nineteenth century presidential campaigners were incorporated into quilts, as were 1876 Centennial prints with views of the Philadelphia exposition, and yardage glorifying Queen Victoria's Jubilee in 1897. For more information on American commemoratives, see Herbert Ridgway Collins's *Threads of History: Americana Recorded on Cloth, 1775 to the Present,* a catalog of hundreds of patriotic textiles (21).

ROBE PRINTS

A robe print is an end-of-the-century fabric that is an exception to the rule that large-scale prints were not popular in post-Civil War quilts and comforters. They were used as backing fabrics for quilts and tied comforters and as scraps in patchwork designs. Although they came in other shades, red ground with a black figure was the most common color combination. The 1901 Sears catalog described them: "Comforter or robe prints. Large scroll oriental comforter prints. Bright colors. Comes in palm leaf, floral and cashmere designs on red, orange, blue brown or heliotrope grounds." The catalogs advertised them from the mid-1870s (Montgomery Ward sold "Robe prints for comforters" in 1876) into the next century. The last reference I found was in 1917 in the Sears catalog. The catalog listings and observation indicate that robe prints are a clue to a date of 1875-1920.

CRETONNES

In the last quarter of the nineteenth century the

mills produced new styles in large scale cottons meant for furnishings which were sometimes cut up for scrap quilts or used for backing and less often combined to make an anachronism—a late nineteenth century or twentieth century chintz quilt. The fabric was no longer called chintz, however, possibly because the word chintz had, since the advent of roller printed cottons for furnishings, come to mean mass-produced, inexpensive fabric, with all the connotations of the word chintzy. Many of the written references describe late nineteenth-century furnishing fabrics as cretonne, a convention that I will follow in referring to large scale furnishings fabric produced after 1875. The word cretonne apparently replaced the word chintz during the last quarter of the nineteenth century, and today the word chintz has made a comeback.

Cretonne (pronounced kree-tawn' by most of the women who remember when it was popular) is derived from the French village of Creton. It was often used interchangeably with the word chintz. Caulfeild and Saward in their 1882 needlework book (22) and a 1925 *Farm Journal* article (23) referred to cut-out chintz quilts as cretonne applique. Chintz is sometimes narrowly defined as a glazed fabric for furnishings with cretonne, the unglazed version (24). But like most other distinctions in textile terms, the difference between chintz and cretonne is not absolute. In a 1918 definition, George Leland Hunter described chintz as an English word and cretonne as a French word for drapery prints. He mentioned that the French prints are larger designs on a heavier cloth (25).

Larry Schwarm

Cretonne comforter back. This turn-of-the-century roller-printed cotton was called cretonne in the catalogs of the day. Collection: Jan Morris and Bob Nitcher .

The cretonnes produced after 1875 were often rather heavy fabric. Many were printed on twill-weave cotton, something not found in earlier chintzes. Common subject matter was florals and paisleys. More distinctive were commemorative cretonnes; a victory arch inscribed with the name Dewey, honoring the hero of the 1898 Spanish-American war, is one that is easy to date. Typical of the times were scenes such as a circus performance, portraits of women in Japanese costume or peasant girls dreamily swinging. Sentiment and exoticism are two of the hallmarks of these prints.

Distinguishing between the late nineteenth-century American roller printed furnishings fabric (cretonnes) and the earlier wood block and roller printed fabric (chintzes) requires experience with detail, printing technique, color and style. The newer prints have better registration; the colors are more muted, the style is more sentimentalized. Glazing is uncommon. One simple clue to a later date is the twill weave. Cretonnes indicate a date of 1875 through 1925.

CALICOES

The word calico is derived from an Indian port, Calicut. To contemporary American quiltmakers the word means a small scale print, usually a floral. In the nineteenth century calico technically meant a type of cloth defined by its weave, so one finds many references to plain calicoes. Percale is a better weave of fabric than calico; in 1922 Sears offered similar small scale prints as calicoes ("American standard fancy calico") for 10 cents a yard or as percale ("high-grade percale") for 20 cents. Most nineteenth-century quiltmakers, like their twentieth-century counterparts, viewed calico as a print and viewed it as the preferred fabric for quilts.

Calico, an inexpensive, roller-printed cotton, was one of the happy results of the industrial revolution. Manufacturers began printing American calicoes in the 1820s and '30s in New England and the mid-Atlantic states. By 1840 there were 1240 American textile factories (26), many of them devoted to calico production, but much of the calico we see in mid-nineteenth century quilts was imported. In 1830 the United States annually imported 3.5 yards of cloth per citizen. By the 1850s imports had increased to 6.5 yards (27).

The small scale cotton prints we call calico can be generally classified as abstract or figurative. Abstract prints, also called conventionalized prints, include stripes, dots and squiggles and all variety of geometric figures, most of which in themselves

Cretonne quilt, maker unknown. Estimated date: 1884–1910. Pieced, three layers but neither tied nor quilted. Cotton. Collection: Helen F. Spencer Museum of Art, the University of Kansas. The William Bridges Thayer Memorial.

Most quiltmakers working at the turn of the century preferred small scale prints over the large scale cottons used here. Characteristics that distinguish later cretonnes from earlier chintzes include the high-quality registration, the twill weave in many of them, and the subject matter, especially the Japanese influence seen in the costumed figures along the bottom row. Some of the prints are found on sample cards from the Cacheco printworks in 1883 and 1884.

are poor clues to date, because they were produced over such a long period. Other types of figures, however, can be helpful in assigning a date.

FLORALS

Figurative or realistic prints are primarily florals.

Tiny flowers became the staple print for many mills; they printed the same florals decade after decade with little or no change. Even when the prints did change, the clues to different eras are subtle. In general, florals are a poor clue to date, with the exception of floral trails, which differ from standard floral calicoes in that the flowers are not so isolated but are connected by serpentine

Mexican Rose quilt, made by Jane Barr in Pennsylvania. Inscribed in corded quilting: July, 1849. Appliqued, quilted and stuffed. Cotton. Collection: Smithsonian Institution, Negative # 76–2667.

Jane Barr used three calicoes in her *Mexican Rose* quilt.

The red-ground floral print in the petals is a clue to a mid-nineteenth century quilt, as are the stuffed work and the dense quilting— a close filling pattern of parallel lines and stipple work behind the padded letters and numbers.

Check quilt, attributed to the family of Alexander Hamilton. Estimated date: 1790–1825. Pieced and quilted with a fringe. Cotton. Collection: Helen F. Spencer Museum of Art, the University of Kansas. The William Bridges Thayer Memorial.

This simple quilt is pieced of two floral trail prints, one block printed on a light ground, the other on dark. The only evidence for the Hamilton family connection is a note that came with the quilt when it was donated to the University of Kansas by collector Sallie Casey Thayer.

Larry Schwarm

Object or conversational print. Prints such as a life-like fly are sure to cause conversation. A late nineteenth-century rage for insects in decoration inspired several similar prints, which are often seen in scrap quilts from 1875 to 1900. Collection: Muriel Pech Owen.

vines. Floral trails were popular for dresses and quilts from the late eighteenth century through the second quarter of the nineteenth and are a good clue to an early quilt.

OBJECT PRINTS

Object prints are loosely classified as figurative subject matter other than florals. These objects range from animals and human figures to tools, sporting equipment and vehicles of all kinds. Object prints, also called conversationals (28) or conversation prints (29), are small scale realistic renderings, printed by roller in primarily monochromatic color schemes; the fabric is usually a light, plain weave cotton, commonly called shirting. The span of object prints has not been established. There is a blue on white dog head print in Persoz's 1846 guide for printers (30), and the 1920's Sears catalogs showed a horseshoe print— white on navy—advertised as suitable for children's rompers. In the 1940s object prints continued to be popular for children's clothing, and objects as diverse as the Eiffel Tower, Chinese pagodas and Mexican sombreros were printed for adult's clothing. Scraps from all of them appeared in quilts.

One change over time was the detail of the print and the number of colors, with twentieth-century examples having more colors but less detail. A typical late-nineteenth-century object print is a fine line drawing of a bicycle, printed in red on white; a typical mid-twentieth-century object print is a yellow duck with orange bill and feet, printed on pastel green.

Subject matter changed with the years; sporty prints depicting tennis racquets, riding whips, oars and especially horsehoes were popular in the last quarter of the nineteenth century (31). The 1893 Montgomery Ward catalog advertised anchor, sailboat and baseball patterns in shirting prints. Cute animals and foreign costumes were themes in the 1940s.

Object prints were exceptionally popular with quiltmakers collecting swatches for their charm quilts and scrap quilts during the last quarter of the nineteenth century. Any subject seemed a fit figure for calicoes in this era. Sewing tools like thread and needles, thimbles and pins are often found in these prints, as are small children drawn in the manner of Kate Greenaway's illustrations. An example is a little girl, dressed in furs, riding a sled. Printed in black on white, the entire figure is less than an inch. The strangest subjects of all were the flies and honeybees carefully rendered in every entomological detail. The insects on fabric reflected a wider fashion for zoological specimens in the '80s. Bees, spiders and bats were fashioned into jewelry, hat decorations, filet crochet designs and Crazy Quilt embroidery.

ECCENTRIC PRINTS

Within the large classification of geometric cali-

Larry Schwarm

"Lane's Net" was a much-copied eccentric print, produced from around 1840 through the end of the century and found in many variations in many quilts. Collections: Pam Johnson and the author.

coes there is the loosely defined category of eccentric prints (or excentrics, as the word is spelled in England). Pettitt tells the story of the first eccentric print. It happened at the Lane factory in England in 1835 when a simple stripe crimped in the roller, producing jagged angles. Rather than discarding the fabric, the manufacturers marketed it, and the idea of bizarre, complicated geometrics caught on (32). Eccentric prints were popular from 1840 through the end of the century; some became staples, produced season after season.

The definition of an eccentric print is vague. It often has many small stripes broken into acute angles and can look deceptively like the invention of a designer working in 1935 under the influence of art deco and Flash Gordon. Eccentric prints are quite common in quilts from the last half of the nineteenth century.

VERMICULATE, MACHINE GROUND, PICOTAGE AND OTHER DETAILED PRINTS

Early roller printers did many allover patterns of fine line on which a second design might be printed with a wood block. Though wood block and plate printing could give the same effect, the fine-lined background was so suited to the roller printing process that printers could buy pre-engraved rollers with what were called machine grounds—patterns of fine lines and/or dots.

One type of finely detailed print of irregular twisted lines is called a vermiculate ground, a word derived from the Latin for "worm", suggesting worm trails or worm-like writhing. The worm-like lines are a type of background often found in other crafts, such as stone carving.

A common name today for the irregular wavy lines is "seaweed print", because they resemble marine growth. The name has nineteenth-century roots. In 1889 Lucy Larcom recalled a scrap of cotton as a "delicate pink and brown sea-moss pattern on a white ground" (33). Another period name is parsley print, and one authority also uses the terms scribble, maze, web or network pattern for these fine-lined patterns (34).

A variation of the form is flecked with tiny dots rather than lines. The dot designs are called stippling or picotage.

Vermiculate and picotage designs were often monochromatic, usually a color on white. A variation was the "double" print, in which two (or three) shades of a single color were printed on white. Double pinks, as noted previously, were exceptionally popular from the 1840s through the beginning of this century, but we also find references in the 1840s to "double purples" (35) and see evidence of double yellow-oranges. A double print, at first glance, appears to be a pastel plain pink or yellow cotton, but a second look reveals that the fabric is a white ground printed with lines so fine that the eye reads them as solid.

In general, the finely detailed line patterns went out of production in the 1880s with increasing mechanization and cost cutting measures. Grounds to most calicoes from the 1880s to the present are plain colored without the time-consuming detail evident in the nineteenth century vermiculate, picotage or machine-ground prints. An exception is the double pink print, produced through the first half of the twentieth century, although it lost popularity with quiltmakers during the 1920s.

Another exception is the mourning print, a fine black line printed on white in such profusion that the eye reads the fabric as gray. The 1902 Sears catalog offered mourning prints at "5 1/2 cents per yard. Very Best Quality of Mourning Prints. These prints are very swell, and are worn by ladies or misses, are neat and will wash without fading." Mourning prints are a good clue to an 1890-1925 date.

PAISLEYS

Paisley designs are derived from wool shawls that originated in Kashmir, India. The cone shapes,

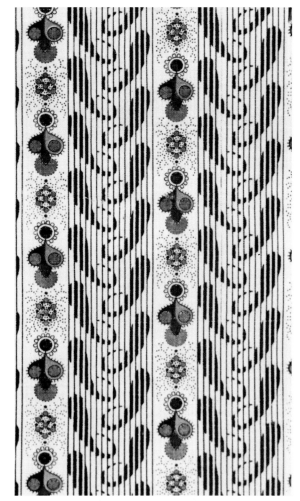

Larry Schwarm

Paisley or shawl prints printed with cones were especially popular in the madder-style color scheme of red, orange and brown in the last half of the nineteenth century. This paisley stripe backed a cotton comforter made between 1875 and 1900. Collection: Pam Johnson.

with their serrated or stepped edges, were a fertility symbol derived from the male organ of the date palm, traditional patterns woven into the shawls that the English began importing in the eighteenth century (36). Kashmir shawls were so fashionable that European weavers began producing copies towards the end of that century with the factories in Paisley, Scotland, producing the best quality reproductions. Textile designers began including the serrated cone shapes in all kinds of printed designs. Paisley prints, also called shawl prints, were printed in every color combination with a madder-style color scheme very popular (resembling the cinnamon reds and oranges in the woolen shawls). Paisley shawls went out of fashion around 1870 and the mills in Paisley ceased production of their version of the fabric in 1886.

By then the town had given its name to both the shawl and the cone shape. Paisley designs were so popular for so long that they are a poor clue in themselves, but the paisley design in madder-style colors in either cotton or wool indicates a date in the last half of the nineteenth century.

Although the shawls were no longer in fashion, paisley designs remained popular until after the turn of the century. One change in style was a black on bright red color scheme. Black cones on red backgrounds appeared in small scale cottons and on large scale robe prints and cretonnes that are often found on quilt backs, in scrap quilts and as whole-cloth comforters. Look for black paisley shapes on red as a clue to a date in the years before and after 1900.

STRIPES AND PLAIDS

Many striped, checked and plaid fabrics are yarn dyed and woven into patterns; they are among the hardest fabrics to date since the same designs were woven over such a long period of time. The process for yarn dyeing and weaving pattern was less dependent on sophisticated technology than the process for printing fabrics. One could produce a yarn-dyed green plaid or a lavender stripe before those colors were commonplace in prints.

However, plaids and stripes can offer weak clues in some cases. Queen Victoria wore the Royal Stuart tartan when she made her first visit to Scotland in 1842. She later had her portrait painted wearing her Scottish tartans and decorated Balmoral Castle with plaid upholstery in 1855, inspiring a fashion for woven and printed plaids in clothing and quilts. The printed plaids we see in mid-century quilts are distinctive because they are often rather unskillfully printed; the cloudy greens and very bright blues, common colors in printed plaids from the 1840s and '50s, were often clumsily applied. Plaids fell out of fashion after the Civil War but appeared again in the 1890 to 1925 period.

Like plaids, stripes are subject to the vagaries of fashion, popular in certain decades, considered passe in others. The color scheme, the scale of the stripe and the skill of the printer are details that offer more information than just the presence of a stripe. Tailored, hard edge shirting stripes are too classic to be especially useful, but stripes incorporating images such as flowers and paisleys and specific details like rainbow grounds and vermiculate patterns are good clues to specific eras.

Large scale chintz stripes were very often used for sets, borders and backs before 1860. Smaller-

Larry Schwarm

Stripes, like paisleys, were popular in madder-style colors of red, orange and brown, good clues to a date between the Civil War and the end of the century. This one backed a cotton comforter made between 1875 and 1900. Collection: Pam Johnson.

scale, madder-style stripes were popular in the 1860-1900 era, when all kinds of printed stripes were fashionable in clothing, furnishings and quilts. Floral and paisley stripes from the '60s through the '80s had an oriental exoticism about them and are, in fact, very much like the stripes available to quilters today, many of which are directly influenced by striped cottons from the last quarter of the nineteenth century.

PRINTED PATCHWORK

The development of printed patchwork is evidence of the popularity of quiltmaking. Both English and American printers produced imitation pieced designs which found their way into quilts. Ruth Finley, who wrote about fabrics in 1929, stated that "geometrical chintz" or "faux patchwork" (faux is French for false) was popular in the 1830s or '40s (37), but the earliest pieces documented go back to about 1850 (38). Dr. William Dunton, a quilt historian of the 1940s, mentioned four pieces he'd seen dated 1854 (39).

Simulated patchwork reflected popular patch-

94

Larry Schwarm

Printed patchwork fabric. This printed Log Cabin yardage is often seen as a backing on pieced Log Cabin quilts. It came in several color combinations and is found in swatch books between 1900 and 1910. Author's collection.

Printed patchwork fabric. This mid-nineteenth century fabric reflects the tastes of the time; calicoes and chintzes are combined in a simple design. The fabric was quilted into a whole-cloth quilt. Collection: Smithsonian Institution, Negative # 75–6405.

work style; the designs from the 1850s imitated chintz patches and those from the turn of the century imitated Log Cabins, Crazy Quilts and charm quilts in madder-style cottons. The 1933 Sears catalog sold cottons in the Grandmother's Flower Garden, Dresden Plate and Double Wedding Ring patterns that were fads at the time.

During the 1930s and '40s fabric designers were occasionally inspired by an old quilt in a book or an exhibit to design printed patchwork that reflected an earlier style; the color schemes in these prints usually shout twentieth century, so that discriminating the fairly recent origins of these revival faux patchwork prints is not difficult.

COMMEMORATIVE CALICOES

Commemorative prints are useful because they can help narrow the dating of a quilt; it could not have been finished before the actual event being commemorated. Most commemorative prints honoring political figures like Benjamin Franklin and Queen Victoria or memorializing events such as the 1893 World's Fair are designed for a large

scale print rather than calico, but during the last half of the nineteenth century, at the height of the calico craze, fabric designers featured small scale commemorative designs too. There are several surviving examples of Civil War calicoes with Union sentiments such as a star design and clasped hands under the slogan "The Union Forever" (40). A tiny stripe featuring a portrait of Ulysses S. Grant and the words "First in War" and "First in Peace" is attributed to 1872 (41). A similar stripe with the initials H.G. and a tophat honors Grant's 1872 opponent, Horace Greeley (42). Both are surprisingly common in scrap and charm quilts of the era.

America's Centennial celebration in 1876 inspired textile designers. Look for red, white, and blue flag-waving versions of Centennial commemoratives. Montgomery Ward sold "flag prints" in 1876 through their catalog—"Small flags 8 cents per yard, large flags 10 cents". More common in quilts are sedate shirtings in colors like brown and green with subtle designs such as a plaid with tiny numerals "1776-1876" printed in one of the lines. Occasionally, the seamstress has trimmed the "1876" half of the legend leaving only "1776". Do not make the mistake of thinking that such a print was produced in the eighteenth century; any such date is undoubtedly a later commemorative design printed in 1876 or even 1976.

Not so literal as the dated Centennial print is a white five-pointed star printed on a navy ground that appears to be from the same time. Most white geometrics on navy ground are poor clues to date, but the field of stars may have been printed only in the years near the Centennial. Could these white stars in a blue field be the flag prints described in the Wards catalog?

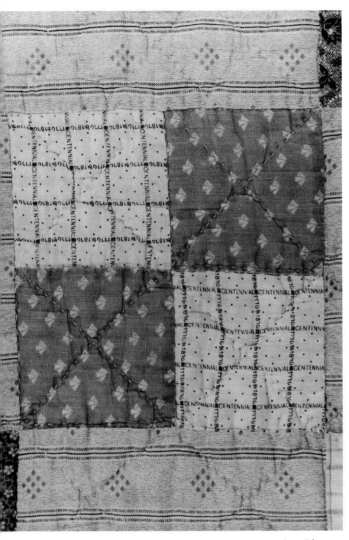

Larry Schwarm

Detail, Nine Patch quilt. Maker unknown. Estimated date: 1890–1925. Pieced and quilted. Cotton. Collection: Cherie Ralston.

The black on white windowpane check reads "Centennial" and "1776-1876". It was probably produced around 1876, but the other fabrics in the quilt look later. This quilt was found inside a cotton comforter where it served as the filler.

96

6

CLUES IN TECHNIQUES

Quiltmakers use a variety of techniques for construction, decoration and finishing. Piecing, applique and quilting are the major techniques; folds and tucks, embroidery, beading and painted embellishments have been incorporated into quilts at various times. Some like the running stitch method of piecing and the buttonhole applique stitch have been used commonly for so many generations that they are of no use for dating, but there are others with narrower spans of use that can be helpful.

Piecing

RUNNING STITCH METHOD

Because the running stitch is the most common method of piecing a quilt in the United States, it is sometimes called the American method. Two pieces of fabric are placed face to face and a seam

Running Stitch

is stitched about 1/4 inch from the edges on the back sides. The joined pieces are then pressed open, with the seams usually pressed to one side or the other. The running stitch can be sewn by machine or hand.

TEMPLATE METHOD

The template method is also called the whipstitch method, the paper template method or the English

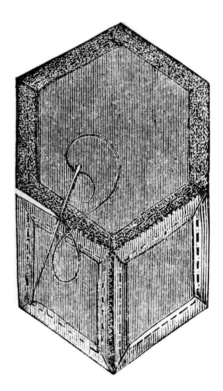

Peterson's Magazine illustrated the template construction method in an engraving in the August, 1880, issue. After the seamstress bastes a fabric diamond over a diamond-shaped paper template, she joins the pieces with an overhand stitch. Later the basting and papers are removed.

patchwork technique. The seamstress cuts paper templates to line each piece in the quilt and bastes the fabric patches over the templates. She whipstitches or overstitches the pieces together by hand and removes the papers. The paper template method was commonly used to construct patchwork organized into mosaic-style patterns, such as hexagon and diamond patchwork, rather than blocks. It can be distinguished on the top of a finished quilt because the evidence of a whipstitch appears tighter and closer together than a running stitch. If the piece has not been backed it is easy

Wreath of Roses quilt (detail). Signed in embroidery: Fannie E. Cole, 1858. Made near Factoryville, Pennsylvania. Appliqued, reverse appliqued and quilted. Cotton. Collection: Sandra Thlick and Katalin Stazer.

Fannie Cole used an applique stitch to tack down the pieces of plain color cottons in her quilt. The centers of the roses and the buds are reverse applique. There is no machine stitching apparent in the quilt or in the back, which is a plain white cotton, brought over to the front for binding. She used red cotton thread and a running stitch to sign her name. The running stitch is less common than the chain stitch or the cross stitch for an embroidered signature.

The dye for the yellow orange is probably chrome orange; the green is probably chrome green and the red in the bud in the lower corner appears to be Turkey red. The dye for the reddish-brown, which may always have been brown, is not as easy to identify.

The *Wreath of Roses* is a common pattern in conventional applique. Fannie's corner blocks show artistic originality, as do the half-wreaths she used to make a border.

98

to determine if the paper template method has been used, especially if the papers remain.

The whipstitch or template method in quilts has been traced back to the early eighteenth century in England. The McCord quilt, date-inscribed 1726, was constructed using that method (1), but early English quilts were also pieced by the running stitch method. By 1850 English quiltmakers, for the most part, had abandoned the running stitch seam in favor of the classic British quilt—hexagon patchwork pieced over paper templates (2). American women also used the template technique, especially when constructing quilts of English mosaic-style design, but the running stitch method was most common here.

In American quilts, the paper template technique is a clue to the nineteenth century. It fell out of use in the twentieth century, although the technique remained popular in England, South Africa, Australia and some other former English colonies. In the United States, hexagon mosaic quilts, likely to have been made in the template method in the nineteenth century, would be typically stitched in the running stitch technique in the twentieth.

If the papers remaining in the top are cut from newspapers or letters they may contain a date, but be careful about taking the date too literally. A case in point: the Saltonstall quilt has papers dated 1710 behind the pieces, but experts who have recently examined the fabrics attribute at least some of them to the last half of the nineteenth century, one hundred and fifty years after the dates on the papers (3). Although this is an extreme case, it is good to remember that earlier generations may have saved scarce paper for quite a while.

FOUNDATION METHOD

In the last quarter of the nineteenth century a new piecing technique called pressed patchwork—or the foundation method—became popular. The seamstress begins with a square of fabric the size of her finished block and bastes a patch to the center. She then places a second patch atop the first, right sides together, and seams these with a running stitch. She presses the patch so the right sides show and adds more in the same fashion, usually working out from the center. After blocks constructed on foundation fabrics are joined, the foundations no longer show being sandwiched between the decorative front and the backing fabric. Only if the piece is unfinished, or if holes have worn in it, can you spot the foundation fabric.

Pineapple, *Windmill Blades* or *Maltese Cross* quilt. Maker unknown. Estimated date: 1880–1920. Pieced to a foundation and tied. Wool, silk and cotton. Collection: Helen F. Spencer Museum of Art, the University of Kansas.

The Pineapple is a variation of the Log Cabin design, popular after 1875. Those made before 1925 are often pieced to a foundation.

Variations of the technique include foundations of triangular or diamond shapes and foundations of paper rather than fabric. The paper is usually removed before the piece is finished, but you may come across a quilt that rustles with the tell-tale sound. Paper added a little extra warmth, which may have motivated some makers during hard times to leave it inside the quilt.

The foundation technique was commonly used with just a few patterns—Crazy Quilts, Log Cabins, Pineapples, and String Quilts. Any of these designs could also be pieced by the running stitch method. One useful clue: there is a general tendency for Log Cabin quilts made in the last third of the nineteenth century to be constructed on a foundation, while those made in the twentieth century were made by the running stitch method. Crazy Quilts and String Quilts do not seem to

Log Cabin spread (detail). Made by Isabella Hardin Hayner in Kentucky. Estimated date: 1875–1900. Pieced to a foundation, bound but unbacked. Cotton. Collection: Dr. William Browning and Susan Browning Pogany.

Isabella Hayner used flour bags as the foundation for her Log Cabin blocks. Since she never backed her spread we can see her technique clearly. She placed a square in the center of a foundation and hand stitched logs around the squares, working out from the center. For a photo of the front see book's cover.

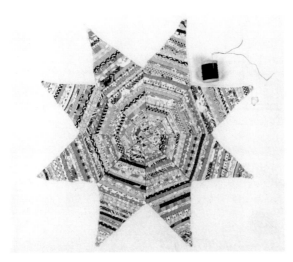

String star (detail), unfinished top. Maker unknown. Estimated date: 1925-1950. Pieced on a foundation and appliqued. Cotton. Collection: Pam Johnson

This string quilt was pieced on a foundation of white sugar or flour sacks and appliqued to blocks of thin white fabric that may also be recycled sacking. Most quiltmakers did not applique their string-pieced patchwork; they found it easier to piece it into a background. This star is unusual in the size of the "strings", which are about 1/4 inch.

follow this rule; foundations were important to their construction whenever they were made.

The Sewing Machine

Consider a hypothetical case: A family brings a Double Wedding Ring quilt to the local historical museum; they believe it to be made by some historical figure like Abraham Lincoln's mother. It is machine-pieced and is said to have been made by Nancy Hanks Lincoln before her death in 1818. Since you are being asked for an opinion (and it is wise to offer one only when asked) you can tactfully discuss fabrics and quilt style with the owners, pointing out that lavender and light green was not a popular color scheme before the twentieth century, and that the Double Wedding Ring pattern was not used before 1920. The family begins to doubt Great-Aunt Maude but suggests that Nancy Lincoln might have been ahead of her time stylistically. Stylistic evidence is debatable; however, there is no question that the sewing machine was not invented until decades after Mrs. Lincoln's death.

The hypothetical problem is not only a bit silly, it is far too easy. Rarely does a dating problem offer such an obvious solution. Mrs. Lincoln's Double Wedding Ring does point out the importance, nevertheless, of looking for machine stitching when examining a quilt.

The development of the sewing machine is attributable to the mid-century era rather than to a particular date. The lock stitch machine with the needle's eye near the point, similar to the machines we use today, was invented by Walter Hunt between 1832 and 1834, but Hunt never patented the machine. Elias Howe patented a more sophisticated model with a horizontal needle in 1846 (4) and began a campaign to change the way the world sewed, but it took Isaac Singer to market the sewing machine on a mass scale. Singer's refinements included a foot treadle and a vertical needle, but his real contribution was promotion. Initially machines cost $500, far out of the reach of the middle class. To make them affordable, Singer developed the installment plan, and prices decreased with competition and volume of manufacture. In 1860 factories were selling 111,000 sewing machines a year, and Singer's home model cost $75 (5). In 1871, when Mary Boykin Chestnut recorded the purchase of her new machine in her account book, the price was $25 (6). Chestnut, an upper-class southern woman whose family fortune had been decimated by the Civil War, typified the many southern women who bought machines in the 1870s.

The two decades between Singer's 1851 patent and Chestnut's 1871 purchase denote the era when the sewing machine became commonplace. A quilt with machine stitching could not have been made before the late 1840s, so any quilt attributed to a pre-1850 date should be checked thoroughly for machine sewing.

Machine stitching is easy to spot in quilting, applique or topstitching of the binding. Check all stages of a quilt's construction, especially the seams in the backing where seamstresses often used a machine even if they sewed all other seams by hand. Remember that hand-stitched blocks might have been set together years later by machine, and that a quilt might have been rebound on the machine by a later generation.

You may want to practice differentiating machine and hand stitching on the right sides of the fabric (where you see it in the finished quilt) by sewing together identical pieces of fabric—one by hand and the other by machine—varying stitch lengths. Press the seams to one side and turn the fabric right side up. Gently spread the seams so that the ends of the stitches show through and see if you can determine which was machine sewn.

Most machine stitching in quilts uses the lock stitch that interlocks top and bottom stitches. There are two other machine stitches you might find in a quilt, the zig-zag and the chain stitch. In the zig-zag stitch the top and bottom stitches proceed in a series of sharp angles. A zig-zag stitch capability has been a feature on modern home sewing machines since the early 1950s, so zig-zag stitching (usually used to anchor applique) is an indicator of recent manufacture. It should be noted that zig-zag machines were in commercial use as early as the 1870s (7), so it is possible that a quilt with zig-zag machine stitching could date from the last quarter of the nineteenth century.

Another machine stitch, the chain stitch, is sometimes used to piece seams. The chain stitch differs from the lock stitch in that it is a series of slip knots. It is not as durable as the lock stitch; if the thread breaks, the chain has a tendency to fall apart. A machine that made chain stitches was patented in 1851 (8) so their presence indicates that the quilt was made after that date. The chain stitch machine was never as popular for home sewing in the U.S. as the lock stitch machine, although quite a few were sold in the 1850s, '60s and '70s. They were more popular in other countries. Pieced quilts from Tahiti and other South Pacific islands typically have chain stitch seams.

Trade cards were a popular advertising medium for sewing machine manufacturers. Author's Collection.

A chain stitch machine seam, especially in a twentieth century quilt, can be a weak clue that the quilt in question may have been made in another country.

In summary, the most important information about machine stitching is that it is a clue to a date after 1850 or so. A machine-stitched seam could not have been sewn before 1845.

Applique

In applique the patches are applied to a background fabric that remains visible as part of the design. The three major categories are reverse applique, cut-out chintz applique and conventional applique.

REVERSE APPLIQUE

In reverse applique two or more layers of fabric are basted together, and the top layer is cut away to reveal the fabric underneath. The technique is also called inlaid applique, with references to this term in quiltmaking going back to the late eighteenth century, when a 1774 newspaper advertisement mentioned a stolen quilt that had in the middle ''a large tree (inlaid work) with a peacock at the root'' (9). Aside from the fact that it is relatively unusual in the twentieth century, reverse applique is of little help in assigning a date since it appears in early applique quilts and nineteenth-century examples.

CUT-OUT CHINTZ APPLIQUE

The technique of cutting printed motifs from fabric and stitching them to a background has been

Cut-out chintz quilt with pieced borders, made by Amelia Heiskell Lauck (1761–1842) in Frederick County, Virginia. Inscribed in the quilting: April 15, 1823. Appliqued of cut-out chintz, stuffed and quilted. Cotton. Collection: The Daughters of the American Revolution Museum. Gift of Anne Arundel Chapter.

Amelia Lauck cut the flowers and birds from block printed cottons and appliqued them with whip stitches of cotton thread. The use of cut-out chintz (also called Broderie Perse) is an excellent clue to a pre-Civil War date.

traced back to the seventeenth century in Europe (10). A number of American quilts and unquilted bedcovers in the technique survive that are attributed to the last quarter of the nineteenth century, and at least six date-inscribed examples between 1782 and 1799 are in the literature. The technique is commonly called Broderie Perse, French for "Persian Embroidery". Caulfeild and Saward used that term in 1882 (11); contemporary needlework historian Susan Burrows Swan believes it to be a late nineteenth-century name for a technique practiced earlier (12). Another late nineteenth-century name is Cretonne Applique (13). Because the term "cut-out chintz" is most descriptive of the technique, I use it to discriminate the technique from conventional applique.

The cut-out chintz technique has a definite correlation to date. It was the most common applique method in the eighteenth and early nineteenth century, but it fell out of use around the time of the Civil War, replaced by conventional applique. In the database, 67 dated quilts made using the technique (often combined with embroidery, conventional applique, reverse applique or piecing) ranged from 1782 to 1873. Only three quilts of the 67 were dated after 1860. Thus, cut-out chintz is a strong clue to a date before 1865.

Further analysis of the cut-out chintz quilts, in terms of block versus medallion format, indicates that seamstresses working before 1840 were far more likely to arrange their cut-out chintz applique in a whole-top, medallion format, and those working after 1840 were more likely to use the block. This change, like many others, probably came about because of the fashion for block-style album quilts which developed around 1840.

CONVENTIONAL APPLIQUE

Most people today have no special name for the applique technique in which the seamstress builds up her own designs in layers of fabric, rather than cutting them from chintz. Caulfeild and Saward distinguish between inlaid (reverse) applique and onlaid applique, but onlaid applique also includes cut-out chintz (14). For the purposes of this book I call this plain old applique ''conventional applique'' to distinguish it from cut-out chintz.

Conventional applique is an old technique used for centuries with embroidery in clothing and other textiles. It appears as a minor technique in eighteenth century quilts, most commonly in border designs made of swags and bows cut from a tiny print or leaves fashioned from a plain cotton to accent cut-out chintz bouquets. Conventional applique began to appear in the block format and as the major design technique in quilts in the early 1840s. It can be traced easily in dated album quilts where it was at first combined with blocks done in the cut-out chintz technique. Gradually but surely, conventional applique replaced the cut-out chintz applique blocks in the album quilts and other quilt styles, so that after 1860 a cut-out chintz quilt is a rarity.

There were 188 quilts made using the conventional applique technique (not a combination of cut-out applique and conventional applique). The range was broad—from 1807 through the 1940s—but the early examples were almost exclusively eagle medallions, indicating that early nineteenth century quiltmakers who wanted a flo-

Floral Basket quilt (detail) made by Mary C. Pickering (Bell) (1831-?) in St. Clairsville Ohio. Estimated date: 1850–1860. Appliqued, stuffed and quilted. Cotton. Collection: Smithsonian Institution, Negative # 81–5761.

According to the family history nineteen-year-old Mary Pickering began her quilt when her husband-to-be left for Oregon. Eight years later he returned and they were married. The technique is conventional applique; she used a buttonhole stitch to anchor the patches, cut from calico and plain cottons. Conventional applique used to construct such block designs is a good clue to a date after 1840. For a full view of the quilt see page 22.

ral or tree-of-life design cut the flowers from chintz fabric, but those who wanted an eagle design had to construct it themselves. It wasn't until the 1840s that the typical seamstress began constructing her own flowers.

Conventional applique has strong ties to the album quilts of the 1840s; the early dated examples tend to be from Maryland, Delaware, New Jersey and Pennsylvania, the same mid-Atlantic states where album quilts were being made (and most of the conventional applique quilts of the 1840s are signature quilts). The album quilt style seemed to have been an important influence on the change from cut-out chintz to conventional applique.

Conventional applique continued strong through the Civil War and the nineteenth century, as the album sampler style faded away. Around 1900 the applique technique abruptly disappeared; of the 188 dated quilts only three were dated in the 25 years between 1900 and 1924. In the late '20s the style was revived, to flower again in the '30s.

Based on this data, the conventional applique technique can be relied upon as a strong clue to date. Its presence in the body of a quilt (rather than merely in the border) is a good indicator of a date after 1840. Although individual exceptions occurred, it was not a popular technique in the first quarter of this century.

APPLIQUE STITCHES

Applique, whether conventional, cut-out chintz or reverse applique, can be done with a variety of stitches. One is the blind stitch, in which no stitches show; they are hidden in the folds of the fabric. More common is an overcast or applique stitch that anchors two layers with tiny visible stitches. A third variation uses embroidery stitches that are decorative as well as functional; sometimes these stitches are purely decorative, embroidered over an applique stitch that anchors the fabric. The most common of these are the interlocking T-shaped stitches—the blanket stitch or buttonhole stitch. Other decorative applique stitches include chain and stem stitches. Few conclusions have been drawn correlating a type of stitch and a specific time.

A rather fine buttonhole stitch in tan or white thread is typical of the eighteenth and early nineteenth century in cut-out chintz applique, but such a stitch is also found in mid-nineteenth century conventional applique. The strongest clue in an applique stitch is a buttonhole stitch in black embroidery thread that is a twentieth century style, common in the 1925-1950 era.

Embroidery

The technique of decorating textiles with thread is far older than the patchwork quilt. Embroidered clothing dating back to the Bronze Age survives (15); embroidery to decorate religious and secular clothing, bed furnishings and other household linens was common in many cultures. When American women began making patchwork quilts in the eighteenth century, they continued to incorporate embroidered accents into their pieced and appliqued designs. As styles of embroidery and thread changed over the centuries, quilt decoration changed, so examination of the embroidery can help with a date.

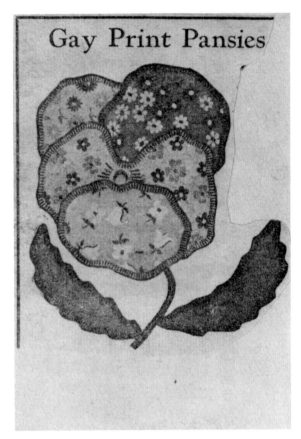

A Pansy design was clipped from a magazine around 1930 for a quilter's scrapbook. The black buttonhole stitching holding down the applique is a strong clue to a date after 1925.

WOOL EMBROIDERY

Crewel yarn, also called crewel thread, is a loosely-plied wool yarn, used for all types of embroidery. Sixteenth- and seventeeth-century English needleworkers, both professional and domestic, used crewel yarn to decorate textiles in a style we often call crewel embroidery but which is also called Jacobean embroidery for the latinized name of King James I who ruled when the style developed. Jacobean wool embroidery was surface embroidery, meaning it does not follow the weave of the cloth as the counted cross stitch used in samplers does. Jacobean embroiderers incorporated motifs drawn from natural forms—fruits, animals and especially flowers—which while recognizable as specific varieties, were more stylized than naturalistic. The motifs were filled in with a variety of stitches and sometimes shaded naturalistically.

Techniques and designs for Jacobean embroidery were carried to America by English immigrants who brought their picture books and design

Chintz quilt (detail). Maker unknown. Estimated date: 1791–1820. Pieced, embroidered and quilted. Collection: Smithsonian Institution, Negative # 45821b.

The Jacobean-style embroidery is one of the clues to an early date in this quilt that combines piecing and embroidery. The flowers are stylized and shaded with a filling stitch, characteristics typical of embroidery on early quilts. For a full-size photo of the quilt see page 15.

references with them. Pattern sheets and reference books survive from the sixteenth century. *A Schole-House for the Needle* was one English design book, written by Richard Shorleyker in 1624. Colonists decorated bedcovers, bed curtains, valances and all manner of textiles with crewel yarn in the Jacobean style and incorporated woolen embroidery into their quilts. They also translated Jacobean design ideas like running vine borders, tree of life medallions, baskets of flowers, isolated roses and pomegranates into quilting and later applique designs.

Wool embroidery lost popularity to silk embroidery styles around the time of the Revolution but made a comeback in the mid-nineteenth century when a fad for the counted thread embroidery known as Berlin work developed. Seamstresses embroidered on a plain weave fabric or canvas, following graphed, tinted patterns to produce fire screens, foot-stool covers, framed mottoes and wallets. German wool yarns, finer and brighter than English crewel yarns, became common for Berlin work. Counted work allowed even the untalented to produce realistic representations of a rose, a cat or a stag. It was heavily promoted by periodicals in the second half of the nineteenth century, until the 1890s when the fad died. The

Berlin work craze never translated to quilts, although some quiltmakers did piece counted thread-covered canvas into their quilts. Berlin work is more commonly reflected in wool surface embroidery in which the naturalistic roses, lilies and other flowers are derived from the naturalistic, florid images found in the counted canvas designs. Berlin-work-inspired borders appear on show quilts of silks and wools, and some contributors to album quilts were obviously influenced by Berlin work to embroider their blocks in wool.

Wool yarn embroidery can be a clue to a quilt's date. The color of the yarn provides some information. Bright, garish aniline dyes would be after the 1850s. The design style is also important. Jacobean-type stylized pomegranates, roses and carnations would be a clue to a pre 1850 date; realistic renderings of flowers more likely would be after 1830, when the Berlin work influence was seen. Outline embroidery and seams covered with linear embroidery patterns would range from 1880 through 1925.

SILK EMBROIDERY

Silk surface embroidery was similar to wool embroidery in the type of stitches used, but silk, due to its expense and the nature of the fiber, was generally used for finer work on a smaller scale. Silk thread comes in many types. Silk floss is a loosely twisted thread; silk ply thread is a cord of several tightly plied yarns. Filoselle is a floss made of waste silk, coarser than floss with less sheen. Chenille is a thick yarn with a fuzzy cut pile nap that gives it a velvet look. Arrasine is also a fuzzy silk thread.

Any and all of these threads might be used to embroider details in an applique block or to embellish a Crazy Quilt. Though a weak clue, the presence of silk thread can indicate that a quilt was made before 1910 when cotton thread generally replaced the more expensive silk thread. As with wool thread, color and embroidery style help to narrow the date.

COTTON EMBROIDERY

Although cotton dominated both the mid-nineteenth century American textile market and mid-nineteenth century American quilts, cotton embroidery thread did not replace silk and wool as the favored decorative thread until the early twentieth century. This lag may have had to do with color fastness; until the years after World War I,

Hexagons and Diamonds quilt. Maker unknown. Estimated date: 1850–1900. Pieced and embroidered, lined with a quilted piece of fabric. Silk. Collection: Smithsonian Institution, Negative # P6381A.

The embroidery in the center and borders of this silk show quilt is a clue to its date. The silk floss and chenille thread indicate a nineteenth-century origin. The naturalism of the roses and buds are more closely related to the realism of mid-century Berlin work than to earlier stylized Jacobean embroidery hence the date can be narrowed to mid- to late nineteenth century.

cotton thread was apparently reliable in only a few colors. In 1882 Caulfeild and Saward indicated that silk threads were available in many colors, but cotton embroidery thread came only in red or blue (16). The Sears catalog in 1902 offered only red, black, navy blue and white embroidery cotton. The red, dyed with the Turkey red process (advertised by a logo of a turkey with the word RED on his chest), was the preferred color, probably because it was considered the fastest.

Some time in the late teens and early twenties, cotton thread in a variety of colors became commonplace. As the price of silk thread rose, cotton thread became the standard for embroidery of all kinds, and the cotton embroidered quilt (with embroidery the major decoration rather than just an accent) became an increasingly popular style.

Cotton thread for embroidery was sold as floss, a loosely plied thread, and as a twist in varying weights. One heavyweight twist, used for crochet and sometimes for quilting and embroidery, was Pearl Cotton, tightly twisted and mercerized to produce a strong, shiny thread. Although cotton thread in a sewing weight had been used before the Civil War for marking quilts with dates and names, heavier cotton twist or floss for signatures or decorative designs is a good clue to a date after 1880.

Crazy Quilt (detail), Maker unknown. Pieced to a foundation and embroidered. Unbacked but bound. Cotton and wool. Collection: James Holmes.

Outline embroidery designs were often traced or transferred from commercial patterns. While the naivete of the sheep and rooster lead one to believe the embroiderer drew animals from her own world, it is more likely she used patterns for the designs on her Crazy Quilt. The thread is cotton twist; most of the reds have faded to pinkish tan (something genuine Turkey red thread would not do).

OUTLINE EMBROIDERY

The technique of outlining a flower or figure became popular as a decorative technique around 1880. Earlier embroiderers, inspired by Jacobean or Berlin work styles, usually filled in their designs, shading with thread. In the early 1880s ladies' magazines, in an effort to encourage artistic endeavors by their readers, who they felt were devoting too much time to Berlin work, began publishing black and white outlines of designs to be embroidered. The esthetically inclined readers were encouraged to fill in the designs with their own skillful shading, but most needleworkers merely copied the outline pattern in a chain stitch, stem stitch or outline stitch. (This last became known as the Kensington stitch after the English needlework school that set the taste) (17). Patterns included naturalistic depictions of flowers, and sentimentalism ran strong. Religious themes, such as a cross on a rock, and nostalgic drawings of children and pets were popular, as were cattails, cranes and fans (exotic images inspired by Japanese design).

Caulfeild and Saward described "outline embroidery" as "an adaptation of Indian and Oriental quilting to modern uses" (18), rather lofty antecedents for a technique that was described in more practical terms in the 1893-4 Montgomery Ward's catalog: "Fancy bed spreads, 2 1/2 yards square, made of good bleached sheeting, unhemmed and stamped in the new 'all over designs' for embroidery in linen floss. Makes a handsome and cheap spread".

The quilt style described in the catalog, in which outline embroidery is the sole decoration, developed soon after the magazines began printing patterns for Kensington embroidery in the early 1880s. Outline embroidered pictures found a place in other styles of quilts; they appeared in the plain blocks set between applique and pieced designs and were essential to the look of Crazy Quilts. Magazines strongly influenced the fashion and the patterns for outline embroidery so the style is easily traced in print. The presence of outline embroidered pictures means the quilt is likely to have originated after the first published patterns in 1880.

Outline embroidery was done in all types of thread on all types of fabrics, but some distinctive combinations of thread and background fibers and colors are helpful in further narrowing the date. Turkey red thread on white cotton was extremely fashionable for bedcovers, quilts, pillows and dresser scarves from 1880 through 1925. Navy blue embroidery on cotton was a less popular variation during those years. Cotton, silk or wool thread outlining designs on woolen comforters was a variation popular in the 1890-1930 era. After cotton thread became available in many

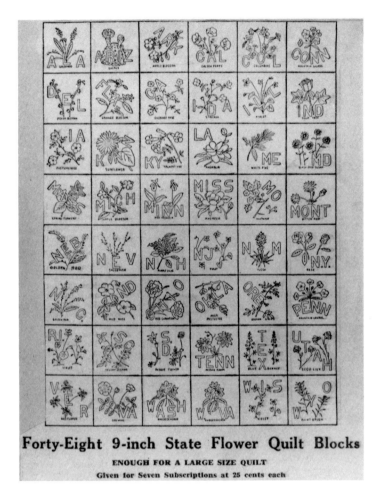

Forty-Eight 9-inch State Flower Quilt Blocks
ENOUGH FOR A LARGE SIZE QUILT
Given for Seven Subscriptions at 25 cents each

Readers of *Good Stories* magazine who sold seven subscriptions in 1937 to their friends and neighbors received 48 stamped muslin blocks to embroider in their state flower design. Outline embroidery has been popular since the 1880s, but the state flower and state bird series seem to have begun in the 1920s.

colors following World War I, outline embroidery in a variety of colors on white cotton grounds became the characteristic embroidered quilt style, still popular today. Floral baskets and bouquets, state birds and nursery rhymes are typical subject matter for these quilts, most of which are made from commercial patterns, kits, pre-stamped blocks and iron-on designs.

CROSS STITCH EMBROIDERY

Cross stitch embroidery is common in pre-Civil War quilts and in mid-twentieth century quilts, but you can quickly learn to see the differences between eras since the function, the type of thread and the size of the stitches are quite different. Cross stitch was the common signature or marking

stitch on early quilts. It was not a common decorative technique until the mid-twentieth-century, when pattern companies that wanted to meet the demand for colonial-style quilt designs adapted cross stitch to depict floral and geometric designs.

Early cross stitch was of fine thread, most often a single strand of sewing thread, done as counted thread embroidery. The seamstress covered a specific number of warp and weft threads with each thread; the stitches would be, by necessity, rather

Sampler, made by Polly Hix (ca. 1819 -?), possibly in Homer, Pennsylvania. Inscribed: 1834. Cross stitch. Silk on linen. Collection: Helen F. Spencer Museum of Art, the University of Kansas. The William Bridges Thayer Memorial.

Fifteen-year-old Polly Hix used two counted stitches in her sampler. The top alphabet is the less-often-seen eyelet stitch; the rest is the cross stitch, which was sometimes used to sign and date quilts before the Civil War. Although decorative or pictorial cross stitch is not found on quilts until the mid-twentieth century, many of the images and the design conventions such as the serpentine floral border that were common in samplers were also common in nineteenth-century quilts.

small. Twentieth-century cross stitch is usually of colored multi-strand embroidery thread; the designs have been printed on the cotton by the pattern company (or transferred using a hot iron transfer) and the needleworker—rather than counting the threads on the background fabric—embroiders over each printed X in comparatively large stitches.

Crazy Quilt made by Edna Force Davis in Fairfax County, Virginia. Inscribed in embroidery: 1897 and 1929. Pieced to a foundation and embroidered. Wool. Collection: Smithsonian Institution, Negative # 67633.

Edna Davis began her Crazy Quilt in 1897 but did not finish it until 1929, so she embroidered both dates and two self-portraits in the lower corners. In one she is a Victorian belle in balloon sleeves; in the other a flapper. She used both outline and filled embroidery motifs and covered every seam with a fancy stitch of some kind. Although the quilt wasn't finished until 1929, its heavily embroidered surface is more typical of the end-of-the-century era when she started it.

EMBROIDERY COVERED SEAMS

Seamstresses have used decorative embroidery stitches to tack down applique cutouts since quiltmakers began using applique as a technique; around 1880 a fad developed for an embroidered outline around pieced patchwork. Quiltmakers outlined the patches in Crazy Quilts with fancy stitches like herringbone and feather stitches, which often did nothing to actually hold down the patches. Embroidery for the sake of embroidery reflects the Victorian penchant for covering any unadorned straight line.

Caulfeild and Saward, writing in 1882 at the beginning of the Crazy Quilt rage, gave instructions for what they called Puzzle Patchwork, advising seamstresses to "work round the edge of every patch with herringbone stitches made with brightly colored filoselle" (19). Women making

Crazy Quilts could find instructions and ideas in books, pamphlets and periodicals but also showed remarkable inventiveness in developing variations on the basic stitches. Dorothy Bond has cataloged 400 she found in old Crazy Quilts (20).

The embroidered lines of fancy stitches are also found decorating the seams of other pieced patterns in plain and fancy quilts, such as Log Cabins, Fans and the Brickwork designs of woolen rectangles made from suiting samples. The presence of embroidery-covered seams is a strong clue to a post-1880 date. Another generalization: there is a tendency for the amount and complexity of this embroidery to diminish through the decades. After the turn of the century embroidery became sparser, simpler and less diverse with basic feather and herringbone stitching the standard seam covers.

Tucking, Folding and Other Novelty Techniques

Quilts have a certain three-dimensionality due to the puffiness of the quilting and the layers of applique. Several techniques add to the depth using fabric manipulation beyond the basic techniques of piecing, applique and embroidery, and most of these techniques date to the second half of the nineteenth century.

By taking tucks or gathers in a square, the seamstress can achieve a cup shape. Victorian seamstresses stuffed the cups with batting, turned them over and stitched them together. The Puff Quilt, in satins and velvets, was popular at the end of the nineteenth century. Caulfeild and Saward included instructions in their 1882 book of needlework techniques and called it Raised or Swiss Patchwork (21).

A variation on the gathered patch is the Yo-yo quilt or Marguerite in which the seamstess begins with a flat circle and gathers the edges to make a smaller puckered circle. The Yo-yo technique dates back to the mid-nineteenth century (22), but for quilts the technique was most popular during the 1925-1950 era. Yo-yo quilts are not quilted; usually they have empty spaces between the circles, and are sometimes backed with a colored piece of fabric or sheet.

The Cathedral Window is a folded, rather than a gathered, design. A square is folded and refolded with additional squares inserted between the pieces. No raw edges show, and the piece is not quilted. Variations of the design have been traced

Crazy Quilt (detail) made by members of the Trinity Lutheran Church, Findley, Ohio. Estimated date: 1893–1933. Pieced to a foundation, embroidered and painted. Silk. Collection: Smithsonian Institution, Negative # 76–2671.

Painted designs are common on Crazy Quilts, as are lines of feather stitching like the embroidery outlining the block. The top for this slumber throw was made as a fundraiser in 1893 and presented to the Reverend Stuckenburg; Mrs. Stuckenburg bordered and finished the quilt 40 years later.

"Yo-yos will get you if you don't watch out," warned *Capper's Weekly* on October 8, 1932. Made of gathered circles, yo-yo quilts (which were never quilted) date back to the Victorian era, but were most popular between 1925 and 1950. Author's collection.

back to the teens, but quilts in the Cathedral Window pattern don't seem to exist until the 1960s or 1970s.

Painted Decoration

Painted decoration can be applied to fabric freehand or with a stencil. Free-hand silk painting was taught in eighteenth-century finishing schools. A 1797 advertisement in Philadelphia mentions that silk painting is as elegant but "less trouble and expence (sic) than embroidery" (23). Mid-nineteenth-century quiltmakers painted and inked details on their applique designs, adding stamens and pistils to the flowers, butterflies' antennae, birds' eyes and people's faces. Most of these mid-nineteenth century painted embellishments were rather discreet, but during the late Victorian era, painted designs became more obvious. The same floral and animal motifs that were rendered in thread on Crazy Quilts were also painted. Echoing the advertisement of 90 years earlier, a reader wrote the needlework column of the *Ohio Farmer* in 1884, "I painted flowers on some of the blocks. They are much prettier than embroidery and not so much work" (24).

During the 1920s a minor fashion for a painted or dyed decorative technique developed in which the quiltmaker drew her design on the fabric with wax crayons (the kind children draw with) and colored it heavily. She then ironed the surface, absorbing the wax and leaving the dye in the fabric. This technique was revived in the 1960s for T-shirt decoration, and I must personally attest that the crayons from the 1960s are not nearly so colorfast as the crayons from the 1930s. The three or four quilts I have seen done in the crayon dyeing technique have held up far better than my T-shirts.

110

Another footnote to quilt history is the decorative technique using textile paints that came on the market sometime in the mid-twentieth century, probably in the 1950s. Sold under the brand name Liquid Embroidery, the paints are easily applied and remarkably colorfast, encouraging another generation of quiltmakers to save time by substituting paint for embroidery. The painted designs of the 1950s are characterized by their very bright, fast colors.

Stenciling was a popular decorative art in the first half of the nineteenth century when would-be artists made use of precut paper templates to decorate floors, walls and furnishing as well as to compose pictures. Young ladies learned what was called "theorem painting", using stencils to paint on fabrics. Some used stencils to dye fabrics for spreads and quilts. Diana Church, in a 1983 research paper, noted that 30 stencil spreads have been recorded, made between 1800 and 1850, primarily in New England and the mid-Atlantic states, with the decade 1825 to 1835 as the prime time (25). I have seen an example dated 1867, made in New York (26), which expands the possible time period for stenciled spreads to between 1800 and 1870. The artists used both the medallion and the block style formats for their designs and probably followed applique fashions; the medallion format would probably indicate a date before 1860, the block format a date after 1840.

Quilting and Tying

Quilting (the stitches connecting the top, batting and back) was the only decorative technique on the early whole-cloth quilts and clothing. As patchwork design became more important to the look of the quilt in the nineteenth century, quilting's importance began to fade. By the end of the century an extraordinarily quilted piece was unusual.

Changing living patterns undoubtedly affected the decline of quilting. Late-nineteenth-century women had opportunities for self-expression other than their needlework. Their educations were better; no longer did reading take second place to sewing a fine seam. The time-consuming, elaborate quilting faded in importance as proof of a woman's sewing skills. And tastes changed after the Civil War. A Crazy Quilt with a showy variety of silk, brocade, velvets and taffetas was far more fashionable than a quilt with intricate but subtle quilting. Also, when quilts became more func-

tional, quiltmakers became more interested in producing something warm in a hurry.

Because of these changes, the amount and the quality of quilting in a piece can be a general indicator of date. Quality is characterized by several things, including the closeness of the quilting lines, the size and regularity of the stitches, and the complexity and sophistication of the design. Closeness of quilting lines is a clue to age; generally quilts in the first half of the century were more closely quilted than those in the last half. Quilts that have very close quilting, even when quilted only in lines or grids, are more likely to be pre-Civil War.

Size of the stitches is dependent on the quilter's skill as well as on the thickness of the batting. The closest stitches, up to 22 stitches per inch (that's 22 on the top side!!) can be obtained only with very thin batts or when no batting is used at all, as in stuffed and corded quilting. The number of stitches per inch (averaging 7 to 8) cannot really be correlated to a specific time, although the closest stitches are generally found in stuffed and corded pieces, which tend to originate before the Civil War. Since there was a trend at the end of the nineteenth century to thicker batting, the presence of large quilting stitches is a weak clue to a late-nineteenth-century or twentieth-century origin.

Despite the development of the sewing machine in the mid-nineteenth century, machine quilting is most common in the twentieth century. Machine jig patterns (for example, a regular, cresting wave-like design) are a good twentieth century clue; the machine quilting attachment seems to be an early-twentieth-century development. Keep in mind that many nineteenth-century tops have been machine quilted at a later date.

The presence of colored rather than white quilting thread is not a useful dating tool, as nineteenth-century quilters used thread to match the patchwork (red quilting in red areas, white in the white), in the same way some twentieth-century quilters have. Colored thread specifically advertised for quilting has been sold since the 1920s. The 1935 Sears catalog sold Grandma Dexter brand quilting thread in "dark pink, yellow, reseda (green), light blue, dark blue, cream or white" for eight cents a spool.

Fancy Quilting

The motifs and patterns found in what can be called fancy quilting are generally poor clues to

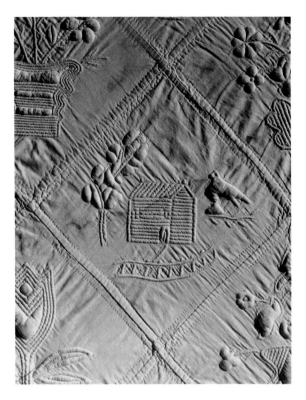

Stuffed whitework quilt (detail). Maker unknown. Estimated date: 1850-1875. Stuffed and quilted. Cotton. Collection: Smithsonian Institution, Negative # 81–13395.

This stuffed and corded white quilt is unusual in its format (block samplers are far less common than medallion style white quilts) and in the machine quilting that encloses the stuffed work and cording. The quilting that frames the blocks is hand stitched.

The log cabin motif appears related to William Henry Harrison's 1840 presidential campaign, which inspired log cabin images in quilted, appliqued and printed textiles; but the machine stitching could not have been done before the invention of the sewing machine in 1845. It seems most likely this quilt dates from the tail end of the era when stuffed and corded quilting was popular—around 1865.

date since they have been used across the centuries. Feathers, cables, leaves, flowers and hearts are typical of seventeenth-century English quilting and remain so today in both England and America. A reliable clue in quilting motifs is the quilting sampler in which each plain block had a different motif. Sampler quilt designs, like sampler applique designs, appear to be a nineteenth-century fashion that faded after the Civil War.

Stuffing and Cording

Certain techniques are surer clues for dating. Stuffed and corded quilts in which the quilting

motifs are raised with additional padding were made from around 1800 through the Civil War. The techniques appear in both whole-cloth and patchwork quilts.

Raised quilting has a number of names; it is a form of whitework, a category of white on white design for bedcoverings that includes embroidery and candlewicking (27). Corded quilting is also called Italian quilting, probably because the earliest surviving examples of the technique are from fourteenth-century Sicily (these three quilts are in fact the oldest surviving quilted textiles) (28). There is little evidence that cording originated in Italy because later examples from Portugal, Germany and England also survive (29). Stuffed and corded quilting today is often called trapunto, an Italian word that means "quilt", another possible reference to its supposed Italian origin. A second geographical allusion is the name Marseilles Quilt, derived from the French port through which many seventeenth-century corded quilts passed on their way from the quiltmakers of Provence in France to the traders in England. A Marseilles Quilt came to mean any stuffed and corded quilt, and later any woven variation on a whitework quilt (30). For more on Marseilles Quilts see page 133.

Stuffed quilting and corded quilting are probably the most descriptive terms as they describe the processes used to obtain the increased dimesionality in the quilting. The seamstresses would stuff shapes such as cherries, leaves and petals and cord linear design elements like vines and stems.

There are two general techniques used to stuff and cord a quilting design. In the first, the extra padding is added before the regular quilting; in the second, it is added after the quilting process. In the first the seamstress bastes a piece of coarsely woven cotton, linen or combination fabric directly to the back of her top. She quilts these two layers together in a technique called flat quilting that allows her to take minute stitches (31). Floral motifs, leaves and other enclosed shapes are contained on all sides by quilting; she then pads them by working small bits of cotton through the coarse backing fabric. To cord the linear elements she threads a large needle with cotton yarn or cord and runs it through the tunnel created by quilting either side of the line.

Once she completes the cording and stuffing, she can also quilt the piece by adding batting and a back to the padded top and quilting a filling pattern in the spaces around the motifs. Parallel lines, a grid or stipple quilting are typical filling patterns. She binds the quilt when it is finished like any other quilt.

Whole-cloth pieces without patchwork could

Stuffed whitework pillow sham (detail of back). Maker unknown (initials MMc). Estimated date: 1800–1860. Stuffed, corded and quilted. Cotton. Author's Collection.

Because the back of this sham was left uncovered, tails of the cording and bits of cotton batting can be seen popping out. The seamstress quilted a fine cotton top and a coarser back together without any batting. She later padded the designs, stuffing the fruit and leaves and cording the stems. The piece never had a batting or additional quilting.

Historian Rachel Maines has theorized that the development of thread-intensive quilting styles was dependent upon an inexpensive and plentiful supply of cotton thread, which came on the market around 1810 (32), a theory supported by the date-inscribed examples of stuffed quilts. The earliest example in the database is dated 1796 (a whole-cloth white cotton quilt). Of the 37 stuffed and corded quilts, 33 (89%) were made between 1800 and 1866, indicating that the presence of stuffed and corded quilting is a strong clue to these decades. There are, as with any other fashion, individual and regional exceptions. The Quilts of Tennessee survey team found many stuffed quilts made in Rhea County and reliably attributed to the last half of the nineteenth century and into the twentieth, indicating that quilters in some areas clung to tradition (33).

During the twentieth century a few exceptional quilters revived the stuffed and corded

Mexican Rose quilt made by Jane Barr in Pennsylvania. Inscribed in corded quilting: July, 1849. Appliqued, corded and quilted. Cotton. Collection: Smithsonian Institution, Negative # 76–2665.

Jane Barr corded her name and the date into her *Mexican Rose* applique. The rest of the quilting, a sampler of motifs, was not padded. The *Mexican Rose* design has been linked to patriotic fervor surrounding the Mexican-American War of 1846–1848.

be left as two layers with the roughly finished back exposed. A look at the back of these two-layer quilts reveals the process. If the quilter added a batting and back, you can still see evidence of this technique if you hold the quilt up to the light. Shadows around each of the stuffed and corded motifs indicate that a fourth layer of fabric is part of the quilt's construction.

In the second common padding technique the seamstress sandwiches top, batting and back together as with any other quilt, and stitches her quilting design with a running stitch through all three layers. When finished, she pads selected areas by working from the back, inserting batting through the fabric by prying apart the threads, or by snipping a small slash in the back. Evidence of the slashes are sometimes apparent on the backs of the quilts stuffed this way. Determining which technique the seamstress used is, unfortunately, of little use in dating a quilt. No correlations between certain years and either technique have been found.

work. Rose Good Kretsinger, Mattie Black, Jeannette Dean Throckmorton and Bertha Stenge won many local and national contests in the second quarter of this century with their trapunto quilts. Although Kretsinger, Black and Stenge hired anonymous women to do their quilting, all four appear to have stuffed and corded their designs.

Carpenter's Wheel (variation) quilt (detail), made by Jane Winter Price in Maryland. Estimated date: 1825–1850. Pieced and quilted. Cotton. Collection: Smithsonian Institution, Negative # 73389.

Jane Price combined several quilting designs in this heavily quilted piece. She self-quilted the patchwork blocks (quilting a quarter inch from the seam) and added a simple cross in the corners of the star. She used the plain blocks to show off her fancy quilting, alternating grape and rose designs. To highlight these motifs she quilted a filling pattern of closely spaced parallel lines (12 to an inch). Her quilting stitches are also exceptional, ranging between 11 and 12 to an inch on the top surface of the quilt.

Kretsinger stuffed hers after the quilter returned the finished quilt. Black, whose trapunto *Bluegrass Star* won the 1933 Century of Progress Contest at the Chicago World's Fair, did the stuffing before selling the top to Margaret Caden who hired the quilting.

FILLING PATTERNS AND SECONDARY DESIGNS

Individual motifs, such as feathers and flower pots, cornucopias and cables, were often accompanied by secondary designs filling the areas behind the fancy quilting. Twentieth-century quiltmakers were less likely to use secondary designs behind their fancy motifs than earlier quilters, so the lack of secondary designs is a clue (although a rather weak one) to a twentieth-century quilt.

Typical secondary designs include grids and parallel lines that run diagonally or perpendicular to the edge of the quilt. The secondary designs themselves are not a clue to date. Whole-cloth petticoats from the mid-seventeenth century are as likely to have parallel lines behind the feather designs as a prizewinning applique quilt from the 1930s. The closeness of the lines is more important in dating than the design; lines less than a half inch apart typified the years before the end of the Civil War.

Very closely quilted secondary designs are also called filling patterns (34). Lines a quarter or an eighth of an inch apart (or less) cause the primary motifs to stand out in relief, an effect that was popular in the same years that stuffed and corded quilts were fashionable. Filling patterns can be simple geometrics like straight lines or grids, and also overall designs called stipple or meander quilting. Stipple quilting is hundreds of stitches in a random pattern, placed so closely together that the background puckers. In meander quilting close lines of stitches wander in paths across the background. Stipple quilting and meander quilting seem to have faded from fashion at the same time as stuffed work and close quilting in general, and thus are a clue to a date between 1800 and 1865.

A collection of quilting templates illustrates popular twentieth-century patterns and template materials. Clockwise from the top: Alvina Roll of Wichita, Kansas, used a hole punch and cardboard to mark half of a floral motif. She probably pushed a pencil point through the holes to mark the quilt (1). Harriett Wood of Topeka cut a bay leaf or tea cup design from a cornflakes box (2) and a fleur de lis from plain cardboard (3). The square cable template (4) is cut from sheet tin and is marked ''Wanda Mowrey,

Larry Schwarm

Jeromesville, Ohio''. Above that are two of Alvina Roll's cardboard templates, a dogwood blossom (5) and a sunflower (6) punched into a piece of a Post Toasties box. To the top left is a feather border design (7), cut from a paper Mountain Mist batting wrapper and punched. With punched templates, quilters used a pounce bag full of powder that sifted through the holes onto the quilt top. Author's collection.

115

SELF-QUILTING

Twentieth-century American quilters are likely to "self-quilt" their patchwork, a technique in which the quilting follows the seams of the piecing (also called "quilting by the piece"). The usual style is to quilt around every piece 1/4 inch from the seam line (so as to miss the seam allowances). Self-quilting appears as the only quilting motif, as in the Grandmother's Flower Garden quilts of the 1930s where self-quilting around every hexagon is the standard quilting design, or it is used in conjunction with fancy motifs. A quilter might stitch a feather wreath in the plain blocks between her pieced blocks, using self-quilting in the pieced blocks. Self-quilting was also done in the nineteenth-century but a more typical nineteenth-century format was to quilt secondary designs across the patchwork. These two treatments are not exclusive to the centuries mentioned, but self-quilting is more typical from 1900 to the present, and the secondary pattern across the patchwork is more typical earlier.

A fairly recent form of self-quilting, in which one quilts directly in the seams, is called "in-the-ditch" quilting. It is a post-1950s design, used often with fatter polyester battings.

DOUBLE OR TRIPLE LINE QUILTING

Twentieth-century quiltmakers who want to include a floral bouquet or a feathered heart in their quilting tend to outline the design one time in quilting stitches. Nineteenth-century quilters might have gone around the design with double or triple lines. They also were likely to use double or triple lines as secondary designs behind the primary motifs. They sometimes covered their quilt completely with sets of double or triple diagonal lines. Double or triple line quilting is, in general, an indicator of a nineteenth-century date (although it is also seen in eighteenth-century bed quilts and petticoats). It is not common in twentieth-century quilts.

UTILITY QUILTING

Utility quilting—a repetitive design quilted across the quilt with little reference to the patchwork—is common to all eras. Most of the patterns used for secondary designs—grids, parallel lines, double and triple lines or clamshell motifs—could be used for utility quilting and most are of little use in dating quilts since they developed early and are still in use.

Courtesy of Genevieve Haskin Williams

Church groups like the Ladies' Aid Society of the Lenexa, Kansas, Methodist Church (pictured quilting in the church yard in 1905) often used all-over utility quilting designs like parallel lines, diamonds or fans. They are easy to mark in the frame and allow for many different hands in the quilting.

FAN QUILTING

Fan quilting, in which groups of concentric arcs are quilted across the patchwork, appears to be a good clue to a post-1875 date. Earlier quiltmakers used this design, but they were more likely to use it in combination with other motifs (there are early exceptions). A good deal of observation and a very limited amount of data (16 dated quilts with fan quilting, 13 of which are dated after 1900) indicate that fan quilting is most likely to be from the end of the nineteenth century or from the twentieth.

Other names for the arc design are the English terms wave or sea wave quilting (35), rainbow or double rainbow quilting (36), elbow quilting (as the quilter used the natural arc of her elbow to guide her (37) and the Baptist fan—a possible reference to the circular cardboard hand fans the Baptists use in church, which could be used as a template for the quilting pattern (38). Another unpublished reference is the Methodist fan design, possibly for the same reason—hot weather does not discriminate between religions. The church-related names may also refer to the fact that the pattern is a favorite with church quilting groups who quilt to raise money. The design is easy to mark while the quilt is in the frame; allowances for poor planning can be made by reducing the size of the fans that don't quite fit. The suitability

116

of the fan design for group quilting may explain its end-of-the-nineteenth century popularity, which parallels the growth of the groups who quilted for fundraising purposes.

Tying

Tying a quilt top to its back and batting takes far less time than quilting—less time than even the most basic utility quilting. The economics of tying a quilt or a comforter made it appealing to the women making covers for warmth and economy. Hence, we find the majority of tied quilts during the eras when quilts were at their lowest in terms of social status—from around 1880 through the 1930s.

Tying is a technique commonly used with foundation patchwork like Log Cabins and Crazy Quilts, where an extra piece of fabric is used as a foundation behind the patchwork. This fourth layer of fabric, which added extra bulk to the quilt, may have motivated quiltmakers to abandon quilting in favor of tying. The popularity of tied Log Cabins and Crazy Quilts may have given quiltmakers a new option for all their quilt styles.

The two terms most commonly used for the technique today are "tying" or "tacking", with "tufting" sometimes heard. Tying has been called "Methodist Quilting", sarcasm directed, perhaps, at the speed at which some Ladies' Aid Societies like to work.

Today we call tied—rather than quilted—bedding comforters, with some regional variations on the word. The *Dictionary of Regional English* found "comfortables", "comfort", "hap" and "puff" still in use, when they recently surveyed people around the country (39). How long people have been making the distinction between a quilted "quilt" and a tied "comforter" is not clear. The words "comfort", "comfortable" and "comforter" stem from the mid-nineteenth century, a time for which there is no substantial surviving evidence of tied comforters. An 1853 Pennsylvania estate inventory lists "lots of quilts and comforts" (40). Eliza Leslie's *The House Book*, published in 1846, described "soft, thick quilts used as a substitute for blankets and laid under the bedspread . . . a thick comfortable may be found a convenient substitute for a mattress" (41). Her instructions for making comfortables described a quilted cover, but she advised "you need not attempt to take close short stitches" (42). There are also references describing the tied comforter as we know it. Lucy Rutledge Cooke wrote a letter to her sister in 1853

Larry Schwarm

Charm comforter (detail). Maker unknown. Estimated date: 1875–1900. Pieced and tied. Cotton. Author's collection.

The fabric dated 1776 is deceptive. It is undoubtedly a Centennial print from 1876. The roller printed cotton in madder-style colors, the charm quilt style (with few identical fabrics) and the ties are clues to a late nineteenth-century date. Tied quilts almost always date from after 1875.

The ties here have an extra flourish. Inserted in each are short lengths of brown cotton, white cotton and red wool twist. The edges have fuzzed into a small pom-pom in the center of each hexagon.

mentioning that she was pulling comforters to pieces for washing (presumably she snipped the ties so she could wash the top and backing while she aired or replaced the batting, which was not washable) (43). Myra Inman Carter wrote in her diary in October, 1861, "Pretty day. Tacked a comfort this morning" (44). During the Civil War, women on both sides made quilts and comforters to supply camps and hospitals (45). Since function was of prime importance in producing bedding for war relief, we would expect that the economy of tying was practiced. However, we have very few surviving tied comforters made before the 1880s. A tied comforter made of banners from Henry Clay's unsuccessful 1844 presidential campaign survives; it is attributed to the years soon after the election (46). Two fragments of a tied whole-cloth comforter attributed to the mid-1850s are in the collection of the Kansas Museum of History (47). Both comforters are tied in an unusual manner with circles of cloth behind each knot, presumably to reinforce the area (much like buttons on an upholstered couch).

Of 51 date-inscribed examples of tied comforters in the data base, only two are dated earlier than 1875, which indicates that tying is a strong clue to a post-1875 date. However, this category of quilts illustrates well the limitations of drawing conclusions based on date-inscribed quilts, since lowly utility quilts are rarely dated and signed.

There are a number of variations in the tying techniques and materials. All types of cotton, wool and silk yarn have been used. Children of the Depression remember saving the string pulled from feedsack seams to tack comforters. The ties are often knotted on the front but can be discreetly tied on the back. On many Crazy Quilts and fancy Log Cabins they are practically invisible. One rather weak clue: The more flamboyant the tie, the more likely the quilt is to be from the last quarter of the nineteenth century when yarn pompoms and multicolored rosetttes fit the late-Victorian esthetic. Simple yarn knots or bows have been used longer and are a strong clue to a rather long period of time—anytime after 1875.

Unquilted Spreads

A spread is a single-layer coverlet with finished edges. Today it is commonly called a summer spread, but the origins of the term are unknown. Decorative lightweight spreads were common in the early years of patchwork in both America and England. The printed palampores from India were often used as unquilted spreads, and early embroidered, stenciled and appliqued pieces were commonly left unquilted. In the mid-nineteenth century, Americans were increasingly likely to quilt their patchwork although the English have continued a strong tradition of unquilted spreads. American applique quilts from the mid-nineteenth century were sometimes left unquilted but bound, and an occasional pieced quilt was finished as a spread, although this is less practical than with applique as there are so many exposed raw seams on the uncovered backs.

Foundation patchwork of the late nineteenth century was frequently finished as a spread. Log Cabins and Crazy Quilts were bound, hemmed or ruffled with no backing fabric. These unbacked but bound pieces are technically spreads although the foundation fabric that supports each patchwork block makes them two layers thick. The unbacked state of some Crazy Quilts and Log Cabins is sometimes a cause of concern to their twentieth-century owners, but the makers were apparently following a traditional finishing concept.

Inscriptions

The most helpful inscription in determining the age of a quilt is one with a date, so examine the quilt carefully, looking for an unobtrusive date. Quilted and inked inscriptions are easily missed. Check the quilting, especially in the borders and the center, for breaks in the regularity of the design, which may be a signature or a date. Ink inscriptions fade with washing and may require close examination to determine whether a mark is a smudge or a date. Check corners, front and back, for possible ink inscriptions.

If a quilt is signed but not dated, the inscription can still offer strong clues as to date, since quiltmakers during different eras were partial to different signature techniques.

INK INSCRIPTIONS

Inked inscriptions became common after the development in the mid-1830s of an indelible ink that did not rot fabrics . Earlier inks, homemade or commercial, were colored with iron or tannin, chemicals that deteriorated fabric. Payson's Indelible Ink credited with being the oldest manufactured ink suitable for fabric, came onto the market around 1834. At the end of the century it was still being advertised as the oldest and best ink for "marking linen, silk and cotton with a common pen without preparation. Payson's has been a household word for over 65 years" (48). Reliable marking inks enabled women to sign their names on quilt blocks as easily as in paper autograph albums. Indeed, the development of non-corrosive ink may have contributed to the fad for autograph quilts, which developed soon after Payson's was invented.

Many of the blocks in the early album quilts of the 1840s and '50s featured elaborate ink signatures and small drawings and verses. By the time of the Civil War, album quilt inscriptions had become shorter and were more likely to include only the block maker's name, and perhaps his or her hometown or date.

Ink was used to sign and date quilts from the 1830s through the end of the century. In the database there were 127 quilts with inked dates. Three are dated before the mid-1830s, evidence that inked inscriptions were possible earlier, although not common. Two are from the twentieth century. Because 96% of the quilts with inked inscriptions are between 1830 and 1899, an inked signature is a strong clue to these years.

One caution with inked inscriptions: they may have been added to an early quilt at a later date as a laundry mark or as an attempt by succeeding generations to document an old quilt.

CROSS STITCH INSCRIPTIONS

In 1847, *Godey's Lady's Book* could look back a dozen years and ask with nostalgia, "What lady whose school days were anterior to the use of indelible ink, but remembers the working of her sampler? The ABC's were then the beginning of needlework education, and the accomplishment of the marking stitch was the proud aim of every school girl." Cross stitch, the marking stitch, was considered a basic part of the female curriculum as preparation for managing a house. The tradition of marking sheets and other household linens with a number and the owner's initials goes back to pre-Revolutionary days. Cross stitch is a form of counted embroidery; the seamstress counts the threads of the background fabric and covers a certain number of warps and wefts with a diagonal. After the advent of ink marking, skills in cross stitch were quickly forgotten and the practice of marking linens in any medium soon stopped, despite advice like that of Catherine Beecher and Harriet Beecher Stowe who in 1868 still advocated that "all bed linen should be marked and numbered, so that a bed can always be made properly and all missing articles be known" (49).

Many early quilts were marked just like other bed linens, with numbers, initials and an occasional date. When album quilts became the fashion, seamstresses often used the cross stitch to embroider their names, the dates and short sentiments. *Godey's* was accurate in noting the demise of the cross stitch, however; it disappeared as a quilt signature technique in the 1850s. Of 38 quilts dated with cross stitch in the database, 87% of them were made before 1855; three cross stitch dates were after the Civil War and two were in the twentieth century. Cross stitch inscriptions are a strong clue to a pre-Civil War date.

CHAIN STITCH AND OTHER EMBROIDERED INSCRIPTIONS

While counted cross stitch was the most popular

Album sampler quilt (detail), made by friends of Susan Rogers. Inscribed in embroidery: 1861 or 1867. Appliqued, embroidered and quilted. Cotton. Collection: Smithsonian Institution, Negative # 71–2708.

Embroidery thread often wears poorly. The last number in the date is wearing away as are some of the details in the birds, who seem happily unaware of the cat. The quilt is bound in straight-grain applied binding, a common technique in all eras.

embroidered inscription technique before the Civil War, other embroidery stitches like the chain stitch, the satin stitch and the running stitch were also used. Chain stitch is the most common embroidery stitch for signatures in the last half of the nineteenth century and into the twentieth. Of 72 quilts in the database with chain-stitched dates, 86% were dated after 1875. Seamstresses from all eras might use a chain stitch (there were three instances in quilts made before 1850), but a chain stitch signature is more likely to have been made after 1875, as are satin stitch and other surface embroidery signatures.

PIECED INSCRIPTIONS: SAMPLER ALPHABET

The sampler alphabet that school girls learned to embroider with cross stitch was adapted to pieced quilt design by a few quilters in the northeast. Winifred Reddall, writing in *Uncoverings* in 1980, noted seven nineteenth-century quilts that were inscribed with large letters pieced of squares and rectangles. The lettered quilts she found came from New York, Connecticut and New Jersey (50). Since then, five more dated examples inscribed with similar pieced lettering have been found, four from New York and one from Connecticut. The earliest date-inscribed example is dated 1807, the latest 1877, and the latest date-attributed example is 1891; so it seems that a sampler-style pieced letter inscription is a better indicator of place (the New York, New Jersey, Connecticut area) than of date. An 1833 example was pictured in a magazine article in the 1920s. Since they offered a pattern for the alphabet, quilts made after that date cannot be assumed to be from the east coast where the piecing design originated.

APPLIQUED INSCRIPTIONS

Applique has been used as an inscription technique throughout the history of patchwork. Two of the earliest date-inscribed quilts, the *McCord Quilt*, dated 1726, and *Anna Tuel's Marriage Quilt*, dated 1785, are inscribed with applique numerals. Examples from every era survive, but there is a tendency for applique inscriptions to be most popular in the years when conventional applique designs were also popular—from about 1840 through 1900.

STAMPED AND STENCILED INSCRIPTIONS

Signature stamps and stencils were often used to sign album quilts during the prime decades of the album craze, the 1840s and '50s. Indelible ink was forced through a small metal stencil featuring a signature surrounded by appropriate flourishes. A neat, personalized quilt block could also be obtained using a signature stamp of metal, and later of rubber. Most of the stenciled and stamped signatures date from the same years as free-hand ink signatures, from the 1840s through the end of the nineteenth century.

QUILTED INSCRIPTIONS

Quilted inscriptions often go unnoticed, as they are only subtle variations in the subtle designs of the quilting. Quilted signatures have little correlation with any particular era. The 92 examples in the data base ranged from 1746 through 1948

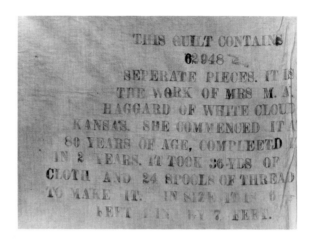

Reverse of a pieced spread made by Martha A. Haggard (1815–1899) in White Cloud, Kansas. Attributed date: 1895–1897. Pieced, bound and backed. Cotton. Collection: Helen F. Spencer Museum of Art, the University of Kansas. Gift of Louise Langworthy.

Either Martha Haggard or her descendants recorded her accomplishments using rubber stamps and ink on the back of the piece the family called *The Wonder Quilt*. For a view of the front see page 27.

with no real patterns of popularity apparent, with one exception. Quilted signatures and dates were a favorite technique of Amish quiltmakers. If one eliminates the Amish quilts from the database there are few twentieth-century examples. Without the Amish (who generally maintained higher standards for their quilting than mainstream quiltmakers during the first quarter of this century) one can conclude that quilted signatures are uncommon in the twentieth century.

Stuffed and corded signatures, like any stuffed and corded quilting, were uncommon after the Civil War, so a padded inscription is a good clue to a date before 1865.

Edging

The manner in which a quilt is finished can provide some information about its age. The quilt's shape, its binding and extra flourishes like fringe or edges of folded triangles were fashionable in different eras; some can be good clues to date.

SHAPE

Most quilts are rectangles or squares; some older quilts and spreads are T-shaped with cutouts in the corners to allow the coverlet to fit around the foot posts of a four-poster bed. Cut-out corners are generally found in quilts attributed to the years before 1860. Scalloped edges are another shape variation, found occasionally in quilts after the 1840s and quite popular in the 1925-1950 period.

BINDING

Applied strips of fabric cut on the bias of the material are a common twentieth-century binding. Although bias strip binding is sometimes found on nineteenth-century quilts (particularly on scalloped edges), it is a good clue to a later quilt. The Missouri Quilt Project examined 703 quilts and found not one example with bias binding attributable to the years before 1890 (51). In my database of date-inscribed quilts I had 187 quilts with plain edges in which I had examined the binding technique. Of these, 68 were dated between 1925 and 1950; 24 of them (35%) were bound with bias. There were 119 dated before 1925; only nine of these (7%) were bound with bias, indicating that after 1925 a quiltmaker was five times as likely to use bias binding as her predecessors. The presence of bias binding is only one piece of evidence to be added to the case for a quilt's date, but it indicates a later quilt.

Quiltmakers used other types of plain edges—applied binding cut on the straight grain of the fabric, bringing the fabric of one side over the other to make a hemmed edge, and folding under both top and back to make a seamed edge. Most of the techniques show a wide range (straight-grain binding ranged from 1781 to 1946 in the database) with no patterns of popularity apparent and so are not clues to date.

A few observations on edges may help build a case for a particular date. Nineteenth-century quiltmakers were more inclined to use a narrow edge; whether it was the back brought to the front or a strip of applied fabric, very little showed on the top. Twentieth-century quiltmakers like a wider edge. Nineteenth-century quiltmakers sometimes added piping to the edge; they inserted a fabric-covered cord in a contrasting color in the seam of the binding on the front of the quilt. This detail seems most common from about 1840 through 1880. Early quiltmakers added a binding of woven tape. The tapes are sometimes woven in a twill pattern and usually have exposed selvages. They are sometimes referred to as hand-loomed tapes, but as with other questions about home-weaving versus factory-weaving, the answers are not clear-cut. Whether woven by hand or machine, a white cotton or linen tape is a good clue to a pre-Civil War quilt. Late nineteenth-century quiltmakers also used wool and silk tapes to bind their show quilts, so don't confuse the early nineteenth-century white cotton tapes with the later colored wool or silk tapes and ribbons.

FANCY EDGES

Fancy edgings include cords and braids, tassels, laces and ruffles, all typical of show quilts from the last half of the nineteenth century. Early quilts may also have wide ruffles.

Fringe is another early edge treatment and one that correlates well with a specific period of time. Of 20 fringed quilts in the database, 19 were dated 1860 or earlier, indicating that fringe (especially a white fringe—knitted, knotted, woven or crocheted) is a strong clue to a pre-Civil War quilt.

Folded triangles inserted into the quilt's edge are known today as prairie points. The technique is derived from clothing decoration; small folded triangles were inserted into the edges of mid-nineteenth-century garments as an alternative to more expensive lace edging. Prairie points, a name that has not been traced in print before the 1970s, implies a midwestern origin, which may not be accurate, since it is found in late nineteenth century English as well as American quilts (52). Evidence that the technique goes back to the mid-nineteenth century are two stuffed-work applique quilts, attributed to sisters in Missouri around 1860 (53). The earliest dated example I have seen is on an 1882 Crazy Quilt. The triangle edge is found in a number of late-nineteenth-century show quilts, but it is most common in cotton quilts made after 1925, and in a cotton quilt is a good clue to that date or later.

Edgings often conflict with clues in the rest of the quilt. In such cases two conclusions are possible. One is that the quilt has been rebound, a common occurrence, since bindings and the areas near the edge are often the first parts of a quilt to wear out. In many cases, new binding has been sewn atop the old, and the presence of the old binding underneath is evidence of the repair. Sometimes the worn areas of the quilt have been trimmed away; a disrupted design repeat may help determine if this is the case. But don't be too quick to attribute every out of kilter border to an over-eager quilt repairer. Many nineteenth-century quiltmakers had entirely different standards for quilt symmetry from ours today. A border on only two or three sides could have been the maker's intention.

A second reason for a conflict between edging and quilt is that the quilting was done at a later date. Thoughtful examination of the edging, the back, the batting and the quilting design can help determine if this is so.

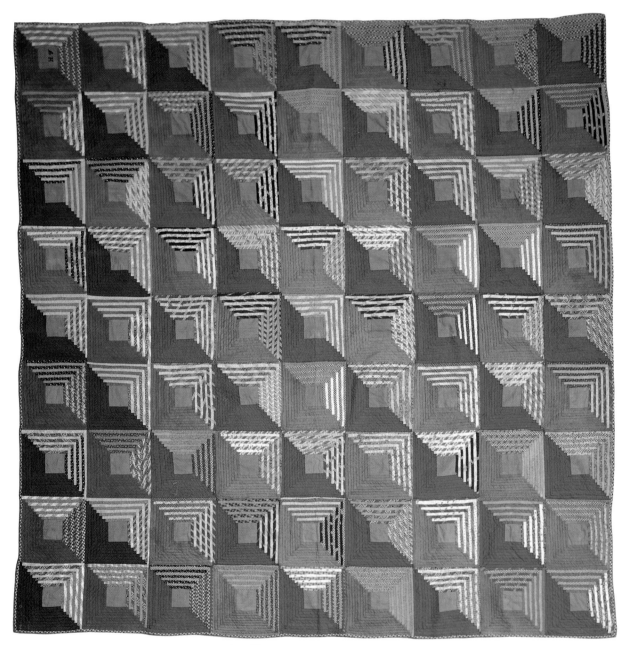

Log Cabin spread (*Sunshine and Shadow* variation), made by Isabelle Hardin Hayner in Kentucky. Estimated date: 1875–1900. Pieced using the foundation method, bound but unbacked. Cotton. Collection: Dr. William Browning and Susan Browning Pogany.

Isabelle Hayner's use of lights and darks is remarkably effective in achieving a three-dimensional look. The Log Cabin is a classic block pattern; quilts and spreads in the design were a nationwide fad after the Civil War.

CLUES IN STYLE

Over the years fashion in quilt styles has changed as dramatically as fashion in clothing. Quilt patterns, colors schemes and borders can help us date old quilts just as hoopskirts, bustles and pants suits help us date portraits. Many quilt styles seem to be as old as patchwork, while others have specific beginnings and abrupt endings—and the latter make the best clues. Keep in mind, however, that fashions don't terminate everywhere at once. Many women continued to make quilts in out-of-date styles just as they continued to wear hairdos that were fashionable in their youth. In this chapter we begin with details of style such as set and borders and proceed to a view of the overall quilt with a guide to distinctive styles.

A magazine illustration, clipped for a quiltmaker's scrapbook around 1930, mixes styles in hairdos, clothing, furniture and quilts. The artist apparently was trying to evoke the 1840s or '50s. The hoopskirted seamstress quilts with a hoop—an anachronism; hoops weren't used until the twentieth century. But the quilt fits—a classic style of red and white blocks in the Nine Patch with a sawtooth border.

Styles in Set

Set is the term for the way the quilt is constructed, the way the patches are organized into a design repeat. There are four major categories of set or quilt design format. The repeat can be organized into a framed medallion, an all-over design, a strip set or a block set (which has several subcategories of set). The two most common sets are the block format that repeats a standard size square unit and the framed medallion format with its central design focus framed by borders.

FRAMED MEDALLION SET

Framed medallion is a twentieth-century term, used by Ruth Finley in 1929 to describe a typical eighteenth-century quilt with a tree-of-life center cut out of chintz, surrounded by pieced and appliqued borders (1).

Quiltmakers working after 1840 were likely to use a block format; earlier quiltmakers preferred the medallion set. Looking at selected periods of time, one sees a shift in popularity from medallion to block format in the second quarter of the nineteenth century. Of the 15 quilts in the database made before 1800 only two (18%) were constructed in the block format. Of 14 quilts made in the 1820s, three (21%) were block style. In the 1830s, 11 of the 19 quilts (58%) were block style; in the '40s 112 of the 140 quilts (80%) were block style. The shift in preference evidently began in the 1830s, possibly opening the way to the fad for the block-style album quilts which flourished in the '40s. Or it may be the album craze that encouraged the change to block-style construction; from our perspective it is difficult to discern the cause and effect. The preference for block style design survived the fading of the album quilt fad. Of the 48 quilts dated in the 1870s, 37 (77%) were

Jon Blumb

Princess Feather quilt, made by Mary Somerville (c. 1801 - ?) Inscribed in cross stitch: May 26, 1818. Appliqued, embroidered and quilted. Cotton. Collection: Helen F. Spencer Museum of Art, the University of Kansas. Gift of Dorothy Jewell Sanders.

Mary Somerville was 17 years old when she made this cut-out chintz quilt, a fact she recorded in the center, along with her name and the date. She used a medallion format (block style chintz quilts were not yet in fashion), and added a series of borders, some made of motifs cut from chintz, others like the stars, and the final feather border constructed of small scale prints. Mary made the best use of her limited amount of chintz. Note the variations in the potted flowers in the third border from the edge. The center design is an early patchwork version of what we call the *Princess Feather*.

block style, a trend that continued throughout the nineteenth and into the twentieth century.

The medallion style never completely died out; some enduring patterns like the Star of Bethlehem and the Princess Feather continued to demand a central focus. Professional quilt designers of the twentieth century revived its use for applique, using a medallion format for realistic floral designs such as sunflowers, poppies and iris.

The medallion format is thus a weak clue to a pre-Civil War date or a post-1925 date (in an applique quilt); it should only be used to support dates established with other, stronger clues. The block format because it ranges over such a long period is scarcely a clue at all. At best it can be used in a negative way, to cast suspicion on an alleged eighteenth-century origin. The true block format is rare in eighteenth-century quilts.

ALL-OVER SET

Finley described the all-over set as one in which the piecework had "neither block nor set" (2). Hexagons are the most common all-over pattern, one that goes back to the early nineteenth century. The earliest date-inscribed example in the database is 1817; the design was in print in *Godey's Lady's Book* in 1835. Variations of hexagon and diamond patterns set in an all-over pattern appear throughout the nineteenth and twentieth centuries. The all-over set is a rather minor clue to a post-1800 date.

STRIP SET

One set not often seen is the strip set, in which the patchwork is organized into strips, usually alternated with plain strips. A variation is pieced of strips of fabric, either printed or solid. The strip set has been more popular in the British Isles than in the United States. I found very few such date-inscribed quilts, but observation indicates that a strip set is a weak clue to a date between 1800 and the Civil War. One exception to that rule is the Wild Goose Chase or Flying Geese design, (right triangles set in strips); this particular pattern was often set in strips throughout the nineteenth and twentieth centuries. Another exception: the strip quilts of the Amish who maintained the style through the mid-twentieth century.

BLOCK STYLES

Blocks, whether applique, pieced or embroidered, can be set together in a number of ways, most of which have been in use so long that they are poor clues. The quiltmaker can seam her blocks side by side in an all-over set; she can alternate decorated blocks with plain blocks in an alternate set, and she can add strips of sashing between the blocks, which can be of patchwork or plain cloth. In any of these sets she can vary the effect by placing her square blocks on point. All these sets for block-style quilts are little more than clues that the quilt was probably made after 1800.

Unpieced sashings, like printed backs, are useful because they offer large pieces of print fabrics for scrutiny. Chintz sashing or alternate blocks of chintz are strong clues to a date before the Civil War. Most patchwork sashing such as Flying Geese triangles and the lattice strips called Garden Maze, generally were too common over too long a period of time to be good clues.

Yankee Puzzle or *Broken Dishes* quilt. Maker unknown. Estimated date: 1790-1825. Pieced and quilted. Cotton. Collection: Smithsonian Institution, Negative # 78037-A.

Most quilts made before 1820 had a medallion format, like this one, in which the seamstress framed the larger center block with smaller blocks to create a design focus. Other clues to an early date are the floral-trail chintz and the T-shaped cutout to fit around the bedposts. The piecing design was recorded in the late nineteenth century as *Hour Glass (Ohio Farmer*, 1894), *Big Dipper* (Ladies' Art Company, 1898) and as *Yankee Puzzle* (Ruth Finley's 1929 book), among many other names. The quiltmaker's name for the design—if she had one—is a mystery.

Sunflowers Bloom on a Quilt

Golden yellow, brown and green —with their friendly nodding heads grow the gorgeous sunflowers, lending brightness to fleeting summer days and to riotous autumn impartially. Here this familiar "Flower of the Sun" stops momentarily to lend year-round brightness to a new and undeniably lovely applique spread. There is a center wreath and a border worked out in clusters of three. Beautifully effective is the diagonal and fan quilting. Pattern No. C8990 includes the necessary transfers for the appliques, for placing them and for the quilting motifs—and costs just 35 cents.

Your quilt will finish to about 90 by 102.

Or, you may have the 90 by 102 top completely stamped (including the quilting) on fine white material as No. C8990M, for $1.95. The yellow, brown and green applique pieces for sunflowers and leaves may be had as No. C8990S, $1 additional. An order for either transfer or stamped quilt will provide many leisure moments of interesting work—repaid in full when your spread, worthy of an heirloom, is finished. Order quilt transfer pattern or quilt materials from Needlework Service, Capper's Weekly, Topeka, Kan.

Larry Schwarm

Realistic flowers, a medallion set, a strong border and a scalloped edge are style characteristics common in appliqued quilts designed by the pattern houses of the 1920s and '30s. This sunflower is from *Capper's Weekly.* Author's collection.

There is one set variation, four large blocks set in the four quadrants of the top, that seems to be typical of the middle of the nineteenth century. The four block set is not as common as a format of smaller blocks. There were only seven examples in the database, six of which were dated between 1850 and 1876, very little evidence to base a case for a date in the third quarter of the nineteenth century, but observation by myself and others does support the theory that the four-block set is mid-nineteenth century fashion. In the Quilts of Tennessee survey, Ramsey and Waldvogel noticed the four-block set primarily in pre-Civil War quilts (3). I should stress, though, that the latest four-

block quilt in my database was dated 1934, so at best, the set is a weak clue, and should only be used as support for an otherwise strong case. There is also some conventional wisdom that the four-block set is a regional variation, found primarily in Pennsylvania quilts. But the Tennessee quilts and the geographic origins of the seven in my database are ample evidence that the set has little regional correlation. Only two were from Pennsylvania; the others ranged from Indiana to South Carolina.

Styles In Borders

CHINTZ BORDERS

Although many of the images used in border designs did not change significantly over the years (florals, vines and swags were popular in both 1780 and 1880), the type of fabrics and the techniques in which the motifs were stitched did. Chintz prints (either cut-out and appliqued or used as unpieced borders) are typical of early quilts; conventional applique borders are more common after 1840. Of 35 quilts in the database with borders of large pieces of floral chintz, 32 (91%) were dated between 1800 and 1860; the remaining three were clustered around 1900, indicating that the fashion waned after the Civil War with a minor revival in the cretonne fabrics at the turn of the century. Based on both data and observation, an unpieced border of chintz is good evidence of a quilt from the Civil War or earlier.

APPLIQUE BORDERS

As we have seen, the applique technique in which flowers, birds and other printed motifs are cut from printed chintzes and applied to a plain background was more popular with earlier quiltmakers than was the conventional self-made applique. Cut-out chintz swags, bouquets, bows and baskets were typical borders for the cut-out chintz quilts. This border technique disappeared after 1860 when conventional applique became dominant.

Conventional applique borders appear earlier than conventional applique block designs. Eighteenth-century and early nineteenth-century cut-out chintz quilts sometimes included conventional applique borders among the more common cut-out chintz and pieced borders, although these conventional applique borders lack the graphic flam-

Strip quilt. Maker unknown. Estimated date: 1825–1850. Pieced and quilted. Cotton. Collection: Helen F. Spencer Museum of Art, the University of Kansas. The William Bridges Thayer Memorial.

Large scale stripes were popular for setting strips and borders before the Civil War. Here the stripe is a rainbow print, with the color shaded from light to dark. The strip set is a weak clue to a date of 1800–1860.

Whig Rose or *Democrat Rose* quilt. Maker unknown. Estimated date: 1840-1900. Appliqued and quilted. Cotton. Collection: Helen F. Spencer Museum of Art, the University of Kansas. Gift of Lizzie Smith.

The use of the four block set for applique quilts is a weak clue to a mid-nineteenth century date, so it may be that this red, white and green quilt is from before 1875 rather than after.

Hexagon or Honeycomb quilt. Maker unknown. Estimated date: 1825–1850. Pieced (English-style template piecing) and quilted. Cotton. Collection: Helen F. Spencer Museum of Art, the University of Kansas. The William Bridges Thayer Memorial.

The hexagon design is one of the most common all-over patterns—those that are not made of square blocks. The quiltmaker cut a green pillar-print chintz into strips for a border. The odd strip along the top edge is a twentieth-century repair, but the quilt doesn't apppear to have been trimmed. The maker intended to have a border on only three sides.

boyance of the high style applique block quilts made after 1840.

A distinctive early border technique, rarely seen after 1850, is an applique Sawtooth or Dog Tooth (4) in which a strip of fabric is cut into jagged peaks and appliqued to the edge of the quilt. This triangular border was used on 15 quilts in the database, dated between 1800 and 1855. A variation resembles a Log Cabin design. The single piece of fabric is carefully cut in a stair-step design that looks like the shading arrangement called Courthouse Steps. Applique Log Cabin borders were made in the first and second quarters of the nineteenth century, long before the pieced Log Cabin blocks became popular for the body of the quilts—another case of border design anticipating a block design. The applique Log Cabin borders disappeared around the Civil War, about the time that the Log Cabin blocks achieved their great popularity.

PIECED BORDERS

Border designs familiar to today's quilters, like the Flying Geese and pieced Sawtooth, were also well used by earlier generations of quilters. One pieced

King's Crown quilt, made by Mary Lawson Ruth McCrea (1835–1880) in Indiana. Inscribed: May, 1860. Pieced, stuffed and quilted. Cotton. Collection: Smithsonian Institution, Negative # 34769.

Sawtooth borders frame the spectacular feather quilting.

128

border that does correlate with date is the strip border, pieced of two or more long pieces of fabric (with no patchwork borders among the plain strips). Of 73 quilts with strip borders in the data base, only nine (12%) are dated between 1840 and 1865 and none before 1840. This indicates that strip borders multiplied with the spread of the sewing machine, and can serve as weak clues to a post-Civil War date.

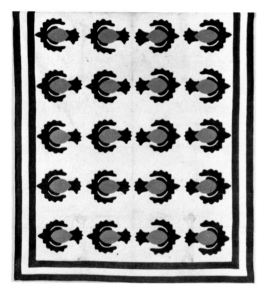

Pineapple quilt. Maker unknown. Estimated date: 1850–1900. Appliqued with pieced border, quilted. Cotton. Collection: Helen F. Spencer Museum of Art, the University of Kansas.

Most quiltmakers never imagined their work hanging on a wall. This pineapple applique with its three-sided strip border and mirror image set was designed for a bed. Pillows covered the unbordered side and the sleeper had a view of pineapples growing left and right. The mitered border corner technique, which requires extra fabric and planning, is not a clue to date.

The corners of these strip borders can be mitered or not, but the mitered corner technique for corners—whether strip, patchwork, applique or plain fabric—is of little use in dating. A quilt top attributed to Martha Washington around 1800 has a nicely mitered border of striped fabric, one that would do credit to any of today's quiltmakers who consider a mitered corner almost obligatory, and an important gauge of craftsmanship.

The border combining isosceles triangles with a scalloped edge is a good clue to the 1925-1950 years. Although it is seen on late-nineteenth century show quilts it was most popular decades later, especially as a frame for Dresden Plate and Fan quilts.

One more observation that can serve as a weak clue to date: the combination of a pieced border on an applique quilt (or vice versa) is more typical of a pre-twentieth century quilt. Quilters in this century are far more likely to match applique border to applique quilts and pieced borders to pieced quilts.

Many quiltmakers felt no compulsion to put symmetrical borders on their quilts. The quilt with a border on three sides, two sides or only one side is surprisingly common throughout the history of patchwork quilts. Collectors are suspicious that an asymmetrical border is evidence the quilt has been cut down (sometimes this is true), but close inspection of the binding fabric often reveals that a quiltmaker never intended borders on all the sides. The three-sided border fits the bed designed for a bolster atop the bedcover, a style that goes back to the eighteenth century (5). Today's quiltmakers usually speculate that the quilt was meant to decorate a bed pushed against a wall. An asymmetrical border probably did not strike the maker as odd, since she never saw her quilt hung on a wall. Because the style stretches across so many decades, an asymmetrical border is of no help in dating a quilt.

Styles in Backing

Most quiltmakers have chosen plain white cotton for the backs of their quilts; so a white cotton, whether coarse or fine, bright white or natural tan, is not a useful clue to age. Other backs, however, have enjoyed more limited spans of popularity and can be helpful. It is important to remember that backs, as well as binding, may have been made later than the quilt top. Many seamstresses let decades slip by before finishing a quilt, and many old tops have been quilted in recent years.

One characteristic of backs that is scarcely any help is the width of the fabrics. Cloth wide enough to back a quilt is not a twentieth-century innovation. The Sears catalogs from 1895 to 1900 sold sheeting in 88-, 90-, 96-, and 104- inch widths, so a wide piece of fabric does not indicate a modern back, nor does a narrow piece necessarily indicate an earlier date.

Some quiltlovers are quick to point out "homespun" backing as a sign of a quilt's age, but true homespun cotton (cotton that was spun at home into yarn and then woven into cloth) was uncommon in America, and a homespun cotton back (or a homespun cotton top) would be a rare exception to the rule that cotton yarn was factory spun and usually factory woven. For more about homespun fabric see Chapter 3.

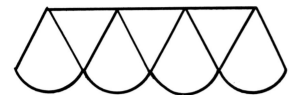

Triangle and Scallop Edge

Many early and mid-nineteenth century quilts have backings of two coarsely woven pieces of cotton, joined at the center. While some of this may have been homewoven fabric, the majority was probably manufactured. An 1839 Pennsylvania inventory lists ''1 piece of muslin for quilt lining'' (value: 50 cents) (6), indicating that fabric was specifically chosen to back or line quilts. The center seam in these older quilts frequently is hand stitched (quilts made before 1850 would, of course, have to have been hand stitched), and the selvages of the fabric are visible on the quilt back rather than being folded into the seam. This characteristic fabric and seam is a clue to a mid-nineteenth century or earlier quilt.

RECYCLED FEED AND FLOUR SACKING

Backs with numerous pieces of white or plain colored cloth are sometimes recycled fabric such as sugar or tobacco sacks. White flour sacks, with information printed, such as the name of the company and the weight of the commodity, appear on the backs of quilts from the mid-nineteenth through the mid-twentieth centuries.

Even an occasional elegant Baltimore Album quilt sports a back of sacking fabric (7), so the mere presence of a plain cotton sack is not in itself a good clue, unless there is a date or a symbol on it (such as the National Recovery Act—NRA—eagle that was used for only a few months in 1933 and 1934). Occasionally one can read enough information about the manufacturer of the flour, sugar or feed to begin a trail of research into the longevity of the company, which may help to pinpoint when the quilt was backed.

Manufacturers introduced patterned cotton sacks for animal feed and flour in the second quarter of this century. Most people who remember recycling patterned feed sacks associate them

Larry Schwarm

The Jack Sprat label is printed on a piece of adhesive paper that will easily peel off this print flour sack, made by the Bemis Bag Company, the largest manufacturer of cotton commodity bags. The bottom and one side of the sack, which was probably made during World War II, is seamed with a chain stitch of heavy cotton cord. Print sacks date from after 1930. Author's collection.

with the Depression; however, they were commonly used for clothing, furnishing fabric and quilts during World War II, and feed and flour are still sold in patterned sacks. The patterned sacking fabrics are a better clue to date than the plain ones, and indicate a post-1925 date.

Several people I have interviewed recall purchasing plain colored cotton feed sacks during the Depression in green, orange and yellow—the popular shades. These plain colored sacks were apparently produced for only a short while; most colored sacking fabric was probably home dyed.

Manufacturers also produced sacking with quilt designs printed on them; sacks with patterns

A stereoscopic photograph from the Keystone View company shows women working for the Arbuckle Sugar Processing Company filling sacks that can be seen moving along the line. The printing on such sacks usually came off with bleaching or soaking, and the white cotton could be used for clothing and quilts. Author's collection.

for applique and false patchwork of pieced designs occasionally turn up in antique shops. These appear to be from the 1930s and 1940s but little has been written about them.

Determining whether fabric on the back or the front of a quilt is from recycled sacks is not easy since the labels are usually not visible. Labels on the patterned sacks were easily removable, often printed on a separate piece of tape that could be stripped off. The plain sacks were bleached by quilters to remove the printing that gave the company name and logo, and sometimes they were dyed to match. The size of the backing pieces can be circumstantial evidence of salvaged fabric. Large feed, flour and sugar sacks were usually about 36" × 22" before they were split open, but smaller pieces might also be sacking. *Sewing With Cotton Bags*, a pamphlet published by the Textile Bag Manufacturers Association around 1930, advised that a six-pound flour sack yielded a 15" × 19" piece of fabric and a ten-pound sugar bag a 16" × 21" piece, although these sizes were not really standardized (8). Exceptionally frugal quilters recycled tobacco sacks, which were only about 4" by 8". In 1942, the Kansas City Star printed a pattern for The Depression Quilt, a top made of dyed tobacco sacks with a back of feed sacks.

Other often-cited evidence for a quilt's sacking origin is the distinctive coarse weave of sacks (es-

pecially printed sacks), but coarsely woven fabric could be purchased off the bolt and it even came in the packages of scraps quilters bought for their scrap-look quilts, so the weave is at best weak circumstantial evidence that the fabric was once a feed sack. The strongest clue to a recycled sack (besides the eyewitness account of someone who remembers ripping open the sack or wearing drawers of the same fabric) is a line of holes that remained after the chain-stitching that orignally held the sack together was pulled out. The thread that held the sack together was usually so coarse that the grain of the fabric did not go back together.

Backs of mismatched fabric (prints or plains) are also found, but are not as common as patched together backs of the same color fabric (which were sometimes dyed to match). Backs of small pieces are better testimony to hard times and scarce fabric than clues to any specific era.

REVERSIBLE QUILTS

Some makers sandwiched two patchwork tops together into a reversible quilt. Little research on two-sided quilts has been done, but there seems to be no pattern as to region or date. It was more likely the maker's idiosyncracy that dictated quilting two tops. An 1811 inventory of a Maryland woman listed "1 Piece Quilt both sides" (value $4.00) (9), and there are a few two-sided quilts in the literature attributed to the early nineteenth century, as well as dozens in the late nineteenth century and beyond.

PRINT BACKS

Backs of printed fabric are often quite a good clue to age, as has been said, because they offer a large piece of yardage for examination. If the fabric is typical of a particular era (for example, a pillar-printed chintz or a black and red robe print) one can quickly pinpoint the era in which the quilt was assembled.

There are no generalizations one can draw about the mere presence of a printed back versus a plain one. Quiltmakers in 1830 seem to have been just as likely to use a print as those in 1880 or 1930. However, print backs were more common on certain styles of quilts, such as Foundation Quilts, and are less commonly found on other styles such as Red, White and Green Applique.

One distinctive backing fabric is a cotton flannel, often a stripe or a plaid, that backs many

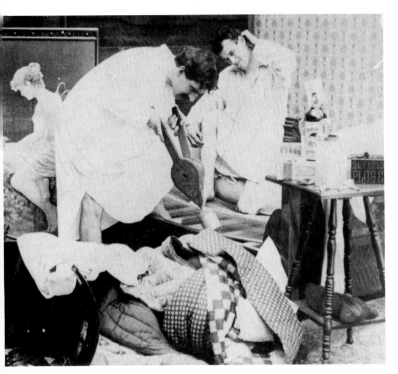

Slightly risque, beds were a common subject for turn-of-the-century stereoscopic cards. This one, copyrighted 1897, shows roommates fumigating their Irish Chain quilt for bedbugs. The quilt is backed with a cotton print. In the pile of bedding on the floor is a whole-cloth quilt, a floral print on one side, the other side plain. Author's collection.

foundation quilts and wool comforters. Cotton flannel backs tend to date from after 1875. Another is plain-colored pastel or bright cotton, a good clue to the 1925-1950 era. Dark, plain colored cottons, silks and wools were common for the backs of show quilts in both the nineteenth and twentieth centuries. It is the combination of the pastel color and the cotton fiber that makes a plain-colored back a twentieth century clue.

FOUNDATIONS

While most quilts and comforters are three layers—top, batting and back—some are constructed as foundation patchwork in which the maker builds the patchwork design on fabric squares, block by block. After each block is constructed it is joined to the others, as all patchwork is, but behind the top there is another layer, visible only through worn spots in a finished quilt or on the reverse of an unfinished top. Exposed foundations are easy to distinguish from finished backs because they are made of blocks of fabric the same size as the blocks in the top, and there are usually raw edges showing in the seams joining the blocks.

Evidence of foundation construction techniques means a likely late-nineteenth-century date. For more information about the technique see Foundation Patchwork in Chapter 6.

Styles in Size

The size of a quilt has not been statistically correlated with dates, but observation by myself and others indicates that large, square quilts (9 or even 10 feet wide) tend to date from before the Civil War or very recently (since the advent of the king-size bed). Quilts about seven-feet square are a rather standard size that gives no indication of date, but smaller quilts, pieces so small they would not cover an adult sleeper, were popular during the last quarter of the nineteenth century. These slumber throws were designed to cover the top of a bed, a piece of furniture or a napper. Even smaller quilts may be children's bedding. In general, size is at best a weak clue for dating.

A Guide to Distinctive Styles

Because style is so useful in quilt dating I have devised this catalog of common styles. Each part includes information about how to recognize the style, its years of popularity, as well as special tips for the collector and references for further reading. Some information summarizes earlier chapters and readers are referred to other parts of the book for more detail. Most quilts can be found in more than one style category. A red and white embroidered child's quilt, for example, will be discussed in at least three categories: Color Schemes (red and white), Children's Quilts and Outline Embroidered Quilts. In dating any particular quilt, you will first want to look through the list below and check out all the stylistic categories that might apply.

Styles in Fabrics

  Whole-Cloth Quilts
    Whitework Quilts
    Wool Whole-Cloth Quilts
  Chintz Quilts
    Pieced Chintz Quilts
    Cut-Out Chintz Quilts
  Charm Quilts
  Wool Utility Quilts & Comforters
  Show Quilts

Styles in Techniques

Nineteenth-Century Applique Quilts (Conventional Applique)
Twentieth-Century Applique Quilts
Crazy Quilts
Foundation Patchwork
Outline Embroidered Quilts

Styles in Function

Album and Friendship Quilts
   Single Pattern Album or Friendship Quilts
   Sampler Albums
Sampler Quilts
Fund-raising Quilts
Commemorative and Patriotic Quilts
Children's Quilts

Styles in Color

Red, White and Green Quilts
Red and White Quilts
Blue and White Quilts
Dark Cotton Quilts
Light, Bright Quilts

Styles Favored by Regional, Ethnic and Religious Groups

Amish Quilts
Hawaiian Quilts

There are several distinctive sub-styles of American whole cloth quilts. A late variation are the rayon satin quilts—often commercially quilted by machine—that were popular in the 1925-1950 era. These came in many pastel colors and were often reversible to a different color. The best clue to their age is the rayon fabric, although a few quiltmakers during these years splurged on silk; one occasionally finds a whole-cloth silk quilt, especially a baby quilt, from the mid-twentieth century.

Another recent style is the Mennonite whole-cloth quilt, which seems to date back to the early twentieth century in midwestern Mennonite communities. The style is currently increasing in popularity, at least among Kansas Mennonites, because the whole-cloth quilts sell well at the Mennonite Central Committee Relief sales, and they are suitable to the group quilting that church members do to make quilts for the annual sales (10). Discriminating between a nineteenth-century and a contemporary whole-cloth quilt (whether made by a Mennonite or not) is easiest if polyester blend fabrics and a polyester batting are in the quilt. The twentieth-century examples sometimes have two shades of fabric, while the nineteenth-century cotton quilts are always white on both sides. The newer examples rarely have stuffing, cording or other padded quilting in them, while the antiques often do.

WHITEWORK QUILTS

Whitework quilts, called Marseilles quilts until the end of the last century and trapunto quilts today, can be traced back to seventeenth-century France (11) and eighteenth-century England (12). However, the surviving hand-made American examples date only from after the last quarter of the eighteenth century.

The coverlets are characterized by elaborate stuffing and cording, often combined with flat quilting. Most have tops of white cotton, but linen is also found. Like other whole-cloth quilts, most whitework quilts are based on the medallion format. The central element is surrounded by geometric and floral borders. Cornucopias, pineapples and serpentine feathers were popular motifs. Many are finished with a cotton fringe, and it is clear they were intended to be both a Sunday-best quilt and evidence of superior needleworking skill.

The style thrived during the first half of the nineteenth century, probably influenced by appreciation of classical Greek design with its white statues and architecture, and by the increasing availability of cotton fabric and the cotton thread necessary for the complex quilting.

Whitework also refers to other kinds of needlework popular during those decades; white on white embroidery and candlewicking made use of similar designs. The techniques for whitework quilting, the stuffing, cording and flat quilting, were also used for clothing and other household linens including pillow shams, furniture covers, and splashers—protective wall covers hung behind a washstand. These smaller pieces are sometimes mistakenly indentified as baby quilts.

The whitework quilts were popular enough to be imitated by machine-woven versions called Marseilles quilts. In 1763 Scottish weavers began producing white spreads that were "quilted in the loom". The Marseilles quilts or Marseilles spreads can look remarkably like a quilted piece. The weaver could add a layer of stuffing and imitate a quilting stitch. The imitations are so good they can fool novice collectors, but they do not have the handmade, rather irregular look of a hand-quilted white quilt. Marseilles spreads were popular through the end of the nineteenth century when decorating trendsetters considered them a tasteful alternative to patchwork quilts. The later

Stuffed whitework quilt made by Elizabeth Holmes Adams (1797–1838) in Peterborough, New Hampshire. Estimated date: 1800–1840. Quilted and stuffed after being quilted. Cotton. Collection: Helen F. Spencer Museum of Art, the University of Kansas. Gift of Mrs. W.H. Sears.

Elizabeth Adams separated the center motif, the corner fans and the borders of her design with double lines of quilting, a design convention more common in British whole-cloth quilts than in nineteenth-century American versions. The stuffed work that emphasizes the feathers, flowers, bowknots and swags is most typical of the years 1800–1860.

at the end of the Civil War, although there were individuals who continued to do the time-consuming work. In 1873 there was still a premium category for "Quilt, white solid work on muslin" at the St. Louis Fair, indicating that people continued to enter them, but these entries may have been older quilts, shown by proud children and grandchildren of the makers (14).

WOOL WHOLE-CLOTH QUILTS

Whole-cloth quilts made of wool are popularly called linsey-woolsey quilts, implying a weave of linen and wool, however the quilt tops are generally all wool, rather than mixed. For more about linsey-woolsey, see chapter 3.

The wool bedquilt is closely related to the quilted wool petticoat, fashionable in the eighteenth century when dresses featured open panels exposing quilted silk or wool undergarments. Some of the whole cloth wool quilts were once petticoats in which the gathers have been removed and the long rectangle of fabric has been divided and sewn into a square format. Salvaged petticoats are recognizable because the seams on the back of the quilt echo the seams in the top.

Wool whole-cloth quilts survive in bold colors: rich indigos, oranges, greens, golds and shocking pink. Most are based on a central medallion format. In most the quilting is elaborate; feathered plumes are important motifs. Fruit and floral designs similar to Jacobean crewel embroidery designs were also popular. Whole-cloth wool quilts differ from their whitework relations in that they

examples were thinner, and did not have the stuffing layer the earlier spreads did (13).

Handmade whitework quilts in America have a definite period of popularity. Of 22 examples in the database, 20 were dated between 1796 and 1865. The style, like several others, disappeared

---

Summary of Whitework Whole-Cloth Quilts

Characteristics: Look for quilts of white cotton with quilting, stuffing and cording as the decorative techniques.

Range: Late eighteenth century through 1865.

Don't be confused by: Twentieth-century whole-cloth quilts. The earlier versions are likely to have stuffing and/or cording; the later ones aren't. Marseilles spreads are machine-woven imitations of hand-quilted whitework.

Related styles: Wool Whole-Cloth Quilts.

For additional examples: See pages 112 and 113.

See also: "Clues In Techniques" (Quilting and Tying), Chapter 6.

For further reading: Federico, Jean T. "White Work Classification System".

Uncoverings 1980. American Quilt Study Group, Mill Valley, California, 1981.

Garoutte, Sally. "Marseilles Quilts and Their Woven Offspring", *Uncoverings 1982*, American Quilt Study Group, Mill Valley, California, 1983.

Osler, Dorothy. *Traditional British Quilts.* B.T. Batsford, London, 1987.

---

have no stuffed work or cording but are all flat quilted.

Few date-inscribed examples of wool whole-cloth quilts survive. Three are in the database (1788, 1807 and 1831). Date-attributed examples range from 1750 to 1840. The wool whole-cloth quilt is an early style that faded as the calico quilt became the dominant fashion in the 1840s.

Courtesy of Joyce Gross

Whole-cloth wool quilt. Maker unknown. Inscribed in the quilting: 1831. Quilted. Wool. Private Collection.

Classic feathering and floral baskets characterize this indigo blue example. The border is glazed wool; the center, unglazed. Time has emphasized the seams in the center, illustrating that these quilts are not truly "whole-cloth", but usually composed of a number of pieces of identical or similar fabric.

Summary of Wool Whole-Cloth Quilts

Characteristics: Shiny glazed wools, fancy quilting, wool batting.
Range: 1750 through 1840.
Don't be confused by: Later Amish quilts, which are always pieced.
Related styles: Whitework Quilts, Wool Utility Quilts.
For additional examples: See page 44.
For further reading: Vander Noordaa, Titia. "The Lindsey Woolseys at the Shelburne Museum". *Spindle, Shuttle and Dyepot.* 16, Spring, 1985. Pages 59-61.

Styles in Fabrics

CHINTZ QUILTS

Because quilts made of small scale cotton clothing prints (calico) became the dominant style in the mid-nineteenth century, the use of large scale furnishings prints (chintz) in a quilt is a good clue to a date before the Civil War. The two major chintz quilt styles are pieced scrap quilts and appliqued cut-out chintz quilts. Both styles are among the earliest types of patchwork quilts and some seamstresses combined the techniques and styles. Dated examples, attributed to American seamstresses, go back to the 1770s and '80s, but several date-attributed examples in England and America may be from the middle decades of the eighteenth century. A conservative estimate of a range on chintz patchwork quilts in America is from 1775 to 1865.

Narrowing the date of a chintz quilt beyond that 90 year span involves examining the chintzes and looking for other style and technical characteristics such as machine sewing and the presence of cotton thread. For more information about fashions in chintz prints see Chapter 5.

PIECED CHINTZ QUILTS

Chintz quilts are generally of simple patchwork—squares, triangles and stars. Mariner's Compasses, Feathered Stars and Stars of Bethlehem are the more complex kinds of patterns pieced in chintz. Other design characteristics one might find in a chintz quilt are the medallion format, a fringed, ruffled or tape edge, and a mixing of silk, linen and cotton fabrics. Color schemes are usually not controlled and scraps of all types of fabrics, colors and print scale are included.

in the database, all were made before 1830. Based on this rather small sample, one can conclude that the tree-of-life central motif, either cut directly from a printed palampore or constructed of design elements from several pieces of chintz, is a good clue to a date before 1835 or 1840.

Of nine chintz quilts with a central vase in the database, all were dated before 1850; the cut-out chintz central vase design is thus a clue to a quilt made before that date. After 1840 the vases, urns and baskets were usually plain and calico cottons, conventionally appliqued. Also quilters were more likely to isolate their vases and pots in blocks rather than highlighting them in the center of the quilt.

CHARM QUILTS

The charm quilt is a version of the cotton scrapbag quilt in which the seamstress includes no two scraps alike. Not all charm quiltmakers met that goal but they certainly tried. Many charm quilts have two other characteristics that set them apart from mere scrap quilts. They are made of a single pattern piece such as a diamond, square, hexagon, clamshell or triangle and, since every piece is a different scrap, charm quilts do not rely on white or a single color for design unity.

Observation indicates that the charm quilt was popular from about 1870 to 1910. Few charm quilts are dated, but most offer many clues in the multitudes of cotton prints, which sometimes include at least one Centennial print (with dates 1776-1876 in the fabric). The late nineteenth-century examples often have a predominantly brown color scheme with many madder-style paisleys, stripes and florals plus white shirting prints and double-pink cottons. As color schemes and print styles changed around the turn of the century, charm quilts became grayer and bluer. The style

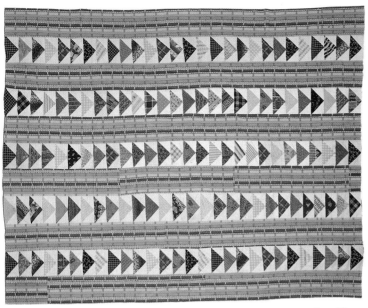

Larry Schwarm

Flying Geese, unfinished quilt top. Maker unknown. Estimated date: 1825–1850. Pieced. Cotton. Collection: Pam Johnson.

The use of prints of different scale from small scale dress calicoes to large scale furnishings chintzes is characteristic of pre-Civil War quilts.

CUT-OUT CHINTZ QUILTS

The cut-out chintz quilt is characterized primarily by the technique of cutting printed designs from one fabric and appliqueing them to another. Seamstresses might use an applique stitch or a buttonhole stitch to secure the motifs. The medallion format was most commonly used, with cut-out chintz in a block format being a strong clue to a date between 1840 and 1865. The two major design themes for the medallion quilts were the tree-of-life and a floral vase or basket.

Of nine date-inscribed tree-of-life quilts that were

Summary of Pieced Chintz Quilts

Characteristics: Look for large scale cotton prints, with or without a glaze.

Range: 1775-1865.

Don't be confused by: Large scale cretonnes as quilt backs at the end of the nineteenth century. The later large scale furnishing fabrics are usually printed with better registration, in more muted colors and often have a twill or sateen weave rather than a plain.

See also: Clues in Printed Cotton, Chapter 5.

For additional examples: See pages 8, 83, 85, 86, 87, 125 and 127.

For further reading: Bullard, Lucy Folmar and Betty Jo Sheill. *Chintz Quilts: Unfading Glory.* Serendipity Publishers, Tallahassee, Florida, 1983. Montgomery, Florence M., *Printed Textiles: English and American Cottons and Linens 1700-1850.* The Viking Press, New York, 1970.

Jon Blumb

Tree-of-Life quilt. Maker unknown. Estimated date: 1800–1825. Appliqued and quilted. Collection: Helen F. Spencer Museum of Art, the University of Kansas. The William Bridges Thayer Memorial.

The quiltmaker included a variety of chintzes. The outer border is a dark ground floral in which the brown ground is shattering. One row of chintzes in the inside ring has several pagodas cut from a piece of Chinoiserie—scenes depicting Western ideas of the Chinese landscape. Both dark ground florals and Chinoiserie were popular in the last quarter of the eighteenth century and first quarter of the nineteenth.

The quilt was pictured 55 years ago in *The Romance of the Patchwork Quilt in America* (Plate XLV). At that time there was no damage evident in the brown chintz in the outer border. The before and after photographs illustrate the conservation problems with some brown dyes.

Album sampler quilt, made by members of the Holden family. Estimated date: 1840–1865. Appliqued (using both the cut-out chintz and the conventional applique methods) and quilted. Cotton. Collection: Woodin Wheel Antiques.

Stylistic differences in the two types of applique are apparent in this album quilt. The simplicity and directness of the rose in the center contrasts with the florid cut-outs in most of the other blocks. Block style cut-out chintz quilts were only popular for a few decades; they were a transition between earlier cut-out chintz medallions and block style conventional applique.

seems to have lost some of its momentum after 1900, fewer true Charm quilts survive in the darker cottons of the 1890-1925 era or the pastel cottons of the 1925-1950 era.

Summary of Cut-Out Chintz or Broderie Perse Quilts

Characteristics: Look for appliqued motifs cut from large-scale furnishings fabrics.
Range: 1775-1865.
See also: "Clues in Printed Cotton", Chapter 6.
Related styles: Signature Album and Friendship Quilts.
For additional examples: See pages 15, 19 and 124.
For further reading: Beyer, Jinny. *The Art and Technique of Creating Medallion Quilts.* EPM Publications, McLean, Virginia, 1982.
Bullard, Lucy Folmar and Betty Jo Sheill. *Chintz Quilts: Unfading Glory*, Serendipity Publishers, Tallahassee, Florida, 1983.
Montgomery, Florence M. *Printed Textiles: English and American Cottons and Linens 1700-1850.* The Viking Press, New York, 1970.

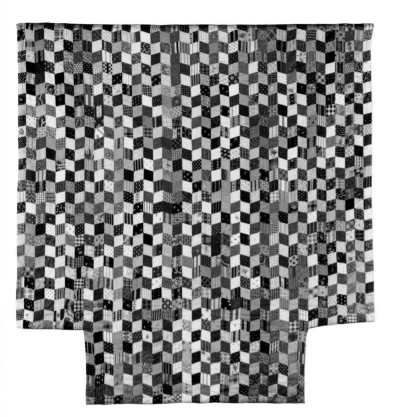

Charm quilts, like other grass roots fashions, received little attention in the nineteenth-century needlework press. Periodicals in the 1920s and '30s attempted to revive the style with patterns, instructions and nostalgic recollections of the fun involved in obtaining hundreds of pieces. The later charm quilts did not make use of a single template, and they were usually more visually cohesive, united with repetitive pieces of identical white or pastel plain fabric.

Nineteenth-century girls and women who collected scraps for charm quilts also collected buttons to thread into charm strings and trinkets to press into charm jars. Other period names for charm quilts are odd fellows or odd feller and beggar's quilts (15).

One of the superstitions associated with charm quilts is that there are sometimes two identical fabrics in a quilt in which no other fabrics match—part of the lucky charm. Another is that the maker collected 999 different fabrics; in reality, few charm quilts have exactly 999 pieces.

Charm quilt. Maker unknown. Estimated date: 1875–1890. Pieced and quilted. Cotton. Collection: Jinny Beyer. The maker included 1,234 different prints cut from a single template, a parallelogram.

Summary of Charm Quilts

Characteristics: Look for a profusion of different cotton prints and a single-template pattern. Twentieth-century charm quilts usually include plain white fabric to unify the design.
Range: 1870-1950.
See also: Chapter 5: Clues in Cotton Prints.
Related styles: Dark Cotton Quilts.
For an additional example: See page 117.
For further reading: Benberry, Cuesta. "Charm Quilts". *Quilters Newsletter Magazine*, # 120.
Benberry, Cuesta. "Charm Quilts Revisited". *Quilters Newsletter Magazine*, #198.
Beyer, Jinny. *The Scrap Look*. EPM Publications, McLean, Virginia, 1985, "Charm Quilts", Chapter 5.

WOOL UTILITY QUILTS AND COMFORTERS

After cotton became the primary fabric for American quilts during the second quarter of the nineteenth century, wool was consigned to the lowly position of fabric fit only for utility quilts and comforters. Wool utility quilts are characterized by simple patchwork patterns, coarse fabrics, batting of thick cotton or wool, and sparse quilting if any quilting at all. Most are tied with yarn. They are generally attributed to the years between 1875 and 1950. It may be that few earlier wool utility quilts survive because wool is so prone to damage from insects, but it seems more likely that functional, everyday wool quilts were not practical until after the Civil War when the American wool and ready-to-wear industries made inexpensive wool clothing and fabrics available.

It is not difficult to distinguish these wool util-

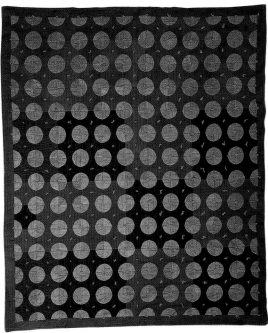

Larry Schwarm

Baseball comforter. Maker unknown. Estimated date: 1925–1950. Pieced and tied. Wool. Collection: James Holmes.

Red wool ties add a sparkle to the grays and blacks of this sturdy comforter.

Larry Schwarm

Brickwork comforter top (detail). Maker unknown. Estimated date: 1900-1950. Pieced and embroidered. Wool with cotton embroidery thread. Collection: Jan Morris and Bob Nitcher.

The rectangles may be wool suiting samples. Feather stitching, called briar stitching in some parts of the country, added a little elegance to these basic bedcoverings. The wools, classic weaves in grays and browns, make it difficult to narrow the date beyond the first half of the twentieth century.

ity quilts from early nineteenth-century patchwork quilts of wool, because the early quilts are of a finer wool, sometimes glazed and often imported and expensive. The early quilts are typically quilted with fancy designs, while the later quilts are primarily tied. The earlier quilts may have backs of wool or wool and linen combination fabric, whereas the later wool quilts are usually thicker and might have backs of cotton flannel or a print cotton cretonne.

Some post-Civil War wool quilts such as string quilts, Log Cabins and Crazy Quilts, are pieced by the foundation method. Seamstresses also used conventional piecing methods to produce simple designs like Four Patches, Bow Ties and Baseballs.

People recall making wool quilts and comforters of used clothing, especially the less worn

Summary of Wool Utility Quilts and Comforters

Characteristics: Look for coarse wools in plain and twill weaves, sparse quilting or tying.

Range: 1875-1950 (most seem to be from about 1890-1925).

Don't be confused by: Wool fabrics that appear to be a synthetic fiber. Many wools available 50 years or more ago do not fit our contemporary ideas of what wools look like, so don't be too quick to judge a strange fabric as synthetic.

Collectors' tips: Peek under the top if you can. You may find a second quilt there, used as filler, which can give you additional help with the date.

See also: "Clues in Fiber and Fabric" Chapter 3, "Clues in Techniques" (Tying) Chapter 6.

For an additional example: See page 73.

For further reading: Lasansky, Jeannette. "The Role of Haps in Central Pennsylvania's 19th and 20th Century Quiltmaking Traditions". *Uncoverings 1985*. The American Quilt Study Group, Mill Valley, California, 1986.

parts of trousers. These "britches quilts" were usually the conservative colors of men's clothing, sometimes livened up with bright embroidery along the seamlines. Rectangular shapes (a pattern called Brickwork in the 1889 Ladies' Art Company catalog) were a common pattern for wool comforters. Many of the bricks were ripped off sample cards. In 1882 Caulfield and Saward described samples "attached to large cards. They are all oblong parallelograms, that is to say the length is double the width . . . these samples are sometimes disposed of for the making of Patchwork quilts or given away in charity for the same . . . purpose." (16).

Whether tied or quilted, of wool or cotton, utility quilts have a number of regional names. Comfort, comfortable and comforter are national; they are called "haps" in England and in parts of Pennsylvania (and possibly elsewhere) (17). In Texas they are "suggans" (18) and in Australia they are "waggas" (19).

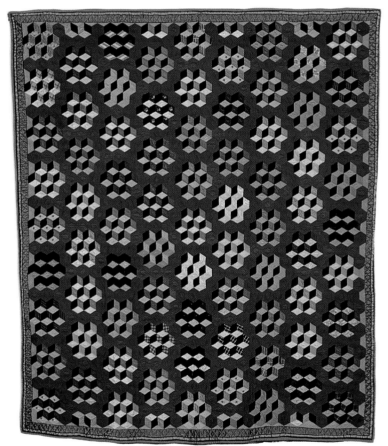

Cubework quilt made by Virginia Price, Blackburn, Missouri. Estimated date: 1880–1900. Pieced and quilted. Silk. Collection of Mary Fairley.

Virginia Price's carefully controlled, yet vibrant quilt is a masterpiece of the silk show quilt style.

SHOW QUILTS

The Victorian conviction that the home was a shelter from the pernicious outside world and that its interior decoration provided both refuge and inspiration for family members contributed to the development of fancy-work quilts, lavished with time-consuming detail and ornament. Sometimes called "slumber throws", these silk and wool quilts were rarely intended to be functional. Too fragile to be slept under, too fancy to be warm, they might serve to cover a napper, to top a white bedspread during the day or to soften the hard lines of a piece of manufactured furniture. Draped over a sofa or a piano, they testified not only to the creativity of the maker, but also to her frugality in using mere scraps of fabric to create a work of art.

The epitome of the style was the Crazy Quilt, which developed around 1880. Heavily embellished silk or wool quilts date back as far as the 1830s and '40s. Allover mosaic designs—diamonds and hexagons—were common patterns from the mid-nineteenth century through its end. Block-style Log Cabins became fashionable in the '70s, and Japanese Fans and string quilts, in the '80s. Most of these patterns crossed from one side of the tracks to the other; they might be made of the cheapest calicoes or the most elegant silks.

The silk show quilt was the style advocated by trendsetters editing the ladies' magazines of the nineteenth century; readers followed the patterns and construction methods of the magazines to produce genteel and tasteful fancywork. The quilts were often pieced using the English-style template method or the foundation method of construction. Many were neither quilted nor tied, and a great many were never backed, possibly because while the scraps for the top might be inexpensive to purchase by the pound, the yards of silk or velvet required for the perfect backing were unattainable.

Some finished show quilts are backed or bordered by pieces of machine-quilted silk, which was commercially manufactured as lining for outerwear of the type described in the 1889-90 Montgomery Ward's catalog: "Quilted satin linings for cloaks and suits. 22 to 24 inches wide in old gold, cardinal, light brown, black, white, light blue, wine or sapphire blue. $1 per yard." Most machine quilting indicates a twentieth-century date, but the quilted silk lining fabric is an exception that dates back to around 1870.

The complex stitches that outlined Crazy Quilts also appear on other show quilts. Some automatically call any fancy quilt covered with embroidery a Crazy Quilt, but technically a Crazy Quilt is pieced of irregular shapes, so a Log Cabin or Tumbling Blocks design with seams covered by embroidery is not a Crazy Quilt. It might better be described as a slumber robe or show quilt. The embroidery-covered seams can help narrow the date of a show quilt, as this embroidery style did not appear until after 1880 or so. Another clue is the heavy use of black in the color scheme. Black silk or wool would be more likely after 1860 than before.

The ups and downs in the supply of silk and fine wools had much to do with the fashion for show quilts, as did the magazine editors, who first encouraged the trend and later advocated a return to the old fashioned, cotton quilt. Observation indicates that show quilts were made between 1830 and 1910; the style was probably most popular in the years 1880-1900.

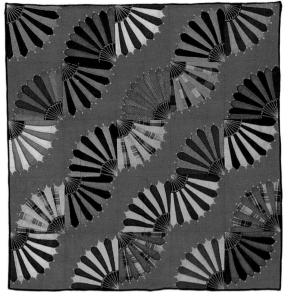

Clay Kappelman

Fan spread, made by Mrs. Ferdinand Siegle of St. Clare, Kansas. Estimated date: 1880–1900. Pieced and tied. Wool. Collection: Lillian Davis.

The line between a plain-Jane comforter and a wool show quilt is fine, mainly a matter of color and embroidered detail. This small piece—a Victorian jewel—was obviously meant for show rather than function.

Summary of Show Quilts

Characteristics: Quilts pieced of silks and fine wools with embroidery and other needlework embellishments. Many of the throws are small, designed to cover only the top of a bed or a table.
Range: 1830-1910.
Don't be confused by: Machine-quilted satin linings. They date back to the last quarter of the 19th century and are usually consistent with the age of the patchwork rather than a recent addition.
Collectors' tips: Collectors should be cautious about buying Show Quilts that have not worn their years well. Silk quilts often have serious deterioration problems due to harsh dyes and additives and no conservation measures can arrest the process. The silks will continue to fracture and flake. Heat, humidity and light accelerate silk deterioration, so silk quilts should be carefully stored and displayed.
See also: "Clues in Fiber and Fabric" (Silk), Chapter 3, "Clues in Techniques" (Embroidery), Chapter 6.
Related styles: Crazy Quilts.
For additional examples : See pages 36 and 106.

Styles in Techniques

NINETEENTH-CENTURY APPLIQUE QUILTS (CONVENTIONAL APPLIQUE)

The technique of applique, securing a decorative piece of fabric atop a fabric base, is as old as patch-work quilts in America. *Anna Tuel's Marriage Quilt*, made in 1785, contains appliqued hearts. For their medallion quilts, seamstresses cut motifs from chintz or constructed their own applique designs out of calico and plain fabrics—conventional applique. Before 1840, few quiltmakers relied on conventional applique as the primary decorative motif. The rise of high-style conventional applique coincides with two closely related styles: the fashions for album quilts and for cotton calico quilts.

Conventional applique quilts fall into two general time periods: 1840-1900 and 1925-1950. (The later quilts will be considered in the next section on Twentieth-Century Applique). The nineteenth-century quilts, whether made in 1840 or 1899, share many common design characteristics. The design figure is colored, constructed on a white ground; red and green are the preferred colors for the motifs. Borders were important. Swags and bowknots, vines or floral trails finish the edges on many of these quilts, although many quiltmakers used the simplest borders of plain strips.

Florals were the standard subject matter, with some abstractions and symbols like hearts, fleurs-de-lis or cut-paper designs. An occasional animal, building or human figure is found, especially in samplers. The flowers were stylized, more closely related to earlier Jacobean or crewel embroidery than to the realistic Berlin work embroidery popular at the same time.

The conventional applique patterns and style seem to have popped up overnight in 1840, but if we look at them in the context of the needlework that was the required training of the cultured woman we find the design influences that shaped the look of applique quilts. There are few motifs or conventions that cannot be traced to earlier sources. The quiltmakers of the 1840s had made cross stitch samplers as children; they slept under Indian palampores in beds hung with Jacobean-style embroidery; they dabbled in cut work, Dresden lace and theorem painting. They transferred their design ideas from these crafts to their applique. The red, white and green color scheme is found in palampores. The ubiquitous Rose of Sharon is an offshoot of the embroiderers' stylized Tudor Rose; the bouquets in the baskets grew from oriental carpets and theorem paintings; the leafy vine borders echo the edges of countless samplers.

Larry Schwarm

Wreath of Roses quilt. Signed in embroidery: Fannie E. Cole, 1858. Made near Factoryville, Pennsylvania. Appliqued, reverse appliqued and quilted. Cotton. Collection: Sandra Thlick and Katalin Stazer.

Fannie Cole included the two flowers most commonly found in nineteenth-century appliqued quilts. The flowers on the wreath are understood to be roses; the name *Rose of Sharon* for this simple, circular shape is found in mid-nineteenth century references. The tulip appeared in more varieties. Her red-brown, green and white color scheme is a variation of the standard red, green and white applique style.

The diversity in nineteenth-century applique is deceptive. Very few designs are unique to the maker; quiltmakers obtained their patterns from family and friends. As the research by America's various state quilt projects extends we will undoubtedly see regional and family histories for many of the unusual applique designs.

Summary of Nineteenth-Century Applique Quilts

Characteristics: Look for motifs constructed by the seamstress rather than cut from floral chintzes. Images are typically rather abstract florals. Color schemes are usually based on red and green on a white background (although blue and white is also popular) and format can be either medallion or block.
Range: 1840-1900.
See also: "Clues in Techniques" (Applique), Chapter 6.
Related styles: Twentieth-Century Applique, Cut-Out Chintz, Red, Green and White Quilts, Album and Friendship Quilts.
For additional examples: See pages 21, 22, 49 and 98.

Twentieth-Century Applique Quilts

In the early twentieth century, commercial pattern designers began excercising strong influence on the look of applique quilts. While most nine-teenth-century floral designs were mere suggestions of a specific flower, the irises, daffodils, waterlilies, roses and pansies that bloomed in the 1920s were anatomically correct—a design trend that makes discriminating between nineteenth- and twentieth-century applique rather easy. Color schemes also changed between 1900 and 1925. Pink and pale green was far more popular with twentieth-century quiltmakers than the bright red and green palette their grandmothers preferred. Another clue to a twentieth-century origin is the medallion format, which had been out of favor since the Civil War.

The distinctive twentieth-century applique style with its naturalism, pastel colors and me-dallion format appeared in magazines in the early teens, but it took a decade or more to reach the pattern-buying public. It is rare to find a twen-tieth-century applique quilt that cannot be traced to a commercial pattern. Many were made from kits containing everything from pre-cut patches for applique to backgrounds stamped with place-ment lines and quilting designs. Knowing the date a pattern was first published can help narrow the date on a modern applique quilt, but unfortu-nately there is yet no comprehensive index to such patterns.

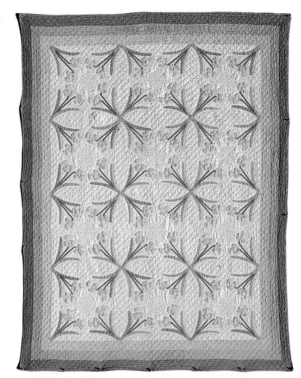

Courtesy of Joyce Gross

Dancing Daffodils quilt, made by Dr. Jeannette Dean Throckmorton (1883–1963) in Iowa. Inscribed in the quilting: 1943. Appliqued and quilted. Cotton. Collection of Jean Martin.

Mountain Mist has been offering the *Dancing Daffodil* pattern since the 1930s. It is similar to an iris quilt from Marie Webster's studio.

Summary of Twentieth-Century Applique Quilts

Characteristics: Look for naturalistic design, pastel colors, and the medallion format, although block style quilts were also common.
Range: 1925-1950 (some may go back to 1910).
See also: "Clues in Techniques" (Applique), Chapter 6.
Related styles: Light, Bright Quilts, Nineteenth-Century Applique.
For additional examples: See pages 33, 62 and 104.
For further reading: Woodard, Thomas K. and Blanche Greenstein. *Twentieth-Century Quilts 1900-1950.* E.P. Dutton, New York, 1988.

CRAZY QUILTS

Crazy Quilts are so recognizable and so common-place they are among the easiest quilts to learn to date, especially since there is a simple rule: There were no Crazy Quilts made before the late 1870s. The Crazy Quilt mania was well documented in the magazines of the day so we can follow the rise and fall of the fashion in print as well as in the quilts. An early reference that describes the hodge-podge of irregularly shaped patches appeared in *Peterson's Magazine* in November, 1879 (20). By 1882, instructions for the technique and the name Crazy Quilt was printed in various sources. Other names were also used at the time, among them mosaic patchwork, puzzle patchwork and Japanese patchwork (after the crazed, asymmetrical look found in Japanese ceramics and other decorative arts).

Magazines greeted the Crazy Quilt with enthusiasm; they offered instructions and sold patterns for the embroidered motifs and the linear seam embellishments. They also sold packets of silk scraps, and some advertisers included patterns showing exactly how the random shapes should be assembled. Penny McMorris in *Crazy Quilts* cites 1884 as the peak year for mention of Crazy Quilts in print (21). Soon after the magazines tired of the craze. In the late 1880s they were criticizing it, and by 1910 there was less print devoted to it, although the silk scraps were still sold in magazines through World War II.

Carol Crabb, who studied the records of the Missouri State Fair, found a parallel pattern of interest in Crazy Quilts in the premium lists. The first year there was a category for "Japanese" patchwork was 1883 and by 1910 the Crazy Quilt category was gone.

Because women made so many Crazy Quilts, and because they dated them (they are among the most commonly dated style of quilt), we can track the trend well through the dated examples. There were 97 date-inscribed Crazy Quilts in the database. (I eliminated two, dated 1846 and 1868, because it is likely these dates were commemorative). The earliest of the 97 were three examples dated 1882. In the years between 1882 and 1889, 36 were made; in the decade 1890−99 there were 29; in 1900−09, 13; in 1910−19, eight; in 1920−29, seven and in 1930−39, four. There was none dated between 1940 and 1950. Most (67%) were made before the end of the century. Few were made during the 1930s, but by then other pattern crazes had captured quiltmakers' imaginations. The dated quilts from the 1880s were most often made entirely of silk; in the '90s more wool and cotton was used in combination with silk and there were more all-wool and some all-cotton examples. It is fairly safe to say that the fabric and the complexity of the embroidery are sufficient clues to narow the dating. Heavily embroidered silk versions may be more likely to date from the nineteenth century while the simpler, more functional wool and cotton examples are possibly from the twentieth.

FOUNDATION PATCHWORK

In the 1860s and '70s a fad for Log Cabin quilts developed. The pattern was new and so was the

Clay Kappelman

Crazy Quilt, made by Mary Williams in Chicago. Inscribed in embroidery: 1882 (but a commemorative ribbon is dated 1889). Pieced using the foundation method, embroidered and tied. Silk. Collection: Mary Lou Humphrey.

Mary Williams was a seamstress, well known for her fine hand. Her childhood nickname was "Dumpling" or "Dump", which she embroidered near the central fans. The edge is pieced of the folded triangles, inserted between the top and backing, that today's quiltmakers call prairie points. They are found on Crazy Quilts and other late nineteenth-century show quilts but are most popular for edging cotton quilts of the mid-twentieth century.

technique. Instead of seaming two rectangular logs together, quiltmakers pieced Log Cabins on a square foundation block, beginning in the center and working out. Variations of the pattern followed: the Pineapple or Windmill Blade, the Crazy Quilt, the string quilt and the Fan, all typically built on a foundation in the nineteenth century.

The foundation is usually not visible unless the quilt is damaged or unfinished. Some foundations were made of paper which was removed before the top was assembled (string quilts were often built on paper foundations), complicating identification. However, if you have determined the quilt has a foundation, you have a strong clue to

Crazy quilts and spirit photographs were two late-nineteenth century fashions. Above the child hovers her guardian angel. The Crazy Quilt has a cotton cretonne back. Author's collection.

String comforter. Maker unknown. Estimated date: 1890–1925. Pieced using the foundation method and tied. Wool, silk and cotton. Collection: Jan Morris and Bob Nitcher.

String quilts made good use of narrow strips of fabric; they were most common in the years 1890–1940.

Summary of Crazy Quilts

Characteristics: A strict definition of a Crazy Quilt requires pieces of irregular shapes and sizes. Many are embellished with embroidered and painted pictures, ribbons, lace, beads, sequins and purchased chenille appliques. Most are covered with linear embroidery patterns covering the seams. The embroidery is not necessary; Crazy Quilts can be completely unembellished. Nearly all Crazy Quilts are constructed on a foundation which is visible only on unbacked or damaged examples. They are not often quilted and rarely contain batting. Crazy quiltmakers showed much inventiveness in their edge treatments, so Crazy Quilts are likely to have fringes, ruffles, scallops, prairie points and other fancy edges not usually seen in quilts during these years.

Range: After 1880 with 1880-1910 the peak years.

Don't be confused by: Commemorative dates before 1880, which are probably wedding or birthdates, rather than the date of the quilt.

Collectors' tips: Like other Show Quilts and silk quilts, Crazy Quilts are subject to silk deterioration. Care in storage and display is a must. Fine net (especially silk crepeline) is recommended to cover flaking silks. Attempts to add new pieces over old silks usually is unsatisfactory and only aggravates deterioration in surrounding patches.

See also: "Clues in Fiber and Fabric" (Silk), Chapter 3. "Clues in Techniques" (Foundation Patchwork, Embroidery and Painted Decoration), Chapter 6.

Related styles: Show Quilts, Outline Embroidered Quilts.

For additional examples: See pages 107, 109 and 112.

For further reading: Gunn, Virginia. "Crazy Quilts and Outline Quilts: Popular Responses to the Decorative Art/Art Needlework Movement, 1876–1893." *Uncoverings 1984.* American Quilt Study Group, Mill Valley, California, 1985.

McMorris, Penny. *Crazy Quilts.* E.P. Dutton, New York, 1984.

date. Foundation quilts in the Log Cabin design date from the 1860s or later. (The earliest date-inscribed example in the database is 1869, but written records trace it back to the early 1860s). Pineapples and Crazy Quilts date from the late 70s or later, Fans and string quilts from the '80s or later. With some patterns—Fans and Log Cabins—the foundation construction method is a clue to a date of 1920 or earlier, since Log Cabins and Fans made after 1925 were likely to be con-structed using the regular piecing seam. String quilts and Crazy Quilts continued to be built over a foundation.

Foundation quilts, probably because they have an extra layer, were often tied rather than quilted. They were made of different fabrics and for a variety of reasons, and range from dazzling Show Quilts lavished with embroidery to the plainest wool quilts meant mainly for warmth.

Summary of Foundation Patchwork

Characteristics: A layer of fabric behind the block indicating the pieces were seamed to this foundation. In unfinished tops you may see shreds of newspapers on the back of seams, indicating a paper foundation.
Range: 1875-present.
Don't be confused by: Quilts made using the English-style template piecing method. In template construction a piece of paper was basted to the back of each piece; in foundation construction a piece of paper was sewn to the back of the entire block.
Collectors' tips: If you find a top with paper still sewn to the back you may want to remove it, as the acid in inexpensive papers like newsprint accelerates aging of the fabric. (If the papers are exceptionally old, you may want to save them—in a separate container.)
See also: "Clues in Techniques" (Piecing), Chapter 6.
Related styles: Crazy Quilts.
For additional examples: See pages 43, 73, 99, 100 and 109.

OUTLINE EMBROIDERED QUILTS

In the early 1880s magazines began printing outline drawings to be embroidered on needlework such as dresser scarves, pillow shams and quilts. A favorite color scheme for outline embroidered quilts was Turkey red thread on a white cotton background. Navy blue and white was also an option, and some quiltmakers used cotton or wool thread on dark wool squares. When cotton embroidery thread became available in a variety of fast colors in the early twentieth century, embroiderers turned to a wider palette including pastel shades.

After 1925, subject matter as well as color schemes changed, and series patterns such as state flowers, state birds or floral baskets became common. Embroidered blocks were often used for friendship quilts during the second quarter of this century.

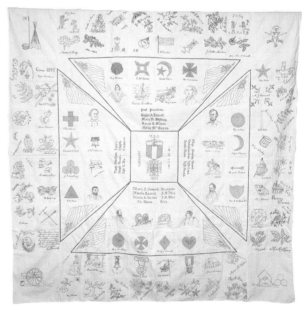

Outline embroidered top (unfinished), made by members of the Women's Relief Corps in Chicago. Inscribed in embroidery: 1892–1893. Embroidered. Cotton. Collection of Woodin Wheel Antiques.

Patriotism is the main theme of the images in this quilt, which appears to be a group effort—possibly a gift for an officer in the organization. Turkey red embroidery on white cotton is a strong clue to an 1880–1925 date.

Summary of Outline Embroidered Quilts

Characteristics: Pictorial motifs as the major decorative techniques.

Range: 1880-present. The earliest date-inscribed example of the red on white cotton in the database is 1889. That color combination was popular from 1880 through 1925; multicolor thread on white has been popular since about 1920.

Don't be confused by: It's tempting to believe that many of these designs are original, but the vast majority were traced or transferred from commercial patterns, and many of the 1925–1950 vintage were stitched from pre-stamped blocks.

See also: "Clues in Techniques" (Embroidery), Chapter 6.

Related styles: Crazy Quilts, Fundraising Quilts, Album and Friendship Quilts, Children's Quilts.

For further reading: Gunn, Virginia. "Crazy Quilts and Outline Quilts: Popular Responses to the Decorative Art/Art Needlework Movement, 1876–1893". *Uncoverings 1984*. American Quilt Study Group, Mill Valley, California, 1985.

Styles In Function

ALBUM & FRIENDSHIP QUILTS

Album and Friendship quilts are group projects. Each block is made or signed by a different person and assembled into a finished quilt which might be presented as a gift or kept by the maker as a tangible reminder of friends and relatives. There are two distinct styles of these signature album quilts: one is a sampler album comprised of a variety of patterns, the other is a single-pattern album (sometimes called a friendship quilt) in which all or most of the blocks are of the same design. Both styles seem to have developed along the eastern seaboard in the early 1840s.

The name "album quilt" goes back to the nineteenth century. "Album patchwork" is mentioned in the *Lowell Offering* in 1837 (22) (two years before any surviving dated examples of signature album quilts), and an 1853 quilt is inscribed "Barclay Reynolds Album Quilt" (23).

Album quilts are close relatives of the autograph albums displayed on parlor tables since the 1820s. Young men and women had cultivated distinctive signatures to grace the pages of friends' albums. Anyone dissatisfied with her own hand could sign with a metal stencil or signature stamp available with an added flourish or two. Those who could not compose a satisfactory accompanying verse could find suggestions in periodicals and etiquette books. The same kinds of verses, drawings, and signatures were inked, stamped and stencilled on the pages of bound albums and the blocks of album quilts.

The development in the 1830s of a permanent ink that would not damage fabrics probably contributed significantly to the album quilt fad. The signature medium can be a clue to the date of an undated album. Ink and cross stitch embroidery were the favored techniques for inscriptions in the first decades of the style; as it continued into the end of the nineteenth century and the twentieth, linear embroidery—especially the chain stitch—became the common technique. Cross stitch signatures indicate a pre-Civil War date; inked signatures indicate a date between 1840 and 1900 and chain stitch signatures can be any time between 1840 and the present but probably are from after the Civil War.

The length and content of the inscription is also an indicator of date. The early album quilts often featured poetry and dedications such as "Should I be parted far from thee/Look at this and think of me." Friends also included religious verses and pieties. "So teach us to number our days, that we may apply our hearts unto Wisdom. Psalms XG,12./Margaretta J. Burden/Medford/New Jersey/1844." One particularly appropriate inscription for a quilt was "Accept our valued friendship/And roll it up in cotton/And think it no illusion/Because so easily gotten," chain stitched on an Ohio quilt made between 1850 and 1880. Post Civil War signers were less likely to include such long sentiments; names and cities were usually sufficient.

Blocks were not necessarily signed by those who made them or made by those who signed them. In some quilts it seems that one or two women might have made the blocks and then obtained the signatures of friends and relatives. In

Baltimore in the 1840s and '50s two exceptional seamstresses are thought to have sold blocks to donors, and this may have been the case elsewhere (24). Often a single individual with graceful penmanship inked the signatures on blocks made by different people.

SINGLE PATTERN ALBUM OR FRIENDSHIP QUILTS

The earliest date-inscribed example of a signature album quilt is a single-pattern album dated 1839-1843. There are a few examples dated 1841, more in 1842 and 1843 and so on through the 1850s, after which the numbers drop off, but the style never died out.

Quiltmakers have used a wide variety of patterns within the constraints of the style. A second pattern might be used in the center or in the corner blocks, a design convention found more often in mid-nineteenth century quilts than in later examples. Techniques included piecing and conventional applique. Several pieced patterns, developed in the early 1840s, have come down to us with only the generic name "Album". Most pieced album patterns featured a white central strip or square for an inscription.

Other characteristics of the first decades of the style are a preference for the red, green and white color scheme, especially in applique. Single pattern album quilts are most commonly of cotton, although silk and wool examples survive. The blocks were often set on point in these quilts,

Jerry DeFelice, Courtesy of Leman Publications

Oak Leaf and Reel friendship quilt, made in Medford, New Jersey. Inscribed in ink: 1844. Appliqued and quilted. Cotton. Private collection.

There are more than 80 inked signatures (all in the same hand) on this friendship quilt, primarily from members of the Hoopes and Eachus families. Although it is quilted, it has no batting. The *Oak Leaf and Reel* design was common in mid-nineteenth century friendship quilts and album samplers. The single odd pattern—a wreath—is not an unusual addition.

which meant that many blocks had to be cut in half to fit along the edge, sometimes cut right through the inscriptions.

Summary of Single Pattern Album or Friendship Quilts

Characteristics: Look for signed blocks of the same design.

Range: 1840-present.

Don't be confused by: Inscribed dates that reflect when the signer was born, married or was graduated rather than the date of the quilt. Album quilts dated before 1840 probably reflect such commemorative dates.

Album blocks were sometimes assembled and quilted long after they were received as gifts.

Quilts with many, many signatures may not be friendship quilts but fundraisers, where donors paid to have their signatures on the quilt.

See also: "Clues in Technique" (Inscriptions), Chapter 6.

Related styles: Sampler Album Quilts, Fundraisers, Red, Green and White Quilts.

For an additional example: See page 60.

For further reading: Kolter, Jane Bentley. *Forget Me Not: A Gallery of Friendship and Album Quilts.* The Main Street Press, Pittstown, New Jersey, 1985.

Lipsett, Linda. *Remember Me: Women and Their Friendship Quilts.* Quilt Digest Press, San Francisco, California, 1985.

Nicholl, Jessica. *Quilted for Friends: Delaware Valley Signature Quilts, 1840–1855.* Winterthur Museum, Winterthur, Delaware, 1986.

SAMPLER ALBUM QUILTS

Like the single-pattern album quilt, the sampler album was most popular in the 1840s and '50s, but it did not continue as strong through the end of the century. Sampler albums have been made using nearly every technique available to the quilt artist. The primary technique in the mid-nineteenth century was applique, both cut-out chintz and conventional applique, with some piecing and a few blocks solely of embroidery. Block makers added folded and gathered flowers and embroidered, inked and painted details on their applique designs; many are small masterpieces.

The quilts made in and around Baltimore in those years achieved the acknowledged heights of the fashion with elaborate applique representing floral wreaths, civic monuments, patriotic designs, fraternal symbols and family pets. These Baltimore Album quilts are among the most collectible of quilts with prices for exceptional examples exceeding $100,000. More than 200 have been recorded, and there are undoubtedly many more still undiscovered in family collections (25).

The fashion for album sampler quilts faded in Baltimore in the early 1850s (26), but it had spread across the country and continued for decades. Sampler album quilts made towards the end of the nineteenth century were less likely to be made of appliqued blocks, more likely to be pieced. Twentieth-century examples of the style in piecework or applique are uncommon. The twentieth-century version of the album sampler (made between 1900 and 1970) is typically done

Courtesy of Julie Silber and Linda Reuther

Baltimore Album Quilt attributed to Mary Evans. Inscribed in ink: 1848. Appliqued and quilted with inked details. Private Collection.

Elegant composition and complex applique characterize the Baltimore Album Quilts of the 1840s and '50s. Made for John and Rebecca Chamberlain, this is one of a dozen attributed to the circle of a Baltimore seamstress thought to be named Mary Evans. Triple bow knots and prominent white roses are hallmarks of her masterful style.

in outline embroidery.

In the twentieth century, friendship quilts were extended to the communities of magazine subscribers in the needlework columns. *The Amer-*

Summary of Sampler Album Quilts

Characteristics: Look for signature blocks in a variety of patterns.

Range: Applique sampler albums 1840–1900; pieced sampler albums 1840-present, embroidered sampler albums; 1920-present.

Don't be confused by: Sampler quilts made by a single maker. To qualify as an album quilt there should be more than one signature.

See also: Chapter 5: Clues in Techniques (Inscriptions).

Related styles: Chintz Quilts, Single Pattern Album Quilts, Red, Green and White Quilts, Sampler Quilts.

For additional examples: See page 137.

For further reading: Katzenberg, Dena S. *Baltimore Album Quilts*. Baltimore Museum of Art, Baltimore, Maryland, 1981.

Kolter, Jane Bentley. *Forget Me Not: A Gallery of Friendship and Album Quilts*. The Main Street Press, Pittstown, New Jersey, 1985.

Lipsett, Linda, *Remember Me: Women and Their Friendship Quilts*. Quilt Digest Press, San Francisco, California, 1985.

Nicholl, Jessica. *Quilted for Friends: Delaware Valley Signature Quilts, 1840–1855*. Winterthur Museum, Winterthur, Delaware, 1986.

ican Woman magazine encouraged readers to collect blocks through the mail from fellow readers. In 1910 in the magazine's "Give and Take Club" column, Eva Wheeler wrote "I am making an *American Woman quilt*, and shall be pleased to receive pieced blocks 12 x 12 inches, each with sender's name". For all the requests placed in such columns very few such national sampler album quilts seem to have been discovered.

SAMPLER QUILTS

Samplers are quilts of many different patterns, but the blocks are not signed and therefore presumed to have been made by a single person. The sampler style developed at the same time as the album quilt and the mid-nineteenth century examples look similar. Applique was the favored technique, although pieced blocks were also included. As applique fell out of fashion, quiltmakers made more pieced block samplers. Observation indicates that a sampler of pieced blocks is more likely to have been made after 1875. After 1875, quiltmakers might stitch together blocks of varying sizes with rather haphazard-looking results. The sampler of different-sized blocks is a weak clue to a date after 1875.

Many of the end-of-the-century samplers look to be "pattern quilts" assembled to record a quilt-maker's file of designs. Quiltmakers often made a pattern block to record a design and to use for drawing templates. Many pattern blocks were sewn together quickly from inexpensive fabrics. Some of the turn-of-the-century sampler quilts share these qualities and one wonders if they were pieced together by a later quiltmaker using blocks the original maker may never have intended to assemble.

Courtesy of the Oral Traditions Project, Lewisburg, Pennsylvania
Sampler quilt top, made by M. Hettinger in Pine Grove Mills, Pennsylvania. Date inscribed in ink: 1897. Pieced and appliqued. Collection of Gloria Braun.

A name for each design was inked in its center, reflecting the growing interest in pattern names at the turn of the century. Many are found in the 1889 Ladies' Art Company catalog, a common source for the patterns in such samplers.

At the end of the nineteenth century, the Ladies' Art Company and other pattern companies sold cotton blocks for any of their hundreds of patterns for about 50 cents each. Some of the later sampler quilts may contain pattern blocks from commercial sources or from magazine pen pals.

Summary of Samplers

Characteristics: Look for a variety of patterns in a block quilt, with no more than one signature indicating that the quilt was made by one person.
Range: Blocks primarily applique: 1840-1900.
　　　　Blocks primarily pieced: 1875-present.
　　　　Blocks primarily outline embroidery: 1880-present.
Don't be confused by: Album sampler quilts in which the blocks are signed by different people.
Related styles: Album Sampler, Outline Embroidered Quilts.
For an additional example: See page 21.
For further reading: Smith, Wilene. "Quilt blocks—or—Quilt Patterns". *Uncoverings 1986*. The American Quilt Study Group, Mill Valley, California, 1987.

FUND-RAISING QUILTS

For generations women have used quilts to raise funds for causes close to their hearts. We find records of quilts made to earn money for abolition, library books, Civil War gunboats and church buildings. The fund-raising function is not always apparent in the quilt itself, as many were conventional quilts—both plain and fancy—that were raffled or auctioned. Some fund-raisers, however, are easily recognizable by their design, a style that is a good clue to the date.

In the last half of the century a fashion for selling names on a quilt spread across the country. Quiltmakers would embroider the name of an individual or a business in exchange for payment—usually a dime. The finished quilt may have been given to a distinguished community member or more money might be raised through auction or raffle.

The early versions of the signature fund-raisers are indistinguishable from album or friendship quilts, but in the 1880s a distinct style developed—the quilts were literally covered with names. In one common style the names are the only pattern on the quilt; the embroidered words commonly form spokes in a wheel. Red on white was the most popular color combination, but blue on white was seen often. The names are usually embroidered with a chain stitch or another straight stitch, although some late nineteenth-century examples have inked names.

There is some mention in the folklore literature of memorial quilts on which the names of an entire community of people and businesses were embroidered as a record rather than as a fund-raiser (the difference being that one did not have to pay the dime to be included), but it is likely that the vast majority of the name-covered quilts were fund-raisers.

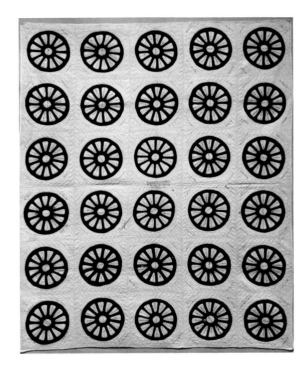

Wheel **fund-raiser quilt** made by members of the Methodist Episcopal Church in White City, Kansas. Inscribed in ink: 1896. Appliqued and quilted. Cotton. Collection of Beth and John Ford. Smithsonian Negative # 74–7893.

Nearly 500 community members paid 10 cents each to have their names inked in the spokes and 25 cents for the hub position in this wheel quilt, which raised money for new church carpeting. The finished quilt was presented to the pastor, the Reverand Dr. John S. Ford, and his wife Sarah Swigart Ford. Under the central wheel is inked, "Presented to Brother and Sister Ford by the Ladies of the Methodist Episcopal Church of White City, Kansas. March, 1896. God Bless You All."

The quilt is a typical late nineteenth-century fund-raiser with inked names, a red and white color scheme and a wheel pattern.

One subgroup is the Red Cross quilt, made during World War I when women, longing to do their part on the home front, devoted time to mak-

---

Summary of Fund-raising Quilts

Characteristics: Look for signatures, far more signatures than on an album quilt. The wheel format was a popular pattern and red or blue and white a popular color scheme.
Range: 1880–1950 (there were 28 dated examples in the database ranging from 1881 to 1944).
See also: "Clues in Techniques" (Inscriptions), Chapter 6.
Related styles: Album and Friendship Quilts, Red and White Quilts, Outline Embroidered Quilts.
For further reading: Cozart, Dorothy. "The Role and Look of Fundraising Quilts 1850-1930". Lasansky, Jeannette (ed.) *Pieced by Mother Symposium Papers.* Oral Traditions Project, Lewisburg, Pennsylvania, 1988. Rowley, Nancy. "Red Cross Quilts for the Great War". *Uncoverings 1982.* The American Quilt Study Group, Mill Valley, California, 1983.

ing warm clothing and bedding for soliders and refugees and raising money for the organization's work through Red Cross quilts, among other projects. The style was inspired by a *Needlecraft* magazine article in 1918. The quilts usually had a Red Cross motif and were pieced, appliqued or embroidered. Among the easiest quilts to date, most were probably made in 1918 (although several of the pieced patterns were recorded in the quilt pattern literature of the 1920s and '30s, which may have inspired a few later examples).

COMMEMORATIVE AND PATRIOTIC QUILTS

Most commemorative, patriotic, political and pictorial applique quilts are one of a kind and thus difficult to date by style, but there are a few common themes that have inspired quiltmakers. Patriotism has been expressed in quilts since the early years of the nation with patchwork eagles and flags and commemorative fabrics.

Earlier writers have mentioned that eagle quilts were most popular around the time of the War of 1812 and later, near the 1876 Centennial, but a look at both the date-inscribed and the reliably-attributed quilts featuring eagles does not support such a generalization. Eagles cover much of the nineteenth and twentieth centuries; the nine date-inscribed examples ranged from 1807 through 1933. Many of the eagle quilts fall into three or four common pattern types, which must have been passed around from hand to hand as no published sources for any of the designs have been found. One of the most intriguing is a pattern of four large eagles arrayed in mirror-image fashion around a small central motif—usually a floral or a sunrise design. Florence Peto, writing in *The Magazine Antiques* in 1940, described the design as a "not uncommon type that goes by the name of Union Quilt . . . popular during the Civil War— north of the Mason-Dixon line of course. In fact, the making of Union quilts seems to have been localized in the state of Pennsylvania." The conventional wisdom today about these eagle quilts is that they are not related to the Civil War but to the Centennial Exposition held in Philadelphia. The only date-inscribed example in the database is dated 1926, long after most of the others were made. Peto's observation about a regional origin seems to hold up. The Oral Traditions Project surveying a four-county area north of Harrisburg, Pennsylvnia, found about 36 examples, the earliest date-inscribed in the 1880s and one reliably attributed to 1876 (27). In their second survey of

Eagle quilt. Maker unknown. Estimated date: 1825–1850. Pieced, appliqued and quilted. Collection: Smithsonian Institution, Negative # 75–15211.

It is tempting to guess that this quilt was made between 1795 and 1818 when there were 15 stars on the United States flag; however the conventional applique flowers and trees appear to be later. Seamstresses did not always match the number of stars on their quilts to the number of stars on their flags.

eight other Pennsylvania counties the researchers found far fewer (28). It may be that these quilts will be traced to a specific region of Pennsylvania.

The flag as a quilt motif does not seem to date as early as the eagle (possibly because the eagle is supposed to symbolize the country in commercial and decorative arts while the flag is reserved for official purposes, a convention rarely respected today). Flags began appearing in the 1840s in blocks in album samplers. By the Civil War the use of stars and stripes as a major motif was established.

Because the number of stars on the flag of the United States has increased as new states have been added, it is tempting to use stars as evidence of quilt date. Fitting the correct number of stars into the field of the flag was not always a priority with quiltmakers, so this method of dating is not 100% accurate. How accurate is it? Of 15 date-inscribed quilts with stars, seven had the correct number of stars for the year the quilt was dated, and eight did not. Three of the eight with the incorrect number had 13 stars, an obvious choice for a seamstress with limited interest in appliqueing stars; but the rest had odd numbers. A flag quilt dated 1887 when there were 38 stars had only 36; an eagle quilt dated 1837, the year the

Commemorative quilt. Maker Unknown. Attributed to 1933. Appliqued and quilted. Cotton.

A century of Chicago history is cleverly symbolized in this quilt entered in the 1933 "Century of Progress in Quiltmaking" contest at the World's Fair. A sub-theme of the fair was summarized in the motto "From teepees to temples", referring to a century of progress in housing. The teepees along the border point to the stockade of Fort Dearborn, the first American settlement in Chicago. Next is the great fire and in the oval are the temples—the skyscrapers of the city with fair buildings in the center.

George Washington quilt made by Carrie Hackett Hall (1866–1955) in Leavenworth, Kansas. Inscribed in applique: 1932. Collection: Helen F. Spencer Museum of Art, the University of Kansas.

Carrie Hall commemorated the 200th anniversary of the birth of George Washington with a quilt she adapted from a pattern sold by a syndicated newspaper column. Note the hatchets around the central medallion and the cherry tree border. The final border design is similar to one the Ladies' Art Company called *Washington Pavement* in their 1889 catalog. Although quilts with fabric celebrating General Washington may date from his time, those with such symbolic or representational patchwork designs date from decades after his death.

Summary of Commemorative and Patriotic Quilts

Characteristics: Look for pictorial motifs in the decorative techniques and the fabrics.

Range: Since the quilts are usually unique there is no definite date.

Don't be confused by: Later quilts commemorating earlier events. Most of the quilts honoring early American history were made as later commemorative designs. Fabric with pictures of George Washington may be from his time, but applique or pieced patterns picturing him are probably from after the mid-nineteenth century.

See also: "Clues in Printed Cottons" (Commemorative Chintzes and Calicoes), Chapter 5.

For additional examples: See pages 23 and 146.

For further reading: Bishop, Robert and Carter Houck. *All Flags Flying: American Patriotic Quilts as Expressions of Liberty*. E.P. Dutton, New York, 1986.

Christopherson, Katy. *The Political and the Campaign Quilt*. The Kentucky Heritage Quilt Society, Frankfort, 1984.

Collins, Herbert Ridgway. *Threads of History: Americana Recorded on Cloth, 1775 to the Present*. Smithsonian Institution Press, Washington D.C., 1979.

26th star was added, had only 24. The number of stars on a quilt obviously should be used only as supporting evidence for a date based on other clues in style, fabric and pattern. See Appendix 3 for a chronological list of the stars on the flag.

The Centennial Exposition and the World's Fair of 1893 were events that inspired many quilts pieced of commemorative fabrics. The New Deal of Franklin Roosevelt in the 1930s prompted a number of quilts, as did the 1933 Chicago World's Fair where Sears, Roebuck and Company sponsored an enormous contest, offering prizes totaling $7500 for quilts commemorating the fair and its theme of a Century of Progress.

CHILDREN'S QUILTS

Children's quilts have been made for centuries. Until the end of the nineteenth century quilts for infants and children were merely cut-down or scaled-down versions of the same designs used in quilts for adults. Whole-cloth quilts, applique florals and scrapbag piecework were adapted to crib or trundle-bed size. Quilts so small they would not cover even an infant are probably doll quilts, which were often made by small children for a first patchwork project. The clues for dating these small quilts are the same ones used for larger quilts with fabric, technique, style and pattern important clues.

In the 1880s a different kind of child's quilt began to appear in periodicals. Patterns designed to appeal to a child's interests featured pictorial representations of images from a child's world. Embroidered outlines drawn in the style of Kate Greenaway, whose old-fashioned children appealed to Victorians in England and America, were first published in *Peterson's Magazine* in 1880. In 1886 the *Dorcus Magazine of Woman's Handiwork* suggested making a Noah's Ark quilt by copying pairs of animals from children's picture books in embroidery or applique. *The Young Ladies Journal* in 1889 offered a pattern for an "appliqued nursery rug or cot counterpane" featuring animals and a toy clown. These early references indicate that style conventions for children's quilts have remained the same since the first patterns were published. Outline embroidery and applique remain the two common techniques.

Patterns for children's quilts increased in the magazines in the first decades of the twentieth century. In the publishing boom of the 1925-1950 years, quiltmakers had dozens of embroidered or appliqued designs from which to choose. Pieced

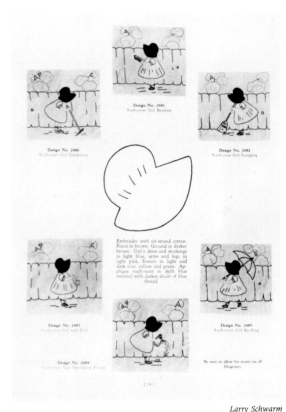

Larry Schwarm

"Grandma" Dexter, a trademark of the Collinghouse Mills in Elgin, Illinois, offered a group of industrious Sunbonnet Sue designs in the early 1930s. Author's collection.

Pieced animal quilts were designed by Ruth Oppenheimer and Wilhelmine Hass in the late '20s. This one, published in *Needlecraft* magazine in March, 1928, featured a dancing bear, a parrot, clowns, Indians and soldiers— images "specially designed for the little ones". Most pieced representational designs date from after 1925.

154

designs were never quite so popular although boats and airplanes became standards and a few pieced animal designs appeared. Most of the specialized children's quilt patterns are traceable to commercial patterns; publication dates can help narrow date spans.

Among the most popular images for children's quilts are the Sunbonnet Children, a design that evolved from illustrations by Bertha Corbett who simplified Kate Greenaway's children, hiding their faces under enormous hats and their bodies under voluminous dresses. Corbett's books appeared in 1900; patterns adapted for outline embroidery were published soon after. By 1912, the *Ladies' Home Journal* was showing an appliqued pastel Sunbonnet Sue quilt and advising a mother to make one out of scraps from her daughter's dresses. Like several other early twentieth-century design innovations, appliqued Sunbonnet children (also called Dutch Dolls) didn't really catch on until the 1925-1950 era when they became one of the fad designs. The Overall Boy (also called Overall Bill and Overall Sam) appears to date from after 1925.

Larry Schwarm

Ocean Wave quilt (variation). Maker unknown. Estimated date: 1925–1950. Pieced and quilted. Cotton. Collection of Larry Schwarm.

Many children's quilts are small scale versions of the same styles and patterns used in quilts for adults and are dated using the same clues. The pastel, plain colored cottons in this small quilt indicate a date after 1925.

Summary of Children's Quilts

Characteristics: Look for sentimental, cute images designed to appeal to children.

Range: 1880-present. Most of the specialized children's designs will date from after 1925.

Don't be confused by: Other small patchwork and quilted items. Not every small piece was meant to be a child's quilt or a doll quilt. Table covers, pillow shams, and splashers (to cover the wall behind a wash stand) were also common small pieces.

Related Styles: Outline Embroidered Quilts, Representational Pieced Designs.

For further reading: Fox, Sandi. *Small Endearments: Nineteenth Century Quilts for Children*, Scribner's, New York, 1985.

Hagerman, Betty J. *A Meeting of the Sunbonnet Children*. Published by the author, Baldwin City, Kansas, 1979.

Shirer, Marie and Barbara Brackman. *Creature Comforts: A Quilter's Animal Alphabet Book*. Wallace-Homestead, Lombard, Illinois, 1986.

Woodard, Thomas K. and Blanche Greenstein. *Crib Quilts and Other Small Wonders*. E.P. Dutton, New York, 1981.

Style in Color

RED, GREEN AND WHITE QUILTS

Applique artists in the nineteenth century favored a limited palette of red and green cottons on a white background. Many used only those complementary colors, while others added accents of bright yellow or pink. Even those who used a variety of colors let the red and green fabrics dominate the design. The same colors were also used for the best pieced designs like Feathered Stars and Rocky Mountain (now called New York Beauty).

We can only speculate as to why the red, green and white color scheme dominated nineteenth-century applique quilts. Since applique is usually an imitation of nature, green leaves and red flowers are a natural choice. Mid-century conventional applique quilts grew from the cut-out chintz applique style of the late-eighteenth and early-nineteenth centuries. The printed palampores and chintzes from which the trees-of-life and the floral motifs were cut were commonly printed in naturalistic reds, pinks and greens on white backgrounds. Red and green calico on white was an extension of that traditional look. On a practical level, Elisabeth Daingerfield, writing around 1920, noted that Appalachian women commonly made their "patch quilts" (applique) in red, green and a "certain rather violent yellow" because of the reliability of those dyes. Only trusted colors were good enough for quilts intended to be heirlooms.

Whether the reason was function, fashion or a combination of the two, red, green and white quilts were popular from about 1830 through the end of the nineteenth century. The earliest date-inscribed examples are cut-out chintz and pieced chintz designs from the 1830s. In the 1840s when block style calico album quilts became the rage, the red, white and green color scheme also became popular. Date-inscribed quilts in those colors range over the rest of the century. Of the 112 such quilts in the database, 108 were made between 1830 and 1900, good evidence that a red, white and green quilt will be from that period of time, although the four twentieth-century versions indicate that some quilters continued to use the old style.

Other design characteristics of red, green and white quilts are the use of small scale calicoes and plain cottons (although many pre-Civil War quiltmakers combined chintzes and calicoes). Combinations of applique and piecing were common. A pieced quilt might have an applique border or vice versa. The color scheme is most associated with quality quilts of intricate design and elaborate

Tim Forcade

Coxcomb quilt, made by Isabelle Wiswall Herman in Herman, New York. Estimated date: 1840–1880. Appliqued, reverse appliqued and quilted. Cotton. Collection of Iris Aller.

Red, green and white applique quilts can be dated 1840 to 1900. Narrowing the date beyond that sixty-year period can be difficult. The overdyed green cotton (fading to yellow), the four-block setting and the serrated applique border were more likely to be used by a mid-century quilter than by one working at the end of the century. However, these clues are, at best, weak. The family history adds support to a mid-century date; they attribute the quilt to the years 1865 to 1880.

A quilt nearly identical to this one is in the collection of the University of Illinois. Most appliqued patterns seem to have been passed around; there are few unique designs.

quilting, but it was also used for everyday quilts with simple pieced design and functional quilting.

Elisabeth Daingerfield's description of red and green as reliable dyes is misleading because by the

---

Summary of Red, Green and White Quilts

Characteristics: Look for applique or pieced quilts in these colors.
Range: 1830–1900.
Don't be confused by: Reds and greens that have faded to brown (green seems to be less reliable than red). Examine plain brown cottons carefully for evidence that they were once another color.
Collectors' tips: Some of the end-of-the-century quilts have not yet been exposed to enough sunlight or washing to begin the fading process; be very careful in washing these quilts and exposing them to light.
See also: "Clues in Color and Dyes", Chapter 4.
Related styles: Applique Quilts, Album and Friendship Quilts.
For additional examples: See pages 8, 22, and 63.

time she was writing about them, they were no longer reliable. It is possible that the red and green style faded because the reds and greens themselves faded so badly. Reds and greens that have faded to tan or brown are a dating clue since they are likely to have been dyed with synthetic dyes, an indication the quilt was made after 1860 and most probably after 1875. When the applique style revived in the 1920s quilters used faster pastels; the red and green quilts were a part of the past.

RED AND WHITE QUILTS

Turkey red and white has been a classic color scheme for quilts since the 1840s. It is closely related to the red, green and white color scheme that developed at the same time and probably for the same reasons, having to do with taste, availability of fabrics and the color fastness of Turkey red cotton. The color scheme is found primarily in cotton quilts, but some red and white wool quilts were also made. The reds in the mid-nineteenth century quilts were both plain and printed fabrics; after 1875, the reds were more likely to be a plain cotton. The background is generally a plain white cotton, but white shirting prints were used from around 1875 through 1925. The color scheme is associated with piecing, applique and embroidery.

Many of the early date-inscribed examples are album quilts from the 1840s, but quilters working alone liked red and white for their star, oakleaf and reel, sawtooth, and fleur de lis designs. Towards the end of the century the color scheme was almost a standard for a number of pieced patterns like the Schoolhouse, Drunkard's Path, Ocean Wave and Sawtooth. The fastness of Turkey red in the era when the new synthetic dyes were so unreliable may explain the popularity of the red and white color scheme until well into the twentieth century. Certainly the reliability of Turkey red cotton embroidery thread contributed to the turn-of-the-century fashion for red on white outline embroidered quilts and fund-raisers.

Jon Blumb

Rob Peter to Pay Paul quilt (variation), made by Nina Ashline in Chicago. Estimated date: 1900–1925. Pieced and quilted. Collection of Susan Ashline.

Among the most difficult styles to date is the red and white quilt of plain cottons—popular fabric from 1840 through 1925. Family history attributes this one to the first quarter of this century.

Red and white quilts lost popularity after 1925. Of 57 examples in the database only one was made in the 1930s. By 1926, the style was obviously considered old fashioned to Elsie Marsh Brandt, who wrote in *The House Beautiful* about "two red and white quilts, left to me by a great aunt . . . Each year we tried to fit them into our bedrooms, but red would just not harmonize with the soft colorings of blue, rose and mauve that had been so carefully blended. So the quaint old quilts were regretfully but invariably laid away in their hiding place in the attic—perpetual white, or rather red elephants on our hands."

Summary of Red and White Quilts

Characteristics: Look for the color scheme in appliqued, pieced or embroidered quilts.
Range: 1840–1925.
See also: "Clues in Color and Dyes", Chapter 4.
Related styles: Outline Embroidered Quilts, Fund-raising Quilts.
For an additional example: See page 146.

One of the enigmas in quilt dating is the pieced quilt of plain red and plain white cottons. The fabric offers little information other than a date of between 1840 and 1925, but there does seem to be a pattern of popularity for this substyle. A look at the dated pieced red and white plain cotton quilts in the database indicates that they were most popular in the last quarter of the nineteenth century. Of 12 pieced quilts made of plain red and white cotton eight (66%) were made in that quarter. One was made before 1875 (in 1848) and three after 1900. The evidence is weak; twelve quilts is a small sample, but the information may help in a case where there is little else to go on.

BLUE AND WHITE QUILTS

Patches of blue cotton appear in scrap quilts from the beginning of American patchwork, but around 1840 a distinctive blue and white color scheme became a style. Blue and white quilts were both pieced and appliqued. Pieced designs included mid-nineteenth-century Feathered Star and Mariner's Compass designs and end-of-the-century Bow Ties and Drunkard's Paths. Appliqued designs included florals and leaves.

The blue and white color scheme was also a standard for woven coverlets being made the same years as the earlier blue and white quilts; some of the mid-century quilts seem directly inspired by the Jacquard-woven coverlets with their geometric centers and flowery borders.

The earliest blue and white quilt in the database is dated 1833; twenty-four examples date from 1844 to 1929. A general range for the style would seem to be 1830 to 1930, and narrowing it beyond that is a matter of examining details such as quilting, pattern and fabrics. Dark blue cottons with small white figures (or yellow-orange figures) are such common prints across so many decades that dating them takes experience. One clue to a date from around 1875 through 1925 is a printed white shirting fabric. In earlier blue and

Clay Kappelman

Feathered Star quilt, made by Mary Elizabeth Togers Harvey in Lewisburg, Pennsylvania. Estimated date: 1840–1875. Pieced and quilted. Cotton. Collection of Patricia Boyer.

Blue and white was a popular choice for a Feathered Star quilt, which was often a woman's best quilt. This one with its willow border reflects design conventions of nineteenth-century woven coverlets.

white quilts the white was almost always a plain cotton; after 1875 quiltmakers might use a white shirting print instead. Examples from after 1880 were generally less intricate than the masterpiece blue and white quilts of the mid-nineteenth century. Pastel blue and white quilts are likely to be from the twentieth century.

Summary of Blue and White Quilts

Characteristics: Look for navy blue prints and white cottons in pieced and appliqued quilts. After 1880 navy blue thread on a white cotton background was fashionable for outline embroidered quilts.
Range: 1830–1930.
See also: "Clues in Color and Dyes", Chapter 4.
Related styles: Outline Embroidered Quilts.

158

DARK COTTON QUILTS

Turn-of-the-century pieced cotton quilts are characterized primarily by their limited palette. Quiltmakers favored wine red, navy blue, a lighter gray-blue, and black—subdued shades that were often combined with a figured white shirting print or a plain white fabric. Many of the quilts were scrapbag quilts pieced of dozens of similar prints. Although some quilters included bright accents of Turkey Red, yellow-orange or double pink prints, the general look was rather dark.

The pieced patterns were rarely complex; Mariner's Compasses, Feathered Stars and Sunbursts were not done in these fabrics and neither was

Larry Schwarm
Washington Sidewalk quilt. Maker unknown. Inscribed in chain stitch embroidery: 1903–1914. Pieced and quilted. Cotton. Collection of Jan Morris and Bob Nitcher.

The pattern is a variation of a standard album design, but only one block is inscribed—"Robert and Dollie 1903–1914". Red was often the only bright color in the dark quilts of the 1890–1925 era. The gray mourning print in the setting squares, the white shirting prints in the background and the black, navy blue and cadet blue cottons are good clues to a date from 1890 to 1925.

Double Nine Patch quilt, made by Martha E. Gross in McCune, Kansas. Estimated date: 1890–1910. Pieced and quilted. Cotton. Collection: Helen F. Spencer Museum of Art, the University of Kansas.

A casual concern for symmetrical corners enlivens the edge of this quilt made, according to family history, in the first decade of this century. The calicoes are the dark, somber colors typical of turn-of-the-century quilts.

applique. Common patterns were Four Patches, Nine Patches, Bow Ties, and Log Cabins. Quiltmakers using the dark cottons at the end of the nineteenth century and the beginning of this one were the first to be able to choose their quilt patterns from published sources, and many of the patterns can be directly traced to magazines, newspapers and pattern catalogs, an aid in pinpointing a date.

The quilts have a functional air about them; fancy quilting is rare, and many of the tops were made into tied comforters. The dark cotton prints were economical. In the Sears and Montgomery Ward catalogs of the 1890-1925 era, the fabrics found in these quilts were among the least expensive. They were sometimes called "wash goods" or "tub goods", fabrics that held up well to laundering, suitable for children's clothing, aprons, housedresses and men's and women's shirting. Both figure and background had little detail. Figures were simple and spaced far apart without overlap. Small scale florals, sprigs, geometrics and a few sporting prints (especially horseshoes) were popular designs. Dots, rings, stripes, plaids and checks were staple designs that appear over and over again in the quilts.

Dark quilts, like so many other plain-Jane quilts, are rarely date-inscribed, but because they are so recent we know much about the fabrics, which were abundant in dated mail-order catalogs and sample books from 1890 through the 1920s. In the mid-1920s the muted, single color fabrics began to disappear in the catalogs, replaced by the multicolor pastel florals that changed the look of the cotton quilt. A limited line of dark fabrics was available through the 1930s, so a few traditionalists may have continued to make dark quilts, but, in general, the fashion ranged from 1890 to 1925.

Summary of Dark Cotton Quilts

Characteristics: Look for simple pieced quilts featuring single color cotton prints in subdued shades. Gray-blue (cadet blue), wine red (claret) and black-ground prints are fabrics common in these quilts and rare in any other time period.
Range: 1890–1925.
See also: "Clues in Color and Dyes", Chapter 4 and "Clues in Cotton Prints", Chapter 5.

LIGHT, BRIGHT QUILTS

During the 1920s changes took place in every aspect of American life; nothing—including quilts—would ever be the same again. One of the big changes in quilts was in color. Postwar improvements in synthetic dyes gave quiltmakers a wider range of colors. They bought cottons in lavender, peach, tangerine and Nile green to make quilts with a light, colorful look.

Of 33 date-inscribed quilts in the database that were characterized as having a pastel or light, bright color scheme, 31 were made after 1925. The two earliest examples were 1902 and 1922, indicating that some innovators began using lighter color schemes soon after the turn of the century, years before the fashion caught on. Some of the early pastel quilts make good use of chambray fabrics, which have a dark thread running one way and a white thread running the other, so the eye reads the fabric as pastel. Although manufacturers did dye cottons in pastel shades before World War 1 (there were many pastel backgrounds in furnishing fabrics through the end of the nineteenth century), quiltmakers seem not to have been interested in them until the twenties. The light, bright color scheme is a good clue that a quilt was made after 1925.

There are two categories of light-colored quilts. Most are scrapbag style; quilters combined all kinds of color and pattern, pulling it all together with plain white cotton. A few patterns (Grandmother's Flower Gardens, Double Wedding Rings, Sunbonnet Sues, Fans and Dresden Plates) showed off a variety of prints so well they became fads that are still with us.

The second style is more color controlled. Quilters used more plain cottons, some of it cotton sateen, and much of it bought specifically for the quilt. Fabric companies sold cottons for quiltmaking. The 1933 Sears catalog offered "Pastoral Cloth. 25 cents per yard. The best quilting fabric made in shades of orchid, lilac, black, butter yellow, light burnt orange, light blue, copen blue, dark pink, rose pink, chamois, brown, nile green, dark green, honey melon and firebrand white. Many a prize winning quilt will be made from this fine cotton. The colors were chosen with blending in mind. Blue harmonizes with the deeper blue, Nile Green with Dark Green . . . " The pastoral cloth at 25 cents a yard was quite a bit more expensive than the standard quality percale at 8 cents, but many quiltmakers splurged on the best fabric for quilts made during those Depression years. Cotton sateen was also popular for the fancy quilts of the day.

One clue to narrowing the date on a light, bright quilt beyond 1925-1950 is in finding the pattern source and the date the pattern was published. For example: a pieced elephant and a donkey appeared in the *Kansas City Star* in 1931, a fact that helps to date the many midwestern quilts made in the designs by either Republicans or Democrats.

Even when one knows scraps were saved for decades, it is tempting to try to discriminate among the fabrics of the 1920s, '30s and '40s. Dated quilts, the fabric catalogs of the time and the memories of many people still living indicate a darkening of colors at the end of the thirties. The 1939 Sears catalog had a new line of Mediterranean Colors, in shades both grayer and darker than those of the earlier thirties: wine, aqua, Riviera rust, Capri blue, Venetian violet, Adriatic green. The most noticeable difference around this time was an increase in aqua and gray shades (a gray dye rather than the earlier black on white mourning print that the eye read as gray). During

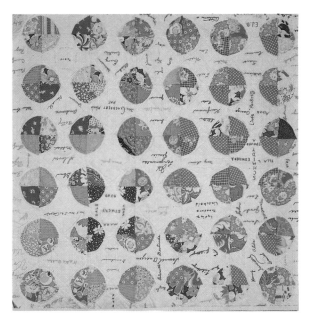

Larry Schwarm

Baseball friendship quilt (detail), made by members of a Mennonite Church in Wichita, Kansas. Estimated date: 1940–1945 (family history). Pieced, embroidered and quilted. Cotton. Collection of James Holmes.

Church members made a going-away gift for minister J.H. Langenwalter and his wife, Jessie. The busy, bright prints are typical of the quilts after 1925.

Courtesy of Joyce Gross

Rose Wreath quilt, made by Dr. Jeannette Dean Throckmorton (1883–1965) in Iowa. Inscribed in the quilting: 1939. Appliqued, stuffed and quilted. Cotton. Collection: Jean Martin.

Jeannette Throckmorton estimated she made 55 to 60 quilts in the last 16 years of her life. This one is from a kit (Paragon #01009), copyrighted 1937 (a fact that would be useful in assigning a date were the quilt not dated). Many of the pastel applique quilts of the 1930s and 40s (and many of the pieced quilts too) were made from kits. The stuffed work, Dr. Jeannette's trademark, carries this example far above the average kit quilt.

the '50s shades brightened up with chartreuse and hot pink. In the '60s olive green, gold and brown cottons were used in the scrap quilts.

Many of the pastel quilts of the 1925-1950 era were impressively quilted, a return to nineteenth-century standards. Those that were quilted plainly

---

Summary of Light, Bright Quilts

Characteristics: Look for clear, light, bright colors in plains and prints. Print cottons often have a number of colors in crowded, splashy patterns.

Range: 1925-present.

Don't be confused by: An odd pastel cotton in a nineteenth-century quilt. Not every pastel green plain or baby pink print is from after 1925. They were available; they weren't yet popular.

See also: Chapter 2: Clues in Color and Dyes, Chapter 3: Clues in Cotton Prints.

Related Styles: Children's Quilts, Outline Embroidered Quilts, Appliqued Quilts.

For additional examples: See pages 62, 70 and 143.

For further reading: The patterns of this period have been well-indexed. If the design originated in a published source, the date of publication can help pinpoint a date for the quilt. For pieced patterns see: Brackman, Barbara. *An Encyclopedia of Pieced Quilt Patterns.* Prairie Flower Publishing, Lawrence, Kansas, 1979–1985.

For applique see: Khin, Yvonne. *The Collector's Dictionary of Quilt Names and Patterns.* Acropolis Books, Washington D.C., 1980.

---

often were self-quilted 1/4 inch away from the seam lines or quilted in an all-over fan design. There was an emphasis on borders and edges. Scalloped edges are most likely to be from this era. Prairie points—triangles folded and inserted into the edge—were also popular. Bias binding became far more important than in the past, a style reflected in the 1935 Sears catalog in which quilters could buy pre-cut bias tape in the same shades as the Pastoral Cloth.

The styles of the 1920s and '30s are still with us. Many quilters working today use an uncontrolled palette of scrap prints coordinated with white. The fad patterns—the Wedding Ring and the Grandmother's Flower Garden—are still the favorites. Discriminating between a quilt made in the 1925-1950 era and one made more recently is a matter of examining the individual cotton prints and looking for polyester in the fabrics and batting (a clue to a date after 1960).

Styles Favored by Regional, Ethnic and Religious Groups

Attention has recently been paid to defining quilt styles favored by communities of quilters who belong to specific religious and ethnic groups and who live in narrowly defined regions of the country. As new data is analyzed, we will learn more about such variations from mainstream styles. The two best-documented variations are the quilts of the Amish and the Hawaiians, which are described here.

Other regional and ethnic style characteristics warrant further study, among them the preference of late nineteenth-century Pennsylvanians for color schemes of pink and green or yellow and blue without the neutral whites that their contemporaries elsewhere used to calm their colors. The Sioux Indians have specialized in making the Star of Bethlehem designs for several generations. Quilts of southern Afro-American women with characteristic strip sets and free-hand pattern construction have been described by several writers.

One problem in analyzing such styles is a tendency to overgeneralize. Southern Black women make many kinds of quilts; some never make an "Afro-American style" quilt and many other quilters who have no Afro-American roots make similar quilts. The same holds true of the Amish, Hawaiians and the Sioux. Because Amish and Hawaiian quilts do appear to differ significantly from

mainstream quilts I have included a section on each. Remember that not all Hawaiian-looking quilts were made by Hawaiians.

AMISH QUILTS

The typical high-style Amish quilt shares many characteristics with mainstream quilts. There are a few major differences, however. One is the heavy use of black. While most mainstream quilters used black only in the 1880-1925 period, the Amish continued to use it after the fashion passed. They also have a preference for plain black cotton, a fabric that mainstream quilters have rarely used until the last decade or so. Many Amish quilters did not use patterned cloth, so their plain cotton quilts stood apart from mainstream calicoes.

Amish quilters continued to quilt their wool quilts long after most mainstream quilters turned to tying wool quilts. The Amish (because they

Variable Star quilt. Made by an unknown Amish woman in Conewango, New York. Inscribed in the quilting: 2–23–63. Pieced and quilted. Cotton. Collection of Esprit.

The "63" in the date could mean 1863 or 1963, but both fall outside the range of such dark Amish quilts, which generally date from between 1880 and 1940. Could it be 1863? Bright, plain cottons are unlikely at that early date, so it must be 1963, a reminder that individuals may carry on a style after the community at large abandons it.

quilted their quilts?) used finer wools well into the twentieth century when mainstream quiltmakers were using coarser, heavier wools. The quilting thread on the dark wool, cotton or rayon Amish quilts is often black, a thread color mainstream quilters did not ordinarily use.

Most Amish communities used the same patterns as mainstream quilters, but some Amish communities (especially in Pennsylvania) had a preference for designs such as the center diamond (a medallion set) and the bars pattern (a strip set), which were not often used by mainstream quiltmakers after the Civil War. Not every center diamond quilt is Amish. Both center diamonds and bars are seen in early quilts and in England, Scotland and Wales, where the designs persisted longer than in mainstream America.

The earliest date-inscribed quilt in the database attributed to an Amish quiltmaker is a Pennsylvania Bars quilt dated 1892, but there are a number of Amish-style quilts attributed to the 1880s. In most Amish communities quiltmakers began making quilts more like mainstream quilters in the 1960s. Fine wool quilts and those made in the center diamond and bar patterns are no longer made, but a few communities still use the dark colors, although they now prefer the polyester and blends from which their clothing is sewn.

Summary of Amish Quilts

Characteristics: Look for black as a color, lack of patterned fabric, fancy quilting (especially significant in wool quilts) and the typically Amish designs such as center diamond and bars.

Range: 1880−1940 for highstyle Amish wool quilts, but dark quilts are still being made in some communities.

Don't be confused by: Black wool quilts that were popular with everyone around the turn of the century. The major difference between Amish dark wool quilts and mainstream dark wool quilts is that the Amish quilted theirs.

Collectors' tips: These quilts are so collectible that some Amish are now making new wool quilts of old wool clothing.

For an additional example: See page 74.

For further reading: Bishop, Robert and Elizabeth Safanda. *A Gallery of Amish Quilts: Design Diversity from a Plain People*. E.P. Dutton, New York, 1976.

Haders, Phyllis. *Sunshine and Shadow: The Amish and Their Quilts*. Universe Books, New York, 1976.

HAWAIIAN QUILTS

Missionaries brought American quiltmaking to the Hawaiians. At some point the islanders adapted the conventional applique techniques to their own flowers and symbols and developed their own style. The Hawaiian quilt appears to be derived from the folded, cut-paper designs found in mid-nineteenth century sampler album quilts.

Na Wai O Maunaolu (The Waters of Maunaolu). Hawaiian quilt. Maker unknown. Estimated date: 1875−1900. Appliqued and embroidered. Cotton. Collection: Shelburne Museum, Shelburne, Vermont.

The mirror-image design covering the whole top, the two-color design (dark blue on white) and the lines of quilting echoing the applique are clues to a Hawaiian quilt. Clues to date are more difficult to find. The museum's records attribute the quilt to the end of the nineteenth century, a date the plain cottons do not dispute. Hawaiian patterns are often symbolic. The area called Maunaolu, mentioned in the pattern name, is on the island of Maui.

In the mainland version, the designs are generally block size, although some examples cover the whole top with a single design as the Hawaiians do. Hawaiians cut the design from what looks to be a single large piece of fabric and applique it to a bed-size background fabric. The quilts are usually a dark color on a light ground, but any high-contrast combination of two plain-color cottons is used. The pieces are often quilted in a distinctive style, with quilting lines echoing the applique like pond ripples radiating from a dropped pebble.

These quilts are rarely date-inscribed. Most attributed versions date from the mid-nineteenth century or later. Since there are no cotton prints for clues, dating can be difficult, but the colors are a clue. Pastel plains would likely be after 1925; nineteenth-century versions would be brighter or darker with Turkey reds, indigo blues and over-dyed greens.

A second type of Hawaiian quilt is the "Ku'u Hae Aloha" (My Beloved Flag), using the Hawaiian flag (which looks much like the British flag) as a major part of the design. The Hawaiians were forbidden to fly their flag after an 1893 coup against Queen Liliuokalani, so patriots incorporated the design into their quilts. A Ku'u Hae Aloha quilt would thus date from after 1893.

Summary of Hawaiian Quilts

Characteristics: Look for plain cotton applique designs cut from folded cloth in the medallion format. Echo quilting is typical. The Hawaiian Flag is a sub-category of Hawaiian quilt, dating from the last decade of the nineteenth century.
Range: 1840-present.
For further reading: Akana, Elizabeth A. *Hawaiian Quilting: A Fine Art*, The Hawaiian Mission Children's Society, Honolulu, 1981.
Jones, Stella May. *Hawaiian Quilts*. Honolulu Academy of Art and Daughters of Hawaii, Honolulu, 1930, second edition, 1973.

CLUES IN PATTERNS

There are thousands upon thousands of quilt patterns and each has a name— or two or three or more. In *An Encyclopedia of Pieced Quilt Patterns* I recorded about 4000 designs and 6000 published names (1). Appliqued designs are not as well-recorded nor as well-indexed, but there are also thousands of them. Today's quiltmakers have far more designs in their repertoires than quiltmakers of the past. In compiling an index to pieced patterns in date-attributed quilts I counted only 380 in use by 1875, 200 before 1850 and 86 patterns in quilts made before 1825—a fraction of those in use 150 years later (2). The rise of the album quilt in the 1840s probably caused an increase in designs, and the emergence of the published pattern in the 1890s began another surge that continues today. Competition in the commercial pattern market demands diversity; copyright considerations demand changes in designs originated by others, and marketing demands clever names—all of which have lead to a long list of patterns and pattern names.

Early pieced designs were relatively simple, pieced of triangles, diamonds and squares with few pieces per block, the kind today's quiltmakers call beginner's blocks. Checks, simple stars and the all-over pattern of right triangles we call Yankee Puzzle or Broken Dishes are the most common pieced designs in early quilts, with just a few complex exceptions—most notably the Mariner's Compass. Complexity gradually increased through the first half of the nineteenth century as many of the difficult designs (made difficult with a multitude of small pieces and/or curved seams) appeared. Whig's Defeat, Rocky Mountain (now called New York Beauty), and Feathered Star date from the mid-nineteenth century and they are still among the hardest patterns to piece. By the end of the century most of the standards, the Log Cabin, the Fan, the Drunkard's Path, the pieced tree and the pieced house were in use. Twentieth-

century quiltmakers and designers added to the list by drafting variations of the older patterns. The Double Wedding Ring, born in the 1920s, is a variation of the older Pickle Dish. The many versions of the Dresden Plate rework a set of four of the fans popular in the late Victorian years. The designers of the 1920s and '30s also developed designs for more complex sets, advocated setting pieced blocks side by side to produce fascinating secondary designs, and brought more of the real world into pieced designs, selling patterns for everything from coffee cups to airplanes.

The majority of the standard applique patterns, Rose Wreaths, Fleurs-de-lis, Whig Roses, Tulips and Pineapples, developed during the album quilt fad. After the Civil War, few new applique designs developed until well into the twentieth century when designers updated applique with realistic daffodils, dahlias and dogwoods.

Quilt Names

The lyricism of the pattern names—Solomon's Puzzle, Devil's Claws and Rocky Road to Kansas—is one of the charms of American quilts. These names seem to be put us in touch with our past; they are a folklore that evokes a simpler time. However, it is important to realize that we know of these names primarily through the print media, a business concerned with selling patterns rather than accurately recording folklore. Our knowledge of pattern names is incomplete because it has filtered down to us through the happenstance of editors' whims, readers' letters and advertising copywriters' creativity.

We do not know what nineteenth-century quiltmakers actually called their designs. Only on rare occasions do we find pattern names in their

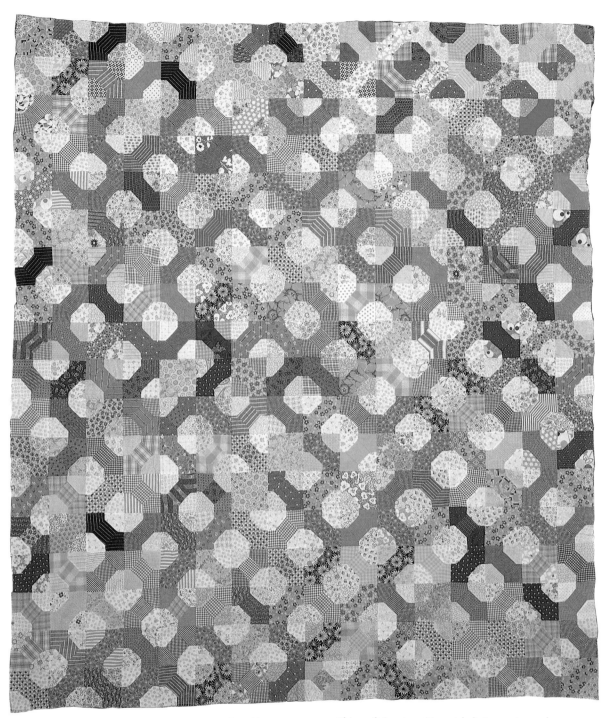

Bow Tie, unfinished top. Maker unknown. Estimated date: 1920–1950. Pieced. Cotton. Collection of Larry Schwarm.

This quilt is a transition style between two color schemes, the dark colors of the turn-of-the-century and the lighter, brighter colors popular after 1925. The pattern dates from after 1880.

letters and diaries or inscribed on their quilts. When we find a pattern name, too often we do not recognize it. We know—or think we know—the pattern described in an 1849 story as Irish Chain (3) or in an 1850 reference to Saw Teeth (4). But what did Nancy Holman mean in 1869 when she wrote in her diary of her Bird Comfort (5)? What pattern was Alice Morse Earl recalling in her 1898 memories of the Blue Brigade design (6)? These patterns and many more are not in our indexes. It is doubtful that the patterns have been lost, but rather that the names have changed across the decades.

Mariner's Compass

An examination of the sources for the name for one common pattern—the design today's quilters call Mariner's Compass—illustrates the discrepancies between our names and those of the past. The design, a circular pattern of radiating points, is one of the oldest in patchwork. It may be derived from the wind roses or compass roses found on sea charts and maps (7) or from the symbol for the sun.

Although Mariner's Compass is a common name in today's quilt books and conversations, few pattern references printed before 1960 have included it. The 1889 Ladies' Art Company catalog, Webster's 1915 book (8), Finley's 1929 book (9), and Hall's 1935 index to patterns (10) included the design but used other names. The earliest published reference to the name was printed at the end of the nineteenth century in Eliza Southgate Bowne's letters, a source familiar to few quiltmakers at the time. In a letter dated January 9, 1798, she mentioned Mariner's Compass patchwork but did not sketch the design (11). The earliest published reference that I have been able to find with pattern and name combined is in *The Oklahoma Farmer Stockman's* 1929 quilt pattern column. Two years later Finley used the name Mariner's Compass in a *Country Gentleman* magazine article.

There are two possible reasons the name did not appear in the quilt literature until the late 1920s. Either earlier quiltmakers did not use it, or the name somehow slipped through the haphazard system for recording names until 1929.

There do seem to be a number of other names for the design, some in use today and others forgotten. The Kansas Quilt Project found a signed and dated quilt from 1878, with the name Virginia Beauty written on the back, a name that never appeared in print. Finley in her 1931 *Country Gentleman* article said it had earlier been called The Explosion, a name inspired by railroad accidents. Other names never heard from today's quilters include Merry Go Round from *Capper's Weekly's* pattern column in 1928 and Gig Prong from *Country Gentleman* in the early 1940s. Variations (with six points rather than four or eight) were Cog Wheels in the Ladies' Art Company catalog (1889); Topeka or the Pennsylvania Wheel Quilt from *Hearth and Home* magazine in the early twentieth century, and Rolling Pinwheel in Ickis's 1949 book (12).

Names still heard, although less frequently than Mariner's Compass, include The Ladies' Art Company's Slashed Star from 1889 and Chips and Whetstones, first published in 1931.

The most common names in the print sources before 1950 refer to the sun rather than the compass. Two of the earliest references are Sunburst by Marie Webster writing in *The Ladies' Home Journal* in 1908 and Rising Sun in Ruth Finley's 1929 book. Both names were often repeated in later books, magazines and patterns. Finley's reference to the Rising Sun calls to mind a group of names that appeared (without accompanying designs) in the nineteenth-century literature. In 1849 T.S. Arthur mentioned a Rising Star in *Godey's* (13); in 1888 *Good Housekeeping* complained about the "gay red, green and yellow abominations known as the Rising Star and Setting Sun" (14); Alice Morse Earl recalled a Rising Sun as a favorite old design in 1898 (15) and so did the fictional Aunt Jane of Kentucky the same year (16). It may be that these mysterious heavenly bodies are the quilts we call the Mariner's Compass. Such confusion doesn't apply to every old pattern, but the more I study the subject the more I realize there is no such thing as a single, correct pattern name.

Patterns—whatever their names—can be excellent clues to date. Below are two dozen of the patterns often seen in quilts. The names I chose to use with each seem to be the most recognizable today. Some of the old standards—the Nine Patch and the Grandmother's Flower Garden—are clues to broad eras, and others—the Double Wedding

Ring and the Fan—can help pinpoint narrower spans.

Guide to Common Patterns

PIECED PATTERNS

Baskets

Pieced baskets probably developed from the appliqued baskets that appeared on so many chintz medallion quilts and album samplers. The earliest date-inscribed pieced basket in the data base is 1855. Range: 1850-present. For another example see page 61.

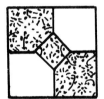

Bow Ties

Called Necktie in the 1898 Ladies' Art Company catalog, it dates from the 1880s, with two date-inscribed examples in that decade. Range: 1880-present. For another example see page 166.

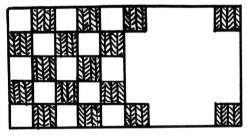

Double Irish Chain

Of ten date-inscribed Irish Chain quilts in the database, the earliest is 1814. Dated examples appear consistently across the decades, indicating the design's popularity throughout the nineteenth and twentieth centuries. Most Irish Chain quilts are made of two blocks, one pieced in a check pattern; the other plain with squares appliqued to the corners. With 25 checks in the pieced square, it is a Double Irish Chain; with 49, a Triple Irish Chain. The name was recorded in the mid-nineteenth century; it may be derived from a similar weaving pattern. Range: 1800-present. For another example see page 18.

Double Wedding Ring

The earliest date-inscribed examples of this popular design and the first published patterns are from the late 1920s, but several quilters I have interviewed recall making them in the early '20s. Range: 1920-present. For another example see page 70.

Fans

In January, 1885 *Peterson's Magazine* printed a pattern saying, "The design of Fans, for patchwork, is something entirely new" (17). There is one dated 1884, the earliest in the database, that includes eight examples. It was inspired by the fashion for Japanese decoration, which also inspired the Crazy Quilt. The early versions tend to be of wools and silks in dark colors. In the 1920s the Fan was revived as a cotton scrap design. Range: 1880-present. For another example see page 141.

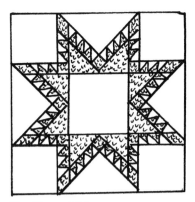

Feathered Star

A variation of the basic eight-pointed star design, it is among the complex patchwork designs that developed in the second quarter of the nineteenth century. Of twelve examples in the database, the earliest is 1838. Range: 1830 - present. For other examples see pages 8, 63 and 67.

Flowers - Pieced Lilies, Peonies and Tulips

Diamonds and triangles symbolize the flowers; the stems and leaves may be pieced, appliqued or a combination of techniques. Of 15 date-inscribed variations the earliest is 1841. Nineteenth-century records as to names are diverse. The Shelburne Museum owns a version with a three-lobed flower of eight pointed stars, dated 1857 and inscribed "Peony and Prairie Flower". The same design was called Tree Quilt Pattern in the *Ohio Farmer* in 1896 and Double Paeony in the Ladies' Art Company catalog in 1889. In the 1880s they were associated with President Grover Cleveland; the version pieced of eight-pointed stars was called Cleveland Tulip (*Household Magazine*) and the President's Quilt (Ladies' Art Company); the four-pointed flower was Cleveland Lilies (Ladies' Art Company). Its common name today is North Carolina Lily, but no geographical link has been established. Range: 1840-present.

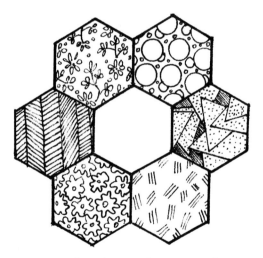

Grandmother's Flower Garden

The hexagon mosaic design arranged in florets has been the most popular quilt pattern since 1925; many women who never made another quilt finished a Grandmother's Flower Garden. The pattern dates to the early nineteenth century. The earliest of nine examples in the database is dated 1817. In 1835 *Godey's* called it Honeycomb, Hexagon or Six-Sided Patchwork. The design sustained its popularity across the decades, changing from chintz to silk to wool to calicoes, first in brown cottons, then grays and then pastels. Technique is a clue to date; template piecing typifies the nineteenth century; running stitch piecing is likely in this one. Range: 1800 - present. For other examples see pages 24, 30 and 128.

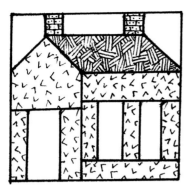

Houses

What we call the Schoolhouse appeared rather late in the nineteenth century. A small house with its gable end to the side was a motif symbolizing the log cabin of William Henry Harrison's 1840 presidential campaign, but cabins appeared on mid-century quilts only in fabric, applique pictures or quilted designs, not pieced patterns. The earliest pieced house in the database is dated 1890. There are only three date-inscribed examples (1890, 1890-92 and 1935-38), a small sample, but observation supports the conclusion that the pattern dates from around 1880 or '90. The earliest printed references to the pieced house call it a Log Cabin (which may relate to Benjamin Harrison's Log Cabin presidential campaign in 1888). Old Kentucky Home, Old Folks at Home, and Lincoln Log Cabin are some of the nostalgic names from the years before Finley called it the Little Red Schoolhouse in 1929. Range: 1880-present.

Log Cabin

The pieced Log Cabin block is a pattern with clear origins. Several examples are dated in the 1870s; the earliest date-inscribed example is 1869. The design is mentioned in the literature of the 1860s; it may be related to Abraham Lincoln's Log Cabin campaign (the second of three). Log Cabin quilts were so popular in the 1870s that fairs opened categories specifically for them (18).

We have a good idea what the quiltmakers called them since the name Log Cabin appears in print with the design several times in those years. Other names were American Patchwork or Canadian Patchwork, Canadian Log Wood and Loghouse Quilting (all in England) and the Log Patch in the 1889 Ladies' Art Company catalog. Unusual English names, Egyptian or Mummy pattern (20), refer to mummy wrappings of dark and light strips in a similar design. Interlocking rectangle designs are found in ornament such as the Greek key and Indian basketry designs. Its earliest quilt antecedents are in the appliqued borders that look much like pieced Log Cabin blocks. These date from the 1840s through the 1860s. Range: (as a pieced block) 1860-present. (As an appliqued border) 1840-1865. For other examples see pages 73 and 122.

Mariner's Compass

A circle composed of radiating points is a common design in many cultures. In patchwork the motif dates to the eighteenth century; an English quilt from 1726 is the earliest date-inscribed example; the earliest date-inscribed American quilt is 1834. Range: (as a medallion center) 1750-present. (As a block) 1825-present. For another example see page 88.

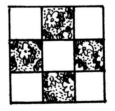

Nine Patch

The arrangement of nine squares in a block is one of the simplest of quilt patterns—one that goes back to the early nineteenth century in date-inscribed examples. Of eight such quilts in the database, the earliest is 1808 with others dated throughout the nineteenth and twentieth centuries. The Nine Patch was often used to teach children to piece and was a favorite for utility quilts. Range: 1800-present. For other examples see pages 83 and 123.

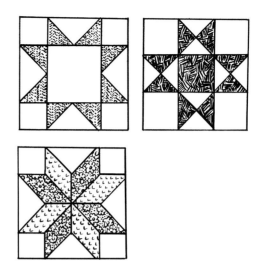

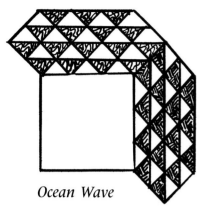

Ocean Wave

The Ocean Wave is a six-sided block pieced of right triangles, usually set with plain squares. The earliest date-inscribed examples are from the 1890s, but several date-attributed examples from the 1870s are in the literature. Range: 1875-present, with 1890-1925 the years it was most often made.

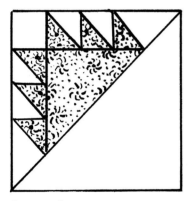

Sawtooth

The sawtooth block appears in many early nineteenth-century quilts, arranged first in strips for borders and later as blocks. The earliest date-inscribed version is dated 1823. Range: 1800-present. For other examples see pages 33 and 102.

Stars

Variations of a simple eight-pointed star with points of diamonds or triangles are among the earliest pieced designs. They appear in borders and blocks dated in the last quarter of the eighteenth century. Range: 1775- present. For other examples see pages 15, 69 and 85.

Star of Bethlehem or Lone Star

The name Lone Star refers to Texas; this large star covering the top of the quilt and the Republic were born around the same time. The earliest date-inscribed example (of six) is Mary Totten's 1835 example, made the year before the fall of the Alamo. There are earlier date-attributed versions, but a date of origin of around 1830 seems most likely.

The early to mid-nineteenth-century versions usually had smaller stars, chintz applique or other designs orbiting in the blank spaces around the central star. Late-nineteenth and twentieth-century quiltmakers were content with true Lone Stars in a blank background. Since the 1920s many pre-cut kits have been sold. Range: 1830-present.

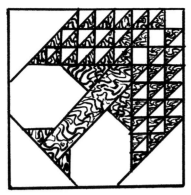

Trees

The tree-of-life design is one of the earliest patch-work patterns; late-eighteenth-century seam-stresses cut limbs and leaves from chintz to construct the flowering trees. A few decades after the cut-out chintz trees fell from fashion before the Civil War, trees pieced of triangles began to appear. The earliest date-inscribed quilt of four in the database is dated 1890, a decade or two after the pattern's probable origin. Pieced trees are often attributed to the colonial era, but such an early date is unlikely. Range: 1875-present.

APPLIQUED PATTERNS

*Coxcomb and Currants or
Flowering Almond*

The eight-lobed flower can be viewed as a cox-comb, an almond blossom, an oakleaf or a poin-settia. The circles on the radiating arms may be currants, almonds or acorns. The pattern, like most appliqued designs, was done in red and green on a white background. It was quite popular for a short period of time. Of the three date-in-scribed examples, two are from the 1850s and one is 1870. The many undated examples are attrib-uted to the same decades. Range: 1850–1880.

Princess Feather

The feather design, a standard quilting pattern for centuries in England and America, was apparently adapted to applique in the early nineteenth century. There are many variations, which can be a central medallion or a block repeat. Flowers or stars appear in the center space and on the ends of the arms. The name may refer to the feathers that symbolize the Prince of Wales; women pre-sented to the Prince at the English court were to wear plumes in their hair. The earliest date-in-scribed example is dated 1818 and many attrib-uted to the mid- and late-nineteenth century. It is one applique design that maintained its popu-larity into the twentieth century, so pastel versions were produced after 1900. Range: 1800-present. For other examples see pages 49 and 124.

Reel, Oakleaf or Turkey Tracks

The basic design has a four-sided center with con-cave curves—a kind of squeezed square—with four arms extending to the corners of the block. Within that broad definition there are dozens of variations. If the arms have the look of an oak leaf the block can be called Oak Leaf or Hickory Leaf; if the arms are a simple oval, as shown, it is called the Reel, and if the arms are triple ovals, it is Turkey Tracks. The simpler versions can be pieced as well as appliqued.

The earliest date-inscribed example of a Reel

172

design is 1818. It was one of the first standard applique designs to be constructed by the quilt-maker rather than cut from chintz. During the 1840s and '50s, oakleaf and reel designs were popular for albums and other applique quilts. The pattern, like most other applique designs, faded away at the end of the nineteenth century, although some quiltmakers continued to piece versions of Turkey Tracks. Range: 1800-1900. For another example see page 148.

Rose Wreath

The Rose of Sharon, a round floral shape with eight scallops on the edges, is the basis of many applique designs, including this wreath of roses and leaves. The earliest date-inscribed wreaths are in album quilts dated 1844; throughout the rest of the century the design was one of the most common applique patterns. It was revived in the

1925-1950 era, so many pastel versions were also made. Range: 1840-present. For another example see page 161.

Whig Rose or Democrat Rose

In this variation of the Rose of Sharon, flowers and stems radiate from a central rose. Stories in the literature attribute the design to the presidential election of 1828 when the newly formed Democrat party first ran against the Whigs, but like most other conventional applique designs, no quilts survive from before the 1840s. Of the six date-inscribed examples in the database, the earliest is in an album quilt dated 1851 (the year of the last Democrat-Whig contest). The pattern, which was not often used in album quilts, was popular throughout the last half of the nineteenth century, long after the Whigs were gone. Range: 1840-1900. For another example see page 128.

NOTES

CHAPTER 1

1. Callahan, Colleen R. "A Quilt and Its Pieces". *Metropolitan Museum Journal*. 19/20, 1984/1985. Page 119.

CHAPTER 2

1. Garoutte, Sally. "Early Colonial Quilts in a Bedding Context". *Uncoverings 1980*, American Quilt Study Group, Mill Valley, California, 1981.

2. Allen, Gloria Seaman. "Bed Coverings, Kent County, Maryland 1710–1820". *Uncoverings 1985*. American Quilt Study Group, Mill Valley, California, 1986.

3. Garoutte. Page 23.

4. Osler, Dorothy. *Traditional British Quilts*. B.T. Batsford, London, 1987. Page 81.

5. Allen, Gloria Seaman. *First Flowerings: Early Virginia Quilts*. DAR Museum, Washington, D.C., l987. Page 6.

6. Garoutte. Page 26.

7. Garoutte. Page 26.

8. Hersh, Tandy. "Quilted Petticoats". *Pieced By Mother: Symposium Papers*. (ed. Jeannette Lasansky). Oral Traditions Project, Lewisburg, Pennsylvania, 1988. Page 6.

9. Winslow, Anna Green. *A Boston School Girl of l771*. Edited by Alice Morse Earl. Reprinted by Singing Tree Press, Detroit, 1970. Page 5.

10. Allen. "Bedcoverings, Kent County, Maryland 1710–1820". Page 20.

11. Swan, Susan Burrows. *Plain and Fancy: American Women and Their Needlework, 1700–1850*. Holt, Rinehart & Winston, New York, 1977. Page 230.

12. Murray, James A.H.; Henry Bradley; W.A. Craigie and C.T. Onions; (editors). *Oxford English Dictionary*. Clarendon Press, Oxford, England, 1933. Page 548.

13. Beaudoin-Ross, Jacqueline. "An Early-Eighteenth Century Pieced Quilt in Montreal". *Canadian Art Revue*. Volume 6, Number 2, 1979. Pages 106–109.

14. Beaudoin-Ross. Page 106.

15. Finley, Ruth. *Old Patchwork Quilts and the Women Who Made Them*. J.B. Lippincott, Philadelphia, 1929. Page 29.

16. Hall, Carrie A. and Rose G. Kretsinger. *The Romance of the Patchwork Quilt in America*. Caxton Printers, Caldwell, Idaho, 1935. Page 53.

17. Philadelphia Museum of Art. *Three Centuries of American Art*. Philadelphia Museum of Art, 1976.

18. Allen. "Bedcoverings, Kent County, Maryland 1710–1820." Page 22.

19. Swan. Page 230.

20. Drinker, Elizabeth. *Extracts from the Diary of Elizabeth Drinker*. Editor, Henry Biddle. Philadelphia, 1889. Quoted in Herr, Patricia T. "All in Modesty and Plainness". *Quilt Digest 3*, The Quilt Digest Press, San Francisco, California, 1985. Page 25.

21. *Oxford English Dictionary*. Page 1875.

22. Phelps, Elizabeth Porter. "The Diary of Elizabeth (Porter) Phelps". Thomas Eliot Andrews, editor. *The New England Historical and Genealogical Register*. Pages 118–122, 1964–1968. Quoted in Bonfield, Lynn A. "The Production of Cloth, Clothing and Quilts in Nineteenth Century New England Homes". *Uncoverings 1981*. American Quilt Study Group, Mill Valley, California, 1982. Page 86.

23. Cooper, Mary. *The Diary of Mary Cooper: Life on a Long Island Farm, 1768–1773:* Oyster Bay Historical Society, 1981. Quoted in Sprigg, June. *Domestick Beings*. Knopf, New York, 1984. Page 97.

24. Nash, Charles Elventon. *The History of Augusta*. Charles E. Nash and Son, Augusta, Maine, 1904. Quoted in Sprigg. Page 89.

25. Hill, Frances Baylor. Journal. Quoted in Allen. *First Flowerings: Early Virginia Quilts*. Page 18.

26. Harbeson, Georgiana Brown. *American Needlework*, Bonanza Books, New York, 1938. Page 27.

27. Winslow. Page 5.

28. Maines, Rachel. "Paradigms of Scarcity and Abundance: The Quilt as an Artifact of the Industrial Revolution". *In the Heart of Pennsylvania Symposium Papers*. Oral Traditions Project, Lewisburg, Pennsylvania, 1986. Page 86.

29. Kane, Joseph Nathan. *Famous First Facts*. H.W. Wilson, New York, l981.

30. Dumond, Dwight Lowell. *Antislavery: The Crusade for Free-*

dom in America. University of Michigan Press, Ann Arbor, Michigan, 1961.

31. Bowne, Eliza Southgate. A Girl's Life Eighty Years Ago: Selections from the Letters of Eliza Southgate Bowne. Charles Scribner's Sons, New York, 1888. Letter dated January 9, 1798. Page 72.

32. Lawton, Sarah Robert. Will. Quoted in Berry, Michael W. "Documenting the Nineteenth-Century Quilt". American Craft. February, March, 1985. Pages 23–27.

33. Allen. "Bedcoverings, Kent County, Maryland, 1710–1820". Page 19.

34. Lasansky, Jeannette. Pieced by Mother: Over 100 Years of Quiltmaking Traditions. Oral Traditions Project, Lewisburg, Pennsylvania, l987. Page 62.

35. Larcom, Lucy. A New England Girlhood: Outlined from Memory. Houghton Mifflin, Boston, 1889. Reprinted by Peter Smith, Gloucester, Massachusetts, 1973. Pages 122 and 123.

36. Brown, Harriett Connor. Grandmother Brown's Hundred Years 1827–1927. Little Brown, New York, 1929. Page 47.

37. Samson, Chloe. Account Book, in Schlesinger Library, Radcliffe College, Cambridge, Massachusetts. Quoted in Bonfield, Lynn A. "The Production of Cloth, Clothing and Quilts in Nineteenth Century New England Homes". Uncoverings 1981. American Quilt Study Group, Mill Valley, California, 1982. Page 88.

38. Colt, Miriam Davis. Went to Kansas. Watertown, New York, 1862. Reprinted by University Microfilms, Ann Arbor, Michigan, 1966.

39. Herr, Patricia T. "Quaker Quilts and Their Makers". Pieced by Mother: Symposium Papers. Oral Traditions Project, Lewisburg, Pennsylvania, 1988. Page 19.

40. Oxford English Dictionary, Pages 1875 and 1876.

41. Trollope, Frances. Domestic Manners of the Americans. 1832. Reprinted by Knopf, Donald Smalley, editor, New York, l949. Pages 415–420.

42. Rix, Chastina W. and Alfred. Diary 1849–1854. In California Historical Society Library, San Francisco, California. Quoted in Bonfield. Page 71.

43. Arthur, T.S. "The Quilting Party". Godey's Lady's Book, Volume 39, September, 1849. Page 185.

44. Letter from Elizabeth Nessly Myer, March 14, 1860. Quoted in Atwood, Kay. Mill Creek Journal: Ashland Oregon, 1850–1860. Published by the author, Ashland, Oregon, 1987. Page 120.

45. Letter from Ellen Reed, March 19, 1856. Quoted in Lipsett, Linda. "A Piece of Ellen's Dress". Quilt Digest 2. Quilt Digest Press, San Francisco, California, 1984. Page 13.

46. Gunn, Virginia, "Victorian Silk Template Patchwork in American Periodicals, 1850–1875". Uncoverings 1983. American Quilt Study Group, Mill Valley, California, 1984.

47. Murphy, Jan. "Design Influences of a Regional Unnamed Applique Pattern". Uncoverings 1987. American Quilt Study Group, San Francisco, California, in press.

48. Personal communication to the author from Merikay Waldvogel. The pattern is pictured in December of the Quilts/88 Poster Calendar from Main Street Press, Pittstown, New Jersey, 1988.

49. The coincidence in pattern was first noted by Louise Townsend in Quilters Newsletter Magazine, November/December, 1983. Page 8. Katy Christopherson noted more examples in her article "Tracings: Quilts and Cousins". In Kentucky, September/October, 1984. Pages 43–45.

50. Kolter, Jane Bentley. Forget Me Not: A Gallery of Friendship and Album Quilts. The Main Street Press, Pittstown, New Jersey, 1985. Page 59. Kolter's thesis that the Chimney Sweep pattern is typical of New York is supported by dated examples in the database. Of five dated in the 1840s and 1850s, four were made in New York; one is attributed to Texas.

51. Shaw Family Papers. In the collection of the Nebraska State Historical Society, Lincoln. Described in Hedges, Elaine. "The Nineteenth Century Diarist and Her Quilts". American Quilts: A Handmade Legacy. Oakland Museum, Oakland, California, 1981. Pages 63–64.

52. Garoutte, Sally. "California's First Quilting Party". Uncoverings 1981. American Quilt Study Group, Mill Valley, California, 1982.

53. Ropes, Hannah Anderson. Six Months In Kansas By a Lady. John P. Jewett and Company, Boston, l856. Page 197.

54. Ropes. Page 217.

55. Benberry, Cuesta. "White Perspectives of Blacks in Quilts and Related Media". Uncoverings 1983. American Quilt Study Group, Mill Valley, California, 1984. Pages 60 and 61.

56. Gunn, Virginia. "Quilts for Union Soldiers in the Civil War". Uncoverings 1985. American Quilt Study Group, Mill Valley, California, 1986. Page 100.

57. Letter from Dolly Lunt Burge, 1862. Quoted in Ramsey, Bets. "The Quilter" in the Chattanooga Times. August 14, 1986.

58. The Household. Vol 7 # 1, January 1874. Page 4.

59. "Bed-Clothes". Arthur's Home Magazine. October 1883, Page 63.

60. Hearth and Home. June 4, 1870. Page 380.

61. Benberry, Cuesta. "Missouri, Twentieth Century Pattern Supplier". Lady's Circle Patchwork Quilts. May 1988. Page 38.

62. Home Needlework Magazine. 1899.

63. Cutler's Red Book of Ready Reference. W.R. Vansant, 1903. Page 135.

64. Ramsey, Bets. "The Quilter". Chattanooga Times. June 26, 1986.

65. Webster, Marie. Quilts: Their Story and How to Make Them. Doubleday, Page and Co., Garden City, New York, 1915.

66. Wallace's Farmer, January 18,1929. Page 91.

67. Undated newspaper clipping from unknown source in a scrapbook kept by Carrie A. Hall, in the collection of the Helen F. Spencer Museum of Art at the University of Kansas.

68. Good Housekeeping magazine's 1978 national contest drew 9,954 entries. Good Housekeeping, March 1978. Page 4.

69. Letter from Ada Schlick to author, November 23, 1982.

70. Hall and Krestinger. Page 261.

CHAPTER 3

1. Dan River Inc. A Dictionary of Textile Terms. Dan River Inc., New York, 1980. Page 89.

2. Callaway Textile Mills. *Callaway Textile Dictionary*. Callaway Mills, La Grange, Georgia, 1947.

3. Bogdonoff, Nancy Dick. *Handwoven Textiles of Early New England, The Legacy of a Rural People, 1640–1880*. Stackpole Books, Harrisburg, 1975.

4. Winslow, Anna Green. *A Boston School Girl of 1771*. Alice Morse Earl, editor. Reprinted by Singing Tree Press, Detroit, 1970. Page 32.

5. Earle, Alice Morse. *Colonial Dames and Good Wives*. Frederick Unger, New York. Reprinted in 1962. Page 242.

6. Vander Noordaa, Titia. "The Lindsey Woolseys at the Shelburne Museum." *Spindle, Shuttle and Dyepot*. Spring, 1985. Pages 59–61.

7. Bogdonoff. Page 99.

8. Bronson, J. & R. *The Domestic Manufacturer's Assistant and Family Director in the Arts of Weaving and Dyeing*. William Williams, Utica, New York, 1817. Reprinted as *Early American Weaving and Dyeing*. Dover, New York, 1977. Page 107.

9. *New Hampshire Patriot and State Gazette*. Concord, New Hampshire, September 28, 1819. Quoted in Federal Writers' Project. *Hands That Built New Hampshire*. Stephen Dage Press, Brattleboro, Vermont, 1940.

10. Partridge, Virginia Parslow. *Made in New York State: Handwoven Coverlets*. Jefferson County Historical Society, Watertown, New York, 1985. Page 9.

11. Letter from John Lawson. Quoted in Holliday, Carl. *Women's Life in Colonial Days*. Corner House Publishers, 1922. Page 133.

12. Letter from Thomas Jefferson dated 1786. Quoted in Walton, Perry. *Story of Textiles*. Tudor Publishing Company, New York, 1925. Page 144.

13. Wilson, Kax. *A History of Textiles*. Westview Press, Boulder, Colorado, 1979. Page 264.

14. Waldvogel, Merikay. "Southern Linsey Quilts". *Uncoverings 1987*. The American Quilt Study Group, San Francisco, California, in press.

15. Bogdonoff.

16. Hollen, Norma, Jane Sadler and Ann Langford. *Textiles* (5th Edition). MacMillan, New York, 1979.

17. Hollen, Sadler and Langford. Page 24.

18. Swan, Susan Burrows. *Plain and Fancy: American Women and Their Needlework, 1700–1850*. Holt, Rinehart & Winston, New York, 1977. Page 20.

19. Garoutte, Sally. "Early Colonial Quilts in a Bedding Context". *Uncoverings 1980*. American Quilt Study Group, Mill Valley, California, 1981. Page 25.

20. Garoutte. Page 25.

21. Philadelphia Museum of Art. *Three Centuries of American Art*. Philadelphia Museum of Art, Philadelphia, 1976.

22. Beaudoin-Ross, Jacqueline. "An Early-Eighteenth Century Pieced Quilt in Montreal". *Canadian Art Revue*. Volume 6, Number 2, 1979. Page 109.

23. Pullan, Eliza, Mrs. *The Lady's Manual of Fancy Work*. Dick and Fitzgerald, New York, 1859. Pages 95–97. Quoted in Gunn, Virginia. "Victorian Silk Template Patchwork in American Periodicals, 1850–1875". *Uncoverings 1983*. American Quilt Study Group, Mill Valley, California, 1984.

24. Caulfeild, Sophia Frances Anne, and Blanche C. Saward. *The Dictionary of Needlework*, L. Upcott Gill, London, 1882. Reprinted by Arno Press, New York, 1972. Page 379.

25. Hartley, Florence. *The Ladies' Hand Book of Fancy and Ornamental Work*, G.G. Evans, Philadephia, 1859. Quoted in Gunn. Page 17.

26. Maines, Rachel. "Paradigms of Scarcity and Abundance: The Quilt as an Artifact of the Industrial Revolution". *In the Heart of Pennsylvania Symposium Papers*. Oral Traditions Project, Lewisburg, Pennsylvania, 1986. Page 87.

27. Maines. Page 87.

28. Bogdonoff. Page 23.

29. Heilbroner, Robert L. and Aaron Singer. *The Economic Transformation of America: 1600 to the Present*. (2nd Edition). Harcourt, Brace, Jovanovich, San Diego, 1984. Page 49.

30. Kalm, Peter. Journals. Quoted in "Travels in North America". *TWA Ambassador*. April, 1988. Page 83.

31. Wilson. Page 256.

32. Tucker, Barbara M. *Samuel Slater and the Origins of the American Textile Industry, 1790–1860*. Cornell University Press, Ithaca, New York, 1984.

33. Carroll-Porczynski, C. Z. *Natural Polymer Man-Made Fibers*. Academic Press, New York, 1961. Page 6.

34. Both Vander Noordaa and Montgomery describe the tops as all wool. Vander Noordaa, page 61 and Montgomery, Florence M. *Textiles in America: 1650–1870*, W.W. Norton and Company, New York, (no date). Page 279.

35. Hersh, Tandy, "Quilted Petticoats". *Pieced By Mother: Symposium Papers*. Oral Traditions Project, Lewisburg, Pennsylvania, 1988.

36. Hollen, Sadler and Langford. Page 34.

37. Bogdonoff. Page 29.

38. Bogdonoff. Page 37.

39. Washington, George. Orders and Invoices. August, 1759, in the collection of the Mount Vernon Ladies' Association of the Union. Quoted in Allen, Gloria Seaman. *First Flowerings: Early Virginia Quilts*. DAR Museum, Washington, D.C., 1987. Page 6.

40. Bogdonoff. Page 115.

41. Waldvogel, Merikay. "Southern Linsey Quilts". *Uncoverings 1987*. The American Quilt Study Group, San Francisco, in press.

42. Caulfeild and Saward. Page 327.

43. Allen, Gloria Seaman. "Bed Coverings, Kent County, Maryland 1710–1820". *Uncoverings 1985*. American Quilt Study Group, Mill Valley, California, 1986. Page 21.

44. Holman, Nancy. Diary. In the collection of the University of Missouri Library, State Historical Society of Missouri, Columbia, Missouri. Quoted in Hedges, Elaine. "The Nineteenth Century Diarist and Her Quilts". *American Quilts: A Handmade Legacy*. Oakland Museum, Oakland, California, 1980. Page 61.

45. Waldvogel.

46. Letter from Abigail Adams dated May 13, 1798. Quoted in Sprigg, June. *Domestick Beings*. Knopf, New York, 1984. Page 83.

47. Miriam Colt recalled paying 37 1/2 cents when she was earning 25 cents per week as a laundress to earn enough

money to buy fabric for a dress. Colt, Miriam Davis. *Went to Kansas*. Watertown, New York, 1862. Reprinted by University Microfilms, Ann Arbor, Michigan, 1966. Page 236.

48. Jeremy, David J. *Transatlantic Industrial Revolution: The Diffusion of Textile Technologies Between Britain and America: 1790–1830*. M.I.T. Press, Cambridge, Massachusetts, 1981. Page 108.

49. Mills, Betty J. *Calico Chronicle: Texas Women and Their Fashions: 1830–1910*. Texas Tech Press, Lubbock, Texas, 1985. Page 24.

50. Priestman, Mabel Tuke. *Handicrafts in the Home*. A.C. McClurg and Company, Chicago, 1910. Page 192.

51. Caulfeild and Saward. Page 59.

52. Wilson. Page 252.

53. Cooper, Grace Rogers. *The Invention of the Sewing Machine*. The Smithsonian Institution, Washington, D.C., 1968. Page 135.

54. Hall, Carrie A. and Rose G. Kretsinger. *The Romance of the Patchwork Quilt in America*. Caxton Printers, Caldwell, Idaho, 1935. Page 263.

55. Hollen, Sadler and Langford. Page 75.

56. Letter from Jeanne Garity of the Stearns and Foster Company to the author, February, 1988.

57. Osler, Dorothy. *Traditional British Quilts*. Batsford, London, 1987. Page 15.

58. "The Stearns and Foster Company," *American Quilter*, Winter, 1985. Page 15.

59. Finley, Ruth. *Old Patchwork Quilts and the Women Who Made Them*. J.B. Lippincott, Philadelphia, 1929. Page 135.

60. Eaton, Allen H. *Handicrafts of the Southern Highlands*. Russell Sage Foundation, New York, 1937.

61. Ferris, William. *Local Color: A Sense of Place in Folk Art*. McGraw Hill, New York, 1982. Pages 181–2.

CHAPTER 4

1. Haynes, William. *Dyes Made In America 1915–1940*. Calco Chemical Division, American Cyanamid Co., Bound Brook, New Jersey, n.d., ca. 1940.

2. Hollen, Norma, Jane Sadler and Ann Langford. *Textiles* (5th Edition). MacMillan, New York, 1979.

3. Hollen, Sadler and Langord.

4. Partridge, William. *A Practical Treatise on Dying Woollen, Cotton and Skein Silk*. New York, 1823. Page 143.

5. Liles, James N. "Dyes in American Quilts Made Prior to 1930, with Special Emphasis on Cotton and Linen". *Uncoverings 1983*. The American Quilt Study Group, Mill Valley, California, 1984. Page 32.

6. Letters to the author from James Liles dated June 23 and August 16, 1988.

7. Finley, Ruth. *Old Patchwork Quilts And The Women Who Made Them*. J. B. Lippincott, Philadelphia, 1929. Page 177.

8. Liles. "Dyes in American Quilts". Page 37.

9. *Bentley's Catalogue of Novelties in Art Needlework, Stamping Patterns, Lace and Etc.* 1884–5.

10. Finley.

11. Fagan Affleck, Diane L. *Just New From the Mills: Printed Cottons in America*. Museum of American Textile History, North Andover, Massachusetts, 1987. Page 55.

12. Katzenberg, Dena S. *Baltimore Album Quilts*. Baltimore Museum of Art, Baltimore, 1981. Page 24.

13. Personal communication from Diane Fagan Affleck , curator at the Museum of American Textile History, who has traced the term to a 1916 speech made by Robert Roech.

14. Bresenhan, Karoline Patterson and Nancy O'Bryant Puentes. *Lone Stars: A Legacy of Texas Quilts, 1836–1936*. University of Texas Press, Austin, 1986. Page 122.

15. Beyer, Jinny. *The Scrap Look*. EPM Publications, McLean, Virginia, 1985. Page 113.

16. Degraw, Imelda G. *Quilts and Coverlets*. The Denver Art Museum, Denver, 1974. Pages 5–6.

17. I am grateful to Frederica Sedgwick for her insights into the source of ethnic references to pink calicoes.

18. One late nineteenth-century reference is in Crookes, Sir William. *A Practical Handbook of Dyeing and Calico-Printing*. Longmans, Green and Co., London, 1874. Page 74.

19. Whitney, Hattie. "Piecing the Quilt", *Good Housekeeping*. March 18, 1888. Page 208.

20. Persoz, J. *Traite Theorique et Pratique de l'Impression des Tissus*. 4 volumes. V. Masson, Paris, 1846.

21. Webster, Marie. *Quilts: Their Story and How to Make Them*. Doubleday, Page and Co., Garden City, New York, 1915.

22. Adrosko, Rita. *Natural Dyes in the United States*. 1968. Reprinted as *Natural Dyes and Home Dyeing*, Dover, New York, 1971. Page 20.

23. Liles. Page 34.

24. Liles. Page 34.

25. Liles. Page 35.

26. *Godey's Lady's Book*. April, 1851. Page 2.

27. Liles. Page 36.

28. Katzenberg. Page 86.

29. Bresenhan and Puentes. Pages 18 and 42.

30. Letter to the author from James Liles dated October 13, 1985.

31. Fagan Affleck. Page 48.

32. Fagan Affleck. Page 26.

33. Liles. Page 36.

34. Pettit, Florence. *America's Printed and Painted Fabrics 1600–1900*. Hastings House, New York, 1970.

35. Corbman, Bernard P. *Textiles: Fiber To Fabric* (5th edition). McGraw Hill, New York, 1975. Page 179.

36. Daumus, Maurice. *A History of Technology and Invention: Progress Through the Ages*. Crown Publishing, New York, 1979.

37. Corbman. Page 179.

CHAPTER 5

1. Hunton, W. Gordon. *English Decorative Textiles: Tapestry and Chintz*. John Tiranti and Company, London, 1930. Page 9.

2. Clouzot, Henri. *Painted and Printed Fabrics 1760–1815*. Metropolitan Museum of Art, New York, 1915. Page 79.

3. Moss, Gillian. *Printed Textiles 1760–1860*. Smithsonian Institution, Washington, D.C., 1987. Page 18.

4. Clouzot.

5. Robinson, Stuart. *A History of Printed Textiles*. M.I.T Press, Cambridge, Massachusetts, 1969. Page 26.

6. Moss, Gillian, *Printed Textiles 1760–1860*. Smithsonian Institution, Washington, DC, 1987.

7. Pettit, Florence. *America's Printed and Painted Fabrics 1600–1900*. Hastings House, New York, 1970. Page 185.

8. Trollope, Frances. *Domestic Manners of the Americans*. 1832. Reprinted, Donald Smalley, editor, Knopf, New York, 1949. Page 158.

9. Letter quoted in Pettit. Page 57.

10. Randolph's 1776 inventory is quoted in Lanier, Mildred. "The Textile Furnishings". *The Magazine Antiques*. January, 1969. Pages 121–127.

11. The 1712 advertisement in the *Boston Newsletter* is quoted in Clouzot.

12. Montgomery, Florence M. *Printed Textiles: English and American Cottons and Linens 1700–1850*. The Viking Press, New York, 1970.

13. Irwin, John and Katharine B. Brett. *Origins of Chintz*. Her Majesty's Stationery Office, London, 1970. See Chapter 5, "The Flowering Tree".

14. Montgomery. Page 160.

15. Montgomery. Page 96.

16. Montgomery. Page 356.

17. Lynn, Catherine. *Wallpaper in America*. W. W. Norton & Co., New York, 1980. Page 507.

18. Montgomery. Page 306.

19. Lynn. Page 507.

20. Montgomery. Page 281.

21. Collins, Herbert Ridgway. *Threads of History: Americana Recorded on Cloth, 1775 to the Present*. Smithsonian Institution Press, Washington, D.C., 1979.

22. Caulfeild, Sophia Frances Anne, and Blanche C. Saward. *The Dictionary of Needlework*. L. Upcott Gill, London, 1882. Reprinted by Arno Press, New York, 1972.

23. "Quilt Patterns to Please All Tastes". *The Farm Journal*. January, 1925. Page 86.

24. *Standard College Dictionary*. Funk and Wagnalls, 1966. Page 317.

25. Hunter, George Leland. *Decorative Textiles*. J. B. Lippincott, Philadelphia, 1918. Page 322.

26. Katzenberg. Page 28.

27. Tucker, Barbara M. *Samuel Slater and the Origins of the American Textile Industry 1790–1860*. Cornell University Press, Ithaca, 1984. Page 191.

28. Yates, Mary Paul. *Textiles: A Handbook for Designers*. Prentice Hall, Englewood Cliffs, New Jersey, 1986. Page 45.

29. Bresenhan, Karoline Patterson and Nancy O'Bryant Puentes. *Lone Stars: A Legacy of Texas Quilts, 1836–1936*. University of Texas Press, Austin, 1986. Page 122.

30. Persoz, J. *Traite Theorique et Pratique de l'Impression des Tissus*. 4 volumes, V. Masson, Paris, 1846.

31. Fagan Affleck, Diane L. *Just New From the Mills: Printed Cottons in America*. Museum of American Textile History, North Andover, Massachusetts, 1987. Page 53.

32. Pettit. Page 231.

33. Larcom, Lucy. *A New England Girlhood: Outlined from Memory*. Houghton Mifflin, Boston, 1889. Reprinted by Peter Smith, Gloucester, Massachusetts, 1973.

34. Katzenberg. Page 20.

35. An 1848 newspaper advertisement announces the arrival of ten cases of London double purple prints. Katzenberg. Page 58.

36. Gernsheim, Alison. *Victorian and Edwardian Fashion: A Photographic Survey*, Dover, New York, 1981. Page 30.

37. Finley, Ruth. *Old Patchwork Quilts and the Women Who Made Them*. J.B. Lippincott, Philadelphia, 1929. Page 68.

38. Montgomery. Page 334.

39. Dunton, William Rush, Jr., M.D. *Old Quilts*. Published by the author, Catonsville, Maryland, 1946. Page 11.

40. Christopherson, Katy. *The Poltical and the Campaign Quilt*. The Kentucky Heritage Quilt Society, Frankfort, 1984. Page 16.

41. Collins attributes the Grant fabric to the 1868 campaign, (page 187), but Christopherson dates it to 1872 (page 22). It seems more likely a match for the Greeley fabric of the later campaign.

42. Collins. Page 188.

CHAPTER 6

1. Beaudoin-Ross, Jacqueline. "An Early-Eighteenth Century Pieced Quilt in Montreal". *Canadian Art Revue*. Volume 6, Number 2, 1979. Page 108.

2. Gunn, Virginia. "Template Quilt Construction and Its Offshoots from Godey's Lady's Book to Mountain Mist". *Pieced By Mother Symposium Papers*. Oral Traditions Project, Lewisburg, Pennsylvania, 1988. Page 69.

3. Beaudoin-Ross. Page 106.

4. Cooper, Grace Rogers. *The Invention of the Sewing Machine*. The Smithsonian Institution, Washington, D.C., 1968. Page 11.

5. Cooper. Page 47.

6. Chestnut, Mary Boykin. Diary. Quoted in Muhlenfeld, Elizabeth. *Mary Boykin Chestnut: A Biography*. Louisiana State University Press, Baton Rouge, 1981.

7. Cooper. Page 63.

8. Cooper. Page 36.

9. Swan, Susan Burrows. *Plain and Fancy: American Women and Their Needlework, 1700–1850*. Holt, Rinehart & Winston, New York, 1977. Page 213.

10. Beyer, Jinny. *The Art and Technique of Creating Medallion Quilts*. EPM Publications, McLean, Virginia, 1982.

11. Caulfeild, Sophia Frances Anne, and Blanche C. Saward. *The Dictionary of Needlework*. L. Upton Gill, London, 1882. Reprinted by Arno Press, New York, 1972. Page 270.

12. Swan. Page 223.

13. Caulfeild and Saward. Page 270.

14. Caulfeild and Saward. Page 270.

15. Bath, Virginia Churchill. *Needlework in America: History, Designs, and Techniques*. Viking Press, New York, 1979. Page 77.

16. Caulfeild and Saward. Page 173.

17. Gunn, Virginia. "Crazy Quilts and Outline Quilts: Popular Responses to the Decorative Art/Art Needlework Movement, 1876–1893". *Uncoverings 1984*. American Quilt Study Group, Mill Valley, California, 1985. Page 140.

18. Caulfeild and Saward. Page 374.

19. Caulfeild and Saward. Page 384.

20. Bond, Dorothy. *Embroidery Stitches From Old American Quilts*. Published by the author, Cottage Grove, Oregon, 1977.

21. Caulfeild and Saward. Page 384.

22. Gunn, Virginia. "Yo-Yo or Bed of Roses Quilts: Nineteenth Century Origins". *Uncoverings 1987*. American Quilt Study Group, San Francisco, California, in press.

23. Swan. Page 69.

24. A letter in the *Ohio Farmer*, July 19, 1884. Page 46. Quoted in McMorris, Penny. *Crazy Quilts*. E.P. Dutton, New York, 1984. Page 21.

25. Church, Diana. "The Baylis Stenciled Quilt". *Uncoverings 1983*. American Quilt Study Group, Mill Valley, California, 1984. Page 75.

26. Nelson, Cyril. *Quilt Engagement Calendar 1985*. E.P. Dutton, New York. Plate 28.

27. Federico, Jean T. "White Work Classfication System". *Uncoverings 1980*. American Quilt Study Group, Mill Valley, California, 1981. Page 68.

28. Orlofsky, Myron and Patsy Orlofsky. *Quilts in America*. McGraw Hill, New York, 1974. Page 4.

29. Colby, Averil. *Quilting*. B.T. Batsford, London, 1972.

30. Garoutte, Sally. "Marseilles Quilts and Their Woven Offspring". *Uncoverings 1982*. American Quilt Study Group, Mill Valley, California, 1983.

31. Colby. Page 23. Swan. page 227.

32. Maines, Rachel. "Paradigms of Scarcity and Abundance: The Quilt as an Artifact of the Industrial Revolution". *In the Heart of Pennsylvania Symposium Papers*. Oral Traditions Project, Lewisburg, Pennsylvania, 1986. Page 86.

33. Ramsey, Bets and Merikay Waldvogel. *The Quilts of Tennessee*. Rutledge Hill Press, Nashville, Tennessee, 1986. Page 63.

34. Colby.

35. Colby. Page 50.

36. Bresenhan, Karoline Patterson and Nancy O'Bryant Puentes. *Lone Stars: A Legacy of Texas Quilts, 1836–1936*. University of Texas Press, Austin, 1986. Page 106.

37. Ramsey and Waldvogel. Page 99.

38. Meyer, Suellen. "The Show Me State". *Lady's Circle Patchwork Quilts*. May, 1988. Page 10.

39. Cassidy, Frederic C. (editor). *Dictionary of American Regional English*. Belknap Press, Cambridge, Massachusetts, 1985. Volume 1. Pages 739–40.

40. Inventory of Henry Bean's 1853 estate. Quoted in Roan, Nancy and Ellen J. Gehret. *Just A Quilt*. Goschenhoppen Historians, Green Lane, Pennsylvania, 1984. Page 31.

41. Leslie, Eliza. *The House Book*. Cary and Hart, Philadelphia, 1846. Quoted in Lasanksy, Jeannette. *Pieced by Mother*. Oral Traditions Project, Lewisburg, Pennsylvania, 1987. Page 26.

42. Leslie. Quoted in Lasanksy, Jeannette. "The Role of Haps in Central Pennsylvania's 19th and 20th Century Quiltmaking Traditions". *Uncoverings 1985*. The American Quilt Study Group, Mill Valley, California, 1986. Pages 88–9.

43. Letters of Lucy Rutledge Cooke. Quoted in Holmes, Kenneth. *Covered Wagon Women: Diaries and Letters from the Western Trails*. The Arthur H. Clark Co., Glendale, California, 5 volumes, 1983–1986. Volume 4. Page 269.

44. Carter, Myra Inman. Diary. Quoted in Ramsey, Bets. "The Quilter". *The Chattanooga Times*. August 14, 1986.

45. Gunn, Virginia. "Quilts for Union Soldiers in the Civil War". *Uncoverings 1985*. American Quilt Study Group, Mill Valley, California, 1986. Page 112.

46. The Henry Clay banner quilt is in the collection of the Old Barracks Museum, Trenton, New Jersey (# 49.1) and is pictured in Christopherson, Katy. *The Political and the Campaign Quilt*. The Kentucky Heritage Quilt Society, Frankfort, 1984. Page 9.

47. The fragments from the tied comforter are in the collection of the Kansas Museum of History in Topeka, # 30.3 and # 41.1.

48. Advertisement in *Home Needlecraft Magazine*. Volume 1 # 4, October, 1897.

49. Beecher, Catherine and Harriett Beecher Stowe. *The American Woman's Home*. J.B. Ford and Co., New York, 1869. Page 359.

50. Reddall, Winifred. "Pieced Lettering on Seven Quilts Dating from 1833 to 1891". *Uncoverings 1980*. American Quilt Study Group, Mill Valley, California, 1981.

51. Havig, Bettina. "Missouri: Crossroads to Quilting". *Uncoverings 1985*. American Quilt Study Group, Mill Valley, California, 1986. Page 51.

52. Osler, Dorothy. *Traditional British Quilts*. B.T. Batsford, London, 1987. Page 96.

53. One of the quilts is in the collection of the Los Angeles County Museum of Art, pictured in their *1989 Quilts Engagement Calendar*. Neves Publishing Co., New York, 1988. See plate opposite December 4th. The other is pictured in Bresenhan and Puentes. Page 54.

CHAPTER 7

1. Finley, Ruth. *Old Patchwork Quilts and the Women Who Made Them*. J.B. Lippincott, Philadelphia, 1929. Page 23.

2. Finley. Page 129.

3. Ramsey, Bets and Merikay Waldvogel. *The Quilts of Tennessee*. Rutledge Hill Press, Nashville, Tennessee, 1986. Page 47.

4. Colby, Averil. *Patchwork*. Charles T. Branford, Newton Center, Massachusetts, 1958. Pages 47–8.

5. Callahan, Colleen R. "A Quilt and Its Pieces." *Metropolitan Museum Journal*, 19/20, 1984/1985. Page 107.

6. Inventory of Ezra Harder, 1839. Quoted in Lasansky, Jeannette. *Pieced By Mother: Over 100 Years of Quiltmaking Traditions*. Oral Traditions Project, Lewisburg, Pennsylvania, 1987. Page 27.

7. Katzenberg, Dena S. *Baltimore Album Quilts*. Baltimore Museum of Art, Baltimore, 1981. Page 47.

8. *Sewing With Cotton Bags*. The Textile Bag Manufacturer's Association, Chicago, (no date).

9. Inventory of Sarah Thompson, 1811. Quoted in Allen, Gloria Seaman. *First Flowerings: Early Virginia Quilts*. DAR Museum, Washington, D. C., l987. Page 8.

10. Koontz, Sandra and Kay Morse, *The Mennonite Central Committee Relief Sale*. Paper presented at the Kansas Quilt Project Symposium, Topeka, Kansas, July 9, 1988.

11. Garoutte, Sally. "Marseilles Quilts and Their Woven Offspring". *Uncoverings 1982*. American Quilt Study Group, Mill Valley, California, 1983.

12. Rae, Janet. *The Quilts of the British Isles*. E.P. Dutton, New York, l987. Page 15.

13. Garoutte.

14. *Thirteenth St. Louis Fair, Premiums, St. Louis, 1873*.

15. Benberry, Cuesta. "Charm Quilts Revisited". *Quilters Newsletter Magazine*. #198, January, 1988. Page 30.

16. Caulfeild, Sophia Frances Anne, and Blanche C. Saward. *The Dictionary of Needlework*. L. Upcott Gill, London, 1882. Reprinted by Arno Press, New York, 1972. Page 434.

17. Lasansky, Jeannette. "The Role of Haps in Central Pennsylvania's 19th and 20th Century Quiltmaking Traditions". *Uncoverings 1985*. The American Quilt Study Group, Mill Valley, California, 1986.

18. Yabsley, Suzanne. *Texas Quilts, Texas Women*. Texas A & M University Press, College Station, Texas, 1984. Page 23.

19. Gero, Annette. "The Folklore of the Australian Wagga". *Pieced By Mother, Symposium Papers*. Oral Traditions Project, Lewisburg, Pennsylvania, 1987.

20. Gunn, Virginia. "Crazy Quilts and Outline Quilts: Popular Responses to the Decorative Art/Art Needlework Movement, 1876–1893". *Uncoverings 1984*. Page 142.

21. McMorris, Penny. *Crazy Quilts*. E.P. Dutton, New York, 1984. Page 17.

22. Quoted in the film by Ferrero, Pat, Elaine Hedges and Julie Silber. *Hearts and Hands*. Ferrero Films, San Francisco, l987.

23. Bishop, Robert and Patricia Coblentz. *New Discoveries in American Quilts*. E.P. Dutton, New York, 1975. Frontispiece.

24. Katzenberg, Dena S. *Baltimore Album Quilts*. Baltimore Museum of Art, Baltimore, 1981. Page 62.

25. Letter from Joyce Gross. *Quilters' Newsletter Magazine*, September, 1988. #205. Page 67.

26. Katzenberg. Page 70.

27. Lasansky, Jeannette. *In The Heart of Pennsylvania*. Oral Traditions Project, Lewisburg, Pennsylvania, 1985. Page 14.

28. Lasansky, Jeannette. *Pieced by Mother: Over 100 Years of Quiltmaking Traditions*. Oral Traditions Project, Lewisburg, Pennsylvania, 1987.

CHAPTER 8

1. Brackman, Barbara. *An Encyclopedia of Pieced Quilt Patterns*. Prairie Flower Publishing, Lawrence, Kansas, 1979–1986.

2. Brackman, Barbara. "A Chronological Index to Pieced Quilt Patterns, 1775–1825". *Uncoverings 1983*. American Quilt Study Group, Mill Valley, California, 1984.

3. Arthur, T.S. "The Quilting Party". *Godey's Lady's Book*, Volume 39, September, 1849.

4. Harris, George Washington. "Mrs. Yardley's Quilting". Anthologized in Robert Penn Warren's *American Literature: The Maker and the Making*, Volume 1. St. Martin's Press, New York, 1973.

5. Holman, Nancy. Diary. Quoted in a letter to the author dated August 14, 1984 from Elaine Hedges.

6. Earl, Alice Morse. *Home Life in Colonial Days*, 1898.

7. Mathieson, Judy. "Some Sources of Design Inspiration for the Quilt Pattern Mariner's Compass". *Uncoverings 1981*. The American Quilt Study Group, Mill Valley, California, 1982. Page 12.

8. Webster, Marie. *Quilts: Their Story and How to Make Them*. Doubleday, Page and Co., Garden City, New York, 1915.

9. Finley, Ruth. *Old Patchwork Quilts and the Women Who Made Them*. J.B. Lippincott, Philadelphia, 1929.

10. Hall, Carrie A. and Rose G. Kretsinger. *The Romance of the Patchwork Quilt in America*. Caxton Printers, Caldwell, Idaho, 1935.

11. Bowne, Eliza Southgate. *A Girl's Life Eighty Years Ago: Selections from the Letters of Eliza Southgate Bowne*. Charles Scribner's Sons, New York, 1888. Letter dated January 9, 1798. Page 72.

12. Ickis, Marguerite. *The Standard Book of Quilt Making and Collecting*. Greystone Press, New York, 1949. Reprinted by Dover Publications, New York, 1959.

13. Arthur.

14. "Beds, Bedclothing and Bedmaking". *Good Housekeeping*. April, 1888. Page 290.

15. Earl.

16. Hall, Eliza Calvert. *Aunt Jane of Kentucky*. Little Brown and Company, Boston, 1907.

17. *Peterson's Magazine*. January, 1885. Pages 86–88.

18. Gunn, Virginia, Stephanie N. Tan and Ricky Clark. *Treasures from Trunks*. The College of Wooster Art Museum, Wooster, Ohio, 1987. Page 6.

19. Whitley, Mary. *Every Girl's Book of Sport, Occupation and Pastime*. London, 1897. Page 102. Quoted in Rae, Janet. *The Quilts of the British Isles*, E.P. Dutton, New York, 1987.

APPENDIX 1

Building A Case

You may want to use the following worksheet to help you organize the dating information about any individual quilt. Down the left margin are the various categories of clues from fiber to pattern. With these reminders you can go through each category methodically looking for significant clues.

Across the top are three levels of clues: Strong Clues, Weak Clues and No Clue. You will want to judge the strength of each of your clues and write it in the proper column. For example, a bias binding is a weak clue to a date after 1900; it goes in the middle column under Weak Clues. The Crazy Quilt pattern is a strong clue to a date after 1875; write it in the first column.

Many aspects of the quilt are going to be of no help at all in building a case for a date. Write things like grid quilting or straight grain binding in the third column—no clues.

You don't need to fill in all the clue categories. Some clues like thread fiber or the presence of machine stitching are only useful if you are trying to determine whether a quilt was made before the 1840s.

Once you have looked at all the relevant as-pects of the quilt's fabrics, construction and style, you must first evaluate the clues in the Strong Clues column. You will have to use your own judgment for there is no formula here. Each clue should have a range and the quilt will probably date from the years when all the clues overlap. For example if the style is Red and White (1840-1925) and the signature is cross stitched (before 1865), the quilt is likely to date from the years when the clues overlap (1840-1865). Determine the earliest possible date based on the overlap of all the strong clues and write it in the blank at the bottom of the page. Then decide upon a latest possible date, again based on clue overlap. Clues in the Weak Clues column may give you a little help in narrowing those dates—but be conservative. They *are* weak clues.

Feel free to photocopy the blank form for Building a Case for your own personal use. Fill it out on a few quilts until you get in the habit of organizing your information in a systematic fashion. To help you learn to use the form there are four examples already filled out describing the four color pictures on pages 184 through 191.

Building A Case

Categories	Strong Clues	Weak Clues	No Clues
Fabric			
Fiber			
Weave			
Batting/Filler			
Thread			
Color & Dyes			
Color scheme in quilt			
Color scheme in individual fabrics			
Damage to color			
Cotton Prints			
Scale of Fabric			
Printing Techniques			
Print Styles			
Techniques			
Patchwork			
Embellishment			
Quilting/Tying			
Inscriptions			
Edging/Binding			
Machine Sewing			

Style

Set/Format

Borders

Backing

Design Style

Pattern

Earliest Date _____

Latest Date _____

Comments:

Building A Case

Blank sheets may be photocopied for individual use

Sample Worksheet # 1

Categories	Strong Clues	Weak Clues	No Clues
Fabric			
Fiber		Cotton—after 1800	
Weave			All plain weave
Batting/Filler			Cotton
Thread	some 6 cord (3 plies of 2)—after 1860		
Color & Dyes			
Color scheme in quilt			Nothing notable
Color scheme in individual fabrics		Madder browns— 2nd half/19th C	
Damage to color			
Cotton Prints			
Scale of Fabric		all calico—after 1840	
Printing Techniques		all roller prints— after 1840	
Print Styles	Shirting prints in whites–1870–1925 Double pinks— 1840–1920 Madder style browns—(these look to be 1870– 1900)		
Techniques			
Patchwork			Pieced
Embellishment			None
Quilting/Tying			Grid quilting
Inscriptions	Ink on reverse—1830–1900	Back over front	
Edging/Binding			
Machine Sewing	Yes—after 1845		

Style

Set/Format	Blocks (pattern is in set; blocks are plain)
Borders	Plain
Backing	Plain white cotton
Design Style	Scrap quilt set with white
Pattern	Variation on Ladies' Art Co.'s Odd Fellows pattern goes back to mid-19th century

Earliest Date _____1870_____
Latest Date _____1900_____

Comments: The strongest clues to date are the combination of the shirting prints (1870–1925) and the madder brown prints which appear to be from about 1870–1900. The overlap in these two clues is 1870–1900. There is nothing to indicate the quilt is older than the Civil War; nothing to indicate it's newer than 1900. This quilt is actually dated in ink on the back: January, 1876.

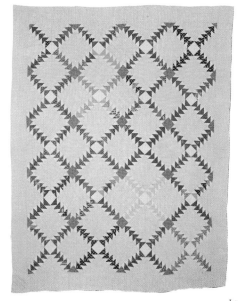

Larry Schwarm

Odd Fellows quilt, signed Dorothy (?) Walker. Pieced and quilted. Cotton. Private collection. See Sample Worksheet # 1.

Building A Case

Blank sheets may be photocopied for individual use

Sample Worksheet # 2

Categories	Strong Clues	Weak Clues	No Clues
Fabric			
Fiber		Cotton—after 1800	
Weave			Plain
Batting/Filler			Cotton
Thread			Didn't check
Color & Dyes			
Color scheme in quilt	Red, green & white— 1830–1900		
Color scheme in individual fabrics		Turkey red plains— after 1840	
Damage to color			None
Cotton Prints			
Scale of Fabric		Only print is green calico—after 1840	
Printing Techniques		roller print—after 1840	
Print Styles			
Techniques			
Patchwork			Pieced
Embellishment	Turkey red outline embroidery— 1880–1925		
Quilting/Tying			Grid quilting
Inscriptions	Turkey red chainstitch 1880– 1925		
Edging/Binding			Didn't check
Machine Sewing			Didn't check

Style

Set/Format			Block/pattern is in set; blocks plain
Borders			Sawtooth
Backing			Plain white cotton
Design Style		Red green & white—1830–1900	
		Outline Embroidered— 1880–1925	
Pattern		Feathered Star 1830–Present	

Earliest _____1880_____
Latest _____1900_____

Comments: Red, green and white quilts, especially those with plain Turkey red fabric are difficult to date beyond the broad range of 1830 or 40 to 1900. The red outline embroidery (1880-1925) on this one is a real help. The overlap in these two clues is 1880-1900, a date which corresponds with the maker's life span (1853-1914) and the family's attributed date (1880).

Larry Schwarm

Feathered Star quilt made by Sarah Maria Grizzel in Barton County, Kansas. Pieced, embroidered and quilted. Cotton. Collection: Mrs. W. Elden Harwood. See Sample Worksheet # 2.

Building A Case

Sample Worksheet # 3

Categories	Strong Clues	Weak Clues	No Clues
Fabric			
Fiber		Cotton—after 1800	
Weave			All plain
Batting/Filler			Cotton
Thread			Didn't check
Color & Dyes			
Color scheme in quilt	Blue & gray scrap look—1890–1925		
Color scheme in individual fabrics	Cadet blue prints 1890–1925		
	Black ground prints 1890–1925		
	White shirting prints 1870–1925		
	Pink and purple plains 1925–1950		
Damage to color			None
Cotton Prints			
Scale of Fabric		Most calico; Some cretonnes—1880–1925	
Printing Techniques		All roller prints—after 1840	
Print Styles	Mourning prints 1890–1925		
	Lots of single color geometrics 1890–1925		
Techniques			
Patchwork		Pieced, not to foundation; in a Log Cabin could mean 20th C.	

188

Embellishment			None
Quilting/Tying	Tied with cotton twist on front— after 1875		
Inscriptions			None
Edging/Binding			Didn't check
Machine Sewing			Didn't check
Style			
Set/Format			Blocks; edge to edge
Borders			None
Backing			Didn't check
Design Style	Dark cotton quilt— 1890–1925		
Pattern	Log Cabin—1860– present	Log Cabins not too popular in 1925– 1950 era	

Earliest Date: _____1890_____
Latest Date: _____1925_____

Comments: The strongest clues here are the Log Cabin design, the tying and the dark cotton color scheme with individual cadet blue, gray mourning prints and black ground prints. The era where all these clues overlap is 1890–1925. The plain pink and lavender cottons are a little confusing; it is important to recall that pastel plains were available before 1925 but were not used too often in quilts.

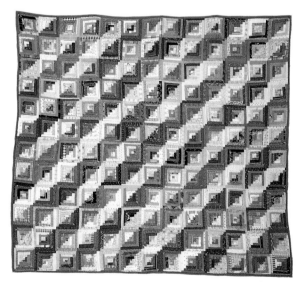

Larry Schwarm

Log Cabin comforter (Straight Furrow variation). Maker unknown. Pieced and tied. Cotton. Collection of Larry Schwarm. See Sample Worksheet # 3.

Building A Case

Blank sheets may be photocopied for individual use

Sample Worksheet # 4

Categories	Strong Clues	Weak Clues	No Clues
Fabric			
Fiber		Wool—before 1840 or after 1875	
Weave	Wool satin—before 1840. Also a twill that looks to be an early wool and a homespun fabric on back—before 1865		
Batting/Filler			Wool
Thread	Wool—before 1840		
Color & Dyes			
Color scheme in quilt			Navy, pink & gold
Color scheme in individual fabrics		Indigo (?) a common color in early wools— before 1840	
Damage to color			
Cotton Prints			None
Scale of Fabric			
Printing Techniques			
Print Styles			
Techniques			
Patchwork			Pieced
Embellishment			None
Quilting/Tying	Fancy quilting on wool quilt could mean before 1840 or an Amish quilt 1880–1940		
Inscriptions			None
Edging/Binding			Straight applied & front over back
Machine Sewing		None-supports date before 1840	

Style

Set/Format	Medallion-before 1865 or may be Amish 1880–1940	
Borders		Plain with corner square
Backing	Pieced of several wools; center of back is same shape as center of front; may be salvaged quilted petticoat 1750–1840 Brown fabric on back is coarse; may be homespun—before 1865	
Design Style	Simple piecing, fancy quilting and wool fabric indicate early wool quilt—before 1840 or Amish quilt 1880–1940	
Pattern	Center Square variation, again either before 1840 or Amish from 1880–1940	

Earliest Date: _____1750_____
Latest Date: _____1840_____

Comments: There are two obvious options here, that the quilt is an early wool quilt or a later Amish-style quilt. Three factors point to the earlier style and thus an earlier date. 1) The recycled petticoat in the middle. 2) The variety of wools ranging from a fine twill and a wool satin weave to a coarse plain weave that may be homespun. 3) The construction and quilting thread are wool. Narrowing the date beyond this 90-year span of time is difficult, but because the center is a petticoat (fashionable in the eighteenth century) one might guess that it was made closer to 1800 than to 1840.

Larry Schwarm

Framed Square quilt. Maker unknown. Pieced and quilted. Wool. Collection of Elizabeth M. Watkins Community Museum. See Sample Worksheet # 4.

APPENDIX 2

Notes on the Database of Dated Quilts

Using a DBase III program and an IBM-PC compatible Leading Edge computer with a hard-disk drive, I entered data on 885 quilts with dates actually inscribed on them. The earliest quilt was dated 1746, the latest 1949. I used quilts I saw in exhibits, museum and private collections, antique shops, and those brought to my classes on dating quilts. I also entered data on date-inscribed quilts pictured in the twentieth-century literature, from women's magazines of the teens and twenties through the recent state quilt project summaries. I used museum catalog cards (often I could not see the quilts themselves) and I read a few of the forms from three quilt surveys (Quilts of Tennessee, the North Carolina Quilt Project and the Kansas Quilt Project).

I analyzed each quilt according to available information about the maker (name, age, city and state) and 13 different characteristics (function, technique, format, style, pattern, scale of print fabric, fiber, shape, color scheme, border, edge treatment, quilting and how the date was inscribed on the quilt). Since the information was gleaned from a variety of sources I often did not have complete information. Books rarely describe the binding technique, so my binding data was limited to about 200 quilts.

Using a database of dated quilts is a reliable way of tracking the changes in style, technique and pattern through the year but with a few limitations. Quilts may be inaccurately dated. There is in the literature an album quilt date-inscribed 1817, 22 years earlier than the next oldest album quilt (1). I have seen a Crazy Quilt dated 1699, 180 years earlier than most of the other Crazy Quilts. The date on the Crazy Quilt must have been 1899, but through accident or overzealous-

ness on the part of a member of the maker's family, the top of the embroidered "8" has rubbed off. The same thing may have happened with the date on the 1817 album quilt, or that date may have signified something other than the date the quilt was made. If a quilt was dated more than 20 years earlier than the other quilts in its category I did not use the information. Thus neither the 1699 Crazy Quilt nor the 1817 album are in the database.

A second limitation to using dated quilts is that certain types of quilts are far more likely to be dated than others. Album and Crazy Quilts are two styles that were frequently dated; wool utility quilts and scrapbag calico quilts were not. The information about the album and Crazy Quilts is more complete and probably more accurate than the information about styles less likely to be dated by their makers.

There is a geographical bias to the information. Since I live in Kansas I have collected a good deal of information on Kansas quilts. But the bias goes beyond those quilts I have personally seen. Most of the information comes from quilts pictured in books, catalogs and magazines, sources that primarily print photographs of antique quilts from a region beginning in the mid-Atlantic states and extending directly west through the plains. Of the quilts in the database with a known or attributed state of origin (only about 30% were from unknown places), Pennsylvania quilts are the best documented; 117 of the quilts were made there. New York was second with 65, followed by Kansas with 63 (my personal geographical bias) and Maryland with 59. The quilts of the Northeastern and Southern states have been poorly recorded in print. There was one quilt each from Alabama and

Mississippi, six from Georgia, five from Maine and two from New Hampshire. It may be that Pennsylvania, New York and Maryland are heavily represented because these are states where dated album quilts were extraordinarily popular; there may be more date-inscribed quilts from these states in the literature, rather than more quilts in general. However, observation indicates that quilts from New England and the deep South are not often seen in books, magazines or exhibit catalogs, an omission that the current regional projects may remedy.

Categories for Database on Dated Quilts

Date:
Second Date: (some quilts have two dates)
Maker's First Name:
Middle Name:
Last Name:
Age when made quilt:
State:
City:

Technique: a = pieced, b = cut-out chintz applique, c = conventional applique, d = both types of applique, e = pieced and cut-out chintz applique, f = pieced and conventional applique, g = pieced and both types of applique, h = embroidered, i = foundation pieced, j = pieced and embroidered, k = conventional applique and embroidered, l = cut-out chintz and embroidered, m = stenciled, n = whole cloth, o = other, p = English template piecing

Format: b = block, m = medallion, s = strip, z = mosaic all over, o = other

Set: a = whole-cloth, b = alternate plain, c = sashing between, d = set edge to edge, e = four large blocks, f = central vase, g = central tree, h = pictorial, i = different size blocks, h = embroidered in alternate blocks, i = pieced and appliqued in alternate blocks, z = mosaic all-over set, o = other

Function: a = single pattern album, b = album sampler, c = sampler, d = fundraiser, e = charm, f = commemorative, g = show quilt, h = baby quilt, o = other

Scale of Fabric: c = calico, h = chintz, b = combination of both, p = plain

Fiber: a = silk & wool, b = cotton and wool, c = cotton, d = silk and linen, e = silk and cotton, f = cotton and linen, g = linen and wool, h = linen, silk and cotton, i = cotton, linen, silk and wool, j = rayon & silk, l = linen, r = rayon, s = silk, w = wool

Corners: c = scallop, s = square, t = cut out in a T-shape, o = other

Color Scheme: a = red, green & white only, b = red, green & white primarily, c = red and white, d = blue and white, e = pastel, f = black as a color, w = white only, o = other

Pattern Name:

Pattern Number: (for pieced patterns I used numbers in *An Encyclopedia of Pieced Quilt Patterns*)

Date Inscription: a = applique, b = stenciled, c = cross stitch, d = painted, e = embroidered (if stitch is unknown), h = chain stitch, i = ink, m = stamped, o = other, p = pieced, q = quilted, r = running stitch, s = satin stitch,)

Border: a = appliqued swags, b = appliqued floral vines, c = appliqued trees, d = appliqued urns or vases, e = other applique, f = single strip of plain or calico fabric, g = embroidered, h = appliqued and embroidered, i = plain strip of chintz, j = pieced sawtooth, k = appliqued dog tooth, l = pieced dog tooth, m = cut- out chintz applique, n = none, p = other pieced, r = sashing continued as border, s = two or more strips)

Edge: b = bound but cannot determine method, e = both back and front turned in, f = fringe, g = rope, h = piping, i = bound with bias strip, k = back over front, p = prairie point, r = ruffle, s = bound with straight grain strip, t = top with no batting or edging, v = front over back, z = tape

Quilting: b = double lines, d = tied, f = fancy motifs rather than just utility quilting, h = fan quilting, i = stuffed, l = triple lines, o = other, p = utility quilting, s = summer spread (unquilted but bound), t = top with no batting or edging

Source for information: Quilt owner

APPENDIX 3

Chronological List of Stars on the U.S. Flag

New stars, representing new states, are added to the flag on the Fourth of July, so there were, for example, 21 between July 4, 1819 and July 3, 1820.

1777–1795	13 stars 13 stripes	1859–1861	33 stars
1795–1818	15 stars 15 stripes	1861–1863	34 stars
1818–1819	20 stars 13 stripes	1863–1865	35 stars
1819–1820	21 stars	1865–1867	36 stars
1820–1822	23 stars	1867–1877	37 stars
1822–1836	24 stars	1877–1890	38 stars
1836–1837	25 stars	1890–1891	43 stars
1837–1845	26 stars	1891–1896	44 stars
1845–1846	27 stars	1896–1908	45 stars
1846–1847	28 stars	1908–1912	46 stars
1847–1848	29 stars	1912–1959	48 stars
1848–1851	30 stars	1959–1960	49 stars
1851–1858	31 stars	1960–present	50 stars
1858–1859	32 stars		

INDEX